STRATUM SERIES

Government in Reformation Europe
1520–1560

STRATUM SERIES

*A series of fundamental reprints
from scholarly journals and specialised works
in European History*

GENERAL EDITOR: J. R. HALE

Published

FRENCH HUMANISM 1470–1600
Werner L. Gundersheimer

THE LATE ITALIAN RENAISSANCE 1525–1630
Eric Cochrane

In preparation

THE RECOVERY OF FRANCE IN THE FIFTEENTH
CENTURY
P. S. Lewis

PRE-REFORMATION GERMANY
Gerald Strauss

SPAIN IN THE FIFTEENTH CENTURY 1369–1516
Roger Highfield

STRIKE

By the same author

United We Stand:
An illustrated account of trade union emblems.

STRIKE
A Live History
1887-1971

R. A. LEESON

LONDON. GEORGE ALLEN & UNWIN LTD
Ruskin House   Museum Street

First published in 1973

© George Allen & Unwin Ltd, 1973

ISBN 0 04 331053 2

Printed in Great Britain
in 11 point Plantin type
by Clarke, Doble & Brendon Ltd
Plymouth

CONTENTS

Abbreviations	*page*	11
Introduction		13
One	1887–1914: Early Starters	21
Two	1914–1925: Heroes and Brothers	51
Three	1926: General Strike and	
	Miners' Lockout	84
Four	1927–1945	112
	Part I Rebellion and Breakaway	114
	Part II The Miners Recover	141
	Part III 'There's a War On'	154
Five	1945–1960: Influence and Affluence	164
Six	1960–1971: Motivated Men	209
Index to contributors		245

ILLUSTRATIONS

facing page

1 Will Dyson cartoon in the *Daily Herald*, 1911   48

2 Liverpool Dock strike, 1911; a docker
argues with troops brought into the city   49

3 'The Cripple Alliance'; cartoon in
The Communist 1921   52

4 Telegram sent out by Ernest Bevin on the
eve of the General Strike, May 1, 1926   64

5 Three blacklegs escorted by police at Garw,
South Wales, in 1929   65

6 Lancashire cotton workers on strike leaving
a mill in August 1932   65

7 Front page of the British Worker, the TUC's
official newspaper for the General Strike,
May 5, 1926   84

8 A mass meeting of airmen at Drigh Road,
RAF station February 1946   112

9 Jack Dash addresses a London dockers'
strike meeting, 1960   113

10 'The Striker's Return', Punch Cartoon,
May 26, 1926   113

11 Seamen on strike demonstrate outside
10 Downing Street, summer 1966   128

12 Harry Hitchings, GKN shop steward, makes
his tower-squatting protest, May 1971   129

13 Giles cartoon on the dock strike, Sunday
Express cartoon, July 24, 1929   164

14 Eccles' TUC Centenary cartoon, Morning
Star, September 1968   211

Acknowlegements

Publisher and author are grateful to the following for permission to reproduce illustrations:

(1) *The Sun*. (2) Ken Sprague Collection. (3) Communist Party
of Great Britain. (4) Transport and General Workers' Union.
(5) *The Western Mail*. (6 & 7) Trades Union Congress. (8)
Arthur Attwood. (9, 11, 12 & 14) *The Morning Star*. (10)
Punch. (13) *Sunday Express*.

ABBREVIATIONS

AEU	Amalgamated Engineering Union
ASCJ	Amalgamated Society of Carpenters and Joiners
ASLEF	Associated Society of Locomotive Engineers and Firemen
ASRS	Amalgamated Society of Railway Servants
ASW	Amalgamated Society of Woodworkers
AUEW	Amalgamated Union of Engineering Workers
BWIU	Building Workers Industrial Union
CSU	Canadian Seamen's Union
ETU	Electrical Trades Union
GKN	Guest, Keen and Nettlefold
IWW	International Workers of the World
JIC	Joint Industrial Committee
MV	Metro Vickers
NATSOPA	National Society of Operative Printers' Assistants
NJIC	National Joint Industrial Council
NUM	National Union of Mineworkers
NUR	National Union of Railwaymen
NUS	National Union of Seamen
RILU	Red International of Labour Unions
TGWU	Transport and General Workers Union
TUC	Trades Union Congress
UCS	Upper Clyde Shipbuilders
UCW	United Clothing Workers (Union)
UMS	United Mineworkers of Scotland
UPW	Union of Post Office Workers

INTRODUCTION

Since the government started to keep count in the 1890s there have been 100,000 strikes in this country, involving millions of people and affecting millions more. Strikes are as much a talking point, a social phenomenon for analysis, as crime or disease; there is usually the same idea in mind, that they ought to be eliminated. Yet they continue, and last year (1971) saw more strikes than in any other year of the century.

At the same time there has been a reluctance, both at the level of popular Press discussion and of academic analysis, to consider strikes as influencing the course of life in Britain. The average social history of the twentieth century admits only one strike (the General Strike of 1926) and that only to imply that it should not have happened and must not happen again.

Both approaches, the analytical and the social historical, have this in common. They are from the outside. Hostile, sympathetic or neutral, they are from the outside. The 'public' view of life and society does not admit that strikes are the means of attempted social change most used by most people, apart from the ballot. In the eyes of many who use it, the strike is a good deal more effective than the ballot, and they use it with more conviction, though it involves them in far more trouble and sacrifice.

Strikes are a force that runs, like an underground river, below the surface of public life, below the level at which governments claim credit for improved living standards and employers advertise higher wages ('recently increased' as the GPO once put it).

Just what difference to Britain have those 100,000 strikes made in the past 80 years? Would Britain have been a better or worse place without them? What caused them? Was it bad conditions, agitators, determination or weakness, calculation or short-sightedness? Were they caused by what people said caused them? Could they have been avoided? Why do young workers today, after generations of counter argument and education, strike so freely, even more freely than did their fathers and grandfathers before them? These questions and many more may be asked by writer, sociologist, industrial relations expert and historian with

13

varying degrees of skill and sympathy. But the crucial answers
elude them, for the vital experience has not been theirs. Apart from
J. Arnison's recent book about the 1966 Roberts Arundel dispute,
I do not know of any study written by someone who actually knows
what it is to go on strike.

This is a remarkable state of affairs, and unparalleled in published work. It is true that civilians write about military tactics, to the
fury of generals. But that does not stop generals' accounts being
published. Even criminals are not obliged to submit in print to
unrelieved analysis by policemen and social workers. Indeed, a
literate burglar will find himself pursued by publishers waving
contracts. But strikers have not been so sought after.

Yet it is not true to say that if writers don't strike, strikers don't
write. Strikers do explain themselves and have done for decades
in leaflets, pamphlets and booklets, most often to fellow trade
unionists. But these works do not find their way into the 'official
record'. They remain part of that underground flow of information
and belief, claim and affirmation which, if it seems not to reach
Westminster or even Congress House, is what runs most strongly
in the docks, shipyards and factories where social history may be
made, if not written.

This book is an attempt to tap that flow, not in a specialised way,
but in a way that is as alive as the experience itself. It assembles the
recollections of some 80 people of some 180 strikes in 20 different
industries over the past 84 years. It reaches back to the time when
the trade union movement numbered less than one million.
Readers may be astonished to discover, as I was, that the Great
Dock Strike of 1889 is still within living memory. But so it is. The
whole development of the trade union movement as we know it
today, 100,000 strikes and all, is still in living memory. The oldest
man who spoke to me was born just after the introduction of the
ballot in Britain and the invention of the telephone. The youngest
was born just as the coal industry was nationalised, and the present
Queen was married.

I did not approach these people with a questionnaire; they are
not that sort of people. I asked them to tell me the story of the
strikes they had seen and pass their own judgement, which they
did freely and frankly. They are people of the Left and of the Right,
and of no political allegiance. There are people whose names will
be familiar, who became Cabinet members, sat on State Boards

and entered Parliament. One man who led 15 unofficial strikes now sits in the House of Lords.

There are many more whose names are unknown save to those with whom they work, and whose opinion is their chief concern. Like the Jewish shop steward who called together his Moslem workmates after the Middle East war and asked if they still wanted him to represent them.

It is their account of this century I have tried to give, in their own words, not grouped by category or industry, but told in the times when these events happened, the times which influenced the strikers and were influenced by them.

The reader will find, when accustomed to the somewhat unusual form of the book, that he is listening to a chronicle tale, with one speaker after another taking up the account, then dropping out, perhaps to re-appear in a new situation, sometimes from a different standpoint. In this way I hope a picture of what has changed and what has not changed in 80 years will emerge.

It may appear that I have given too much space to the miners. But as one of their leaders said 'half the strikes in this country have been in mining', and indeed, out of the 100,000 over 40,000 have been in the pits. And as I am writing this, 50 years after the Triple Alliance was first put to the test, the miners are again on strike and again are calling on the railwaymen and transport workers to help them.

I do not claim that this book is a comprehensive history of industrial dispute, even in coal-mining. But I do believe that it will give something of the flavour, something of the sense of what it was like, what it is like, to go on strike. Part of this account may have been told before in other words. A great deal has never been written down before, though the stories are all well known and have been told in canteens, site huts, miners' welfare halls, working men's clubs and people's homes, much as they were told to me. My strongest wish is that at least some of the power, verve and richness of language that went into the telling of the story has come through.

PEOPLE WHOSE PERSONAL RECOLLECTIONS MADE THIS BOOK

Isaac Angell former chairman, Independent Ladies' Tailors Union.

Albert Arnison rank and file foundry workers' leader, Lancashire.

Arthur Attwood former LAC, RAF, active in the air force demobilisation movement, 1946.

Charles Blackley secretary, Manchester District Council, National Union of Railwaymen.

Lord Will Blyton former Labour MP and Durham miners' leader.

George Bolton Scottish miner, pit official.

Isobel Brown Communist organiser, rank and file leader in 1930 woollen textile strike.

Anette Brownlie shop stewards' convener, BSR factory, East Kilbride.

Les Buck general secretary, Nation Union of Sheet-metal Workers.

Joe Byrne former branch official, Transport and General Workers Union, Liverpool docks.

John Campbell Scottish miner.

Leonard R. Chandler Post Office telephonist, Guildford.

Jack Clements (Jack Melville) music hall artiste (retired).

John Collinson Durham miner.

Frank Cornthwaite shop steward, Lansil Textile factory, Lancaster.

Jim Crump former Birmingham Amalgamated Engineering Union shop steward.

Jack Dash London dockers' rank and file leader (retired).

Ben Davies former lodge official, Banwen pit, Seven Sisters, South Wales.

Bessie Dickenson weaver, Burnley and Nelson (retired).

Harold Dickenson former Burnley Weavers Amalgamation secretary.

Charles Doyle former Battersea power station shop steward, rank and file power workers' leader.

Alf Drury former engineer and regular soldier.

I. Eisenstone former organiser, Independent Cabinet Makers' Union.

Dick Etheridge Austin Motors shop stewards' leader.

Dai Dan Evans general secretary, South Wales area, National Union of Mineworkers (retired).

Edgar Evans of Bedlinog, unofficial leader in strikes at Taff Merthyr pit, South Wales in the 1930s.

Sid Fineman secretary, No. 15 branch, National Union of Furniture Trade Operatives (retired).

Simon Fraser secretary, Liverpool Trades Council.

Jim Gardner former secretary of the Foundry Workers Union.

Alf Garrard former rank and file building worker.

John Green Amalgamated Engineering Union shop steward, Roberts Arundel, Stockport.

Rt Hon. James Griffiths, CH former South Wales miners' president.

Les Gurl Morris Motors, Oxford shop steward, secretary of British Leyland Trade Union Executive Committee.

G. Maurice Hann, CBE former general secretary, National Union of Shop Assistants.

Councillor Finlay Hart shop steward, Clyde shipyards (retired).

Harry Hitchings former convenor of Amalgamated Engineering Union, GKN, Cardiff.

George Hodgkinson former Labour leader, Coventry City Council, and shop steward.

Harriet Hopper shop steward, Plessey, Sunderland.

J. F. Howell branch secretary, National Union of Agricultural Workers, Walsingham.

Fred Hoyle former branch official, Transport and General Workers Union, Avonmouth docks.

Albert Irons, BEM secretary, National Union of Railwaymen, Paddington (retired).

Rt Hon. George Isaacs, JP, DL former Minister of Labour, general secretary of National Society of Operative Printers Assistants.

Frank Jackson rank and file building worker (retired).

George James executive member of National Union of Railwaymen, railway workshop man (retired).

Hywel Jeffreys (Jeff Camnant) retired miner and farmer, Seven Sisters, South Wales.

Hywel Jeffreys retired miner and mining lecturer.

J. W. (Bill) Jones member of Executive Committee, Transport and General Workers Union, former London busmen's leader.

Arthur Kahl branch official, Transport and General Workers Union, Liverpool docks.

Dick Kelley Labour MP for Don Valley, former Yorkshire miners' pit official.

B   17

Peter Kerrigan former Glasgow engineers' leader, Minority Movement and Communist Party organiser.

Arthur W. J. Lewis Labour MP for West Ham North, former General and Municipal Workers' union official.

Mrs H. E. Lewis farmer's wife of Iddesleigh, Devon.

Dr John Lewis former lecturer and Presbyterian minister in Gravesend and Birmingham.

Jack R. Longworth divisional organiser, Amalgamated Engineering Union (retired).

Bob Lovell district secretary, Amalgamated Engineering Union (retired).

Brian Mathers Midlands regional secretary, Transport and General Workers Union.

Jessie McCullough former Lucas factory worker.

Margaret Milligan shop steward, BSR, East Kilbride.

Abe Moffatt Scottish area National Union of Mineworkers president (retired).

E. Mofshovitz former organiser, United Clothing Workers Union.

Megan Morgan daughter of John Morgan, miners' leader, Ynysybwl.

Pat Murphy rank and file seamen's leader, Cardiff.

Dick Nettleton former apprentice leader, 1941 apprentices' strike.

Walter Nugent chairman 6/541 branch, Transport and General Workers Union.

Roger O'Hara former strike leader, Shell Star construction site, Ellesmere Port.

Will Paynter former general secretary, National Union of Mineworkers.

Rev. Simon Phipps, Bishop of Horsham former industrial chaplain.

John Potter strike leader, Pilkington's, St Helens, 1970.

Ernie Pountney former shop assistants' union organiser.

Jimmy Reid Convener of shop stewards, Upper Clyde Shipbuilders.

Councillor Hugh Reynolds former miners' lodge official, Plean, Stirlingshire.

Alex Robson rank and file seamen's leader, Middlesborough.

Ted Rolph, MBE, JP National Union of Furniture Trade Operatives (retired).

R. E. Scouller former official, National Union of Clerks, Glasgow.

Jim Slater official, National Union of Seamen.

Bob Stewart   rank and file building worker of Dundee.

W. H. Stokes, CBE, JP   divisional organiser, Amalgamated Engineering Union. (retired).

Billie Swindlehurst   shop steward, Lansil Textile factory, Lancaster.

Cyril Taylor   former divisional organiser, Amalgamated Engineering Union.

Bill Warman   district secretary of Sheet-metal Workers Union.

Sarah Wesker   (the late) former official of Ladies' Tailors Union.

J. Withers   London machine branch, National Society of Operative Printers and Assistants.

George Wylie   official of Amalgamated Society of Woodworkers, Newcastle.

For information and advice in preparing this book, I am very grateful to the following people: R. Page Arnot, Maurice Blaston, Frank Deegan, David Evans, Eddie Frow, Ken Graves, Horace Green, Gwen Holmes, Julie Jacobs, Idris John, Arthur Jones, Terry Lacey, Alex McCrindle, W. McLafferty, Douglas Miller, Arthur Milligan, Jane Morgan, D. N. Pritt, QC, Eddie Roberts, A. H. Shepherd and Jack Williams.

I am also grateful to the Press Dept, staff of the Department of Employment and Productivity for their help in obtaining strike statistics.

CHAPTER ONE

1887-1914

Early Starters

When this story opens, Queen Victoria is celebrating her Jubilee and Gladstone is Prime Minister; General Booth has coined the phrase 'the submerged tenth' to describe the poor, W. T. Stead has just exposed child prostitution, and, as we shall see, children of ten are still working in the mills. A well-to-do couple may spend 50 per cent more a year on their clothes than on the wages of four servants.

Britain has around one million trade unionists, about one-third the number of domestic servants. This million is split up between nearly a thousand unions, mainly small and exclusive craft unions; their leaders usually vote Liberal and sometimes even serve as minor bureaucrats in Gladstone's administration. Strikes are, where possible, strictly controlled by the union officials. Just over a quarter of a century later, with Victoria and Edward gone, Lloyd George's Liberal government has introduced Labour Exchanges and national insurance and other first moves in the direction of the Welfare State.

The unskilled and semi-skilled have invaded the trade union movement through the new 'general unions', boosting membership to four million. Spurred on by hostile legal judgements depriving them of funds and freedom, the trade union movement has entered the political scene, setting up the Labour Party. The notion of one industry, one union, pioneered by popular leaders like Tom Mann, brings a new element into the craft versus general union struggle. As the cost of living escalates in the three years before 1914, a strike wave of unprecedented size rolls round the country.

BOB STEWART
Rank and file building worker of Dundee

I was an early starter, you might say. I was standing one day
outside Mitchell's jute mill, in Dundee, ready to go in for my
half-time stint. I was ten at the time, which would make it around
1887, and I worked one day at work and went one day to school.
We'd a ten hour day, six to six with two breaks for breakfast and
dinner, and the school was inside the factory grounds. You got
3s 4d in a long week and 2s 9d in a short week. When you were
13 or 14, if you passed the fifth standard, you could start as a full
timer, 56 hours for 6s 8d a week, or thereabouts: the rates were all
different and they were all low.

As I say, we were standing outside the factory when a procession
passed the gates, scholars from the Academy protesting about
homework; they were on strike apparently. It didn't matter to us
little fellers, we just walked off and joined in. We were punished
afterwards by being sent to school, lost our day's pay and got it
from our parents when they found out at the weekend.

All the poor people sent their children as half-timers. Only
craftsmen sent their children to school full-time. We were
'shifters', employed by the bobbin setters to shift the bobbins.
You didn't have a name, all you were called was 'lazy young bugger'
and the shifting wifie had a leather strap to keep you moving. The
shifting wifie also had a spree in her house at the end of the year,
to which the others contributed and this was where the half-
timers learnt to drink.

There were many stoppages that never went outside the mill,
stoppages over bad thread or hard fibres. The women were outside
the unions and notoriously difficult to organise. We shifters had
our own little ways of getting out of work, a little bit of sabotage:
put a match in the right place, get a wee fire going among the waste,
then all run about for water to put it out. This all went on for many
years. It was 1900 or thereabouts before the half-time system was
smashed.

But I started in real earnest when I was apprenticed to the
building trade as a joiner, a wood butcher, and my first strike was
a personal one. It was a terrible winter and I was spending my
time shifting snow off roofs and cleaning gutters. Come Saturday I

got my apprentice pay, four or five bob, and went down to the office to tell them I wanted labourer's pay for labourer's work. 'You'll get your lines,' I was told. 'I'll take my lines', I said and that was my one-man strike finished. It split my apprenticeship in two and I finished it off in the shipyards. In the meantime, though, I helped my brothers form the first carters' union in Dundee. Organising gets into your system. The craftsmen in my home town were well organised, but labourers were thought to be un-organisable. Generally speaking the labourer was regarded as an adjunct to the craftsmen and wouldn't be taken into the union. They were looked down on: I remember one newspaper report 'Accident: two men and a labourer killed'. But this attitude brought its own problems.

Amongst the bitterest strikes in my home town were those between unions, generally arising through a development of technique that made a semi-skilled man capable of looking after a machine. He was cheaper than the craftsman, so the craftsman who thought the machine belonged to him was unseated. I joined the Amalgamated Society of Carpenters and Joiners. There were also the Associated Society and the General Union, and other smaller unions confined to one city. They only amalgamated later after a lot of difficulties.

In the shipyard in Dundee, a man came in to operate a machine the joiners had considered their own. Since the new man was paid a ha'penny an hour less than the craftsman, the joiners struck. The executive committee wouldn't sanction the strike and so we had to give in. Nobody wanted to go to the boss and say we'd given in, so I was sent in as the youngest. I went in to the boss, Mr Charles Gourlay, a real gentleman, beautifully dressed.

'I've come on behalf of the joiners to tell you we've been defeated.'

'That's all right,' he said, 'someone has to win.'

'Yes and it's generally you,' I said. I was a cheeky bugger.

Shipyard or building site it was often the same, the masons out the joiners working, or the joiners out and the painters working. The shops would be well organised within the trades, but there was no concerted action between them and a lot of jealousy about things that didn't matter a damn. Some strikes were official, some unofficial, generally over within an hour after a talk with the foreman. If you were a hard-working delegate there were plenty of opportunities to stop work, if you didn't close your eyes to them. We had an overtime limit of 20 hours a month; anything over had to be sanctioned by the union branch. There was constant friction over that, for the gaffers had their little group of cronies set up in one of the bars, who never came to the branch. I would refuse to sanction more overtime until everyone had had their chance or at least it had been discussed in the branch. Even when foremen were society members they would have their favourites. It was all very puzzling to me as a young fellow, why one section would come out on strike and stop all others, while other conditions would be dealt with by a nod and a wink from the gaffer. If only workers would all come out together. . . .

When the Boer War came, I worked on Salisbury Plain building cantonments. There were men there from all over Britain, out of work in their own towns. You never left the site. You slept on the beds as you put them up. A big proportion of the men were from Belfast and it was Belfast No. 1 branch says this, Belfast No. 1 says that. Well, I thought, Belfast isn't on Salisbury Plain. I called a meeting, got up on a pile of planks and played hell for a penny more an hour. But the Belfast men said 'No: we've agreed on ninepence. I agitated among the Scots, sent a delegation to the boss and he sacked the delegation. So I demanded we should strike the job. But nobody moved and an old fellow, McMasters, said to me 'After what you've said about Belfast, they'll kill you. Best pack your bags.'

So, by 1903 I was in Cape Town, setting up an industrial exhibition. I went on a job, asked what the wages were, 10s, and the standard rate was 14s. Can't have that, I thought. I called a meeting and told them the tale, but all that happened was I got the sack. Men who were good trade unionists then were prepared to blackleg in times of depression. You can scent trouble on a job and you can let it pass; at least it's a job. I never felt like letting things pass. But the union leaders' main aim in life was conserving the funds, bettering conditions short of strikes. Generally men who rose to the top in the union were the ones well screwed down, with steady jobs, wanting to conserve the funds for sick, super-annuation and funeral benefits. They all wanted to be buried decently. The old fellows were always against a strike for fear they'd lose their superannuation. My experience was that far from men dying to go out on strike they didn't want to strike even when they had good reason, wanting a steady job even if it meant giving the gaffer the whip hand. In those days there were no shop stewards and shop stewards' committees in factories or building sites. There would be, in our trade, a delegate elected by the branch and he could only call out the men in his own trade, sometimes after waiting weeks for executive committee sanction.

Then it would be bricklayers out and joiners in, no united action. You didn't take the strike vote on the job in those days, either, but in the branch where you would also have men from other jobs, with other interests. Men had a terrible fear of losing their jobs. It never overcame me. I've never been so in love with work that I wasn't prepared to tell the gaffer to go to hell. The gaffer knows who he's dealing with and often he'll appreciate it if you stand up for the men. You don't lose in the end. At least that's how I found it. Anyhow, I began to get a local reputation and people would call on me whenever there was a strike.

All over the country 1911 was a year of troubles, a cheapening of the price of gold, money losing its value, strikes in Leith, Liverpool; all the ports were out, big and small strikes up and down the country. In Dundee, the carters began it, and when the carters struck it meant jute supplies for the mills stopped. And when the mills stopped there was a tremendous concourse of people; it was a job to keep them out of trouble and keep them entertained. We would start at ten in the morning and go on until ten at night, with relays of speakers in the market, a general tumult all round with lasses from the mills marching up the town. I saw Tom Mann there with half a dozen women on each arm, the first time I ever saw him, singing:

'When the workers take their place at the top of the tree
And the loafer is somewhere down below.'

I went to the music hall and asked the entertainers there to help. Singers and dancers from the theatre came down and performed and helped keep the crowds intact for a whole week. There was one lorry loaded with tins; someone cut the rope and the whole lot came down, so the police hit out and the first casualty was a postman on his round who got a bump on the head. As the strike blossomed out and the town closed down, the mill lasses were running wild, and the authorities got scared and moved troops into the local drill hall. The police got nastier and there was a serious situation. There were dockers in the crowd with bale hooks they used to lift two hundredweight bales, ready to have a rip at the police.

So, while the carters' leaders were in the Town Hall, negotiating with the employers, we kept the crowd in a good humour. We never abused the police, just made fun of them. You talked about anything that came into your head, the strike, the local council, Parliament, teaching them to stand together, come out together and go back together, all in one boat, not to think of one another as Catholic and Protestant but workers. And that was how it was, just before the 1914–18 war, the poor and the unskilled kicking over the traces, though often with little notion of how to organise, and the skilled workers all too often just looking after their own organisation. And so people would turn to whoever would help them.

After 1914 there was more pressure on the worker, more giving away by full-time officials of things already won and more battles to hang on to what you'd got. Wartime saw the beginnings of the shop stewards' movements; works committees they called them. But it also saw other things. It brought people into the factories who'd never been there before, fishermen, farmers. They didn't understand anything of factory discipline. They were used to stopping work when there was no fishing, and if something went wrong at the factory, they'd simply walk out and go home. That's just what happened with fishermen drafted into a foundry near Dundee. Now, during the war, under the Munitions Act, this was treason, and of course these poor fellers were hauled up before the Tribunal. They came to me to ask my help, and I went with them before the Tribunal.

Now the important thing with such bodies, presided over by people who seem so very important, is not to let them imagine you feel inferior, but to treat them like equals. So I would never stand up in front of the chairman, but take out a chair, sit down by him and talk to him like a Dutch uncle, point out that these men were unorganised, and inexperienced, that they were paid less than the rate for that reason. I would suggest to him that what everyone wanted was to get the men back to work and the best way was not to victimise them. And in most cases I would get them off. Afterwards the men would take up a collection and bring it to me and say 'Here's something for your trouble, I'd always say 'No trouble at all, I was enjoying myself'. And I'd tell them to keep their money, and to go and join the union.

And that's the way it went, getting involved, sorting things out. There was always some trouble, large or small; you could get mixed up in it or stay out. Of course I was interfering, but if the union in question had been doing its job, then these men would have been in it. The trouble was that some officials wanted the union no bigger than would keep them in a nice respectable job, which was why most of them shunned strikes. But it is only in a strike you have a chance to see who is a good trade unionist, especially if it brings more people into the union. In the strike each man can play a part, do a job, they become better trade unionists in a week because they are working for the union than they would in a year simply by holding a card. So I never hesitated to go in where my help was asked.

FRANK JACKSON
Rank and file building worker (retired)

Mind your own business, that was what I was taught when I was apprenticed in 1902. Though it didn't make much impression. One day, while I was still an apprentice, I was sent to one job and I was told beforehand, 'There's some trouble on the job; the brickies and labourers have a row on with old "Grumble guts". Take no notice of anyone, just get on and lay the flooring upstairs.' But when I got there, I found the brickies all outside in the street with the boss on a scaffold, haranguing them.

One of the brickies swore at him and challenged him to come down and fight it out. He came down from inside the house, and a labourer swarmed up the scaffolding and, as the boss came out from under, the boards were pushed by the labourer and a load of bricks came down on the boss and knocked him out flat. No work was done that day.

When my own boss complained, I told him I wasn't going on a job when the brickies were outside. But when I told my father about it, I got a bouncing off him. He was President of the Amalgamated Society of Carpenters and Joiners, and he told me I should keep my nose out of other people's affairs. If the brickies stopped work, that was their business and I should keep out.

27

And mind your own business was the rule for us youngsters inside the branch. There were three or four of us apprentices and we were not allowed to take part in the discussion. We had to listen to all the philosophy and wisdom of the older folk. Naturally I rebelled against that and in 1908 I started travelling the country on my own and got a job in the Tredegar Iron and Coal Co. building new offices. While I was there, through a tinplate worker I came in touch with the Industrial Advocates of Great Britain. Their idea was to form groups in various unions advocating unity. They were getting a big response in South Wales and I was all for it. I heard at the time there was a big building job on in Cardiff and so I carted my tools down there and started. I'd been on the job four or five days when a fellow came up to me and said 'You in the union?' 'I'm in the ASCJ.' 'What's that? Never heard of them. It's no bloody good here. This is a General Union job. You'd better join that.'

Well, I'd never heard of the General Union, for Coventry was an ASCJ town. So I refused and heard no more till the following Monday, when the foreman who'd set me on told me I'd have to go or there'd be a strike on the job. I'd no choice but to pack up and move on, but it gave me an even bigger urge to advocate industrial unity. I roamed round Cardiff for two or three weeks before I got a job on a housing estate, where it was all non-union labour. I got one or two of the fellows together and contacted the ASCJ organiser in Cardiff for them to join. But he said he'd have to report the whole matter. He couldn't take new members in just like that. We got fed up with waiting and a bit later came out on strike for a penny an hour increase. We went to the ASCJ branch and the secretary's response was 'You won't get it you know. Why if you get another penny you'll have more than all the other blokes in Cardiff.' Eventually, he came down to the site and took one or two into the union, but then told them 'No benefits till you've been in 12 months'.

Well, the strike ended and the boss wanted us to work an hour extra in the evenings. The others went back on those conditions, but I wouldn't. So I packed in and set off tramping round Wales for two years, and when I got fed up tramping around I landed in London, round about 1910. There was no work in the building trade and so I found a job as a coachbuilder until just before the First World War broke out.

In 1913, I suppose around Christmas time, I got a job on the Pearl Insurance Building going up in Holborn. But while I'd been wandering around changes had been taking place in the ideas of the militants.

The old 'Industrial Advocates', which was a separate organisation, was now dead. Now we had Amalgamation Committees in the various building unions to try and bring them together. We used to meet at break times in a hut on the site and discuss the need for amalgamation. But the foreman on the job was a General Union man and when a new extension was planned, he reckoned to use it to get his own union members on to the job and keep others out. But we had a strike and the foreman got the clip. After this the Master Builders Organisation decided they'd had enough of us. The Pearl site was closed down and the Master Builders demanded that everyone employed had to sign a document saying they would not 'quit their employment because any of their fellow employees is or is not a member of any trade society'. Under a lot of pressure from the members the union officials decided to issue a call not to sign and in February 1914, all the building workers in London were locked out.

Once the lockout started, the militants came to the fore. They knew one another through the amalgamation committees and after the first few days of confusion the districts all over London were electing dispute committees. These in the main were new men, not the old branch secretaries. A central lockout committee was formed, and a financial committee. The official union funds went broke after the first month and the lockout committees carried on for six months raising money with social events, marches with banners, collecting boxes at football matches, organ grinders in the streets. Of course the old officials didn't like it and there were some clashes. One full-time official was thrown down his own stairs by the rank and file.

By August 1914 the bosses had had enough. They withdrew the document, brought the wages up to 9d–10d an hour and when war broke out we were back at work. But there were bigger changes still to come and the funny thing was that the war helped to bring them on, to bring the unions together and bring more men into the unions.

RT HON. JAMES GRIFFITHS, CH
Former South Wales miners' president

'Surely they ought to know that there are only two things you must do in life, join the union, and die.' That's what I recall one old miner saying when he read in the newspaper about a strike somewhere against non-unionists. For us in South Wales, in the anthracite coalfield particularly, the union was the community. Indeed you cannot begin to understand a strike in mining unless you understand the valley communities, each cut off from one another, where everyone, miners, doctors, insurance agents, newsagents, Co-op, everyone is linked to the pit and goes up or down according to its fortunes. People in the valleys were fused together by a suppressed feeling of common danger; it was the essence of good behaviour, for example, that a collier never spoke of the dangers of the pit in front of his boy. This shared feeling found expression in the fellowship of the community, something you grew up with from the time you were a child.

My first strike came in 1904, when I was a boy of 15; my father made me a member of the union when I started work. In the anthracite coalfield the colliers work on the pillar and stall method, leaving a pillar to support the roof and hewing out a stall – sounds like horses. With each collier worked a boy, who had specific duties. One of these was to get clay for ramming the shot, there was a lot of shot firing. For some weeks there had been no supply of clay, and in its place, the boys had to collect stone dust, coal dust, horse droppings, human droppings, and make a mixture of it. The mixture made us sick and we demanded 'smell money', and we got it after a strike of about a week.

So it was natural for anyone growing up in the valleys to become accustomed from the earliest age to disputes, strikes and the importance of the power of the union. I recall very well a meeting which took place in 1905 before the general election campaign that gave the Liberals their landslide victory. It was a ten minute meeting at the head of the slant, where the men always paused for a while before going on towards the coal-face. This period was called in Welsh *mwcin gweld*, 'a spell to see', a period to enable the eyes to grow accustomed to the darkness. On this occasion, the elders of the lodge were reporting to the men that they had interviewed all the Liberal candidates (we had no Labour candidates at that time). All the Liberal candidates had been told that the miners would vote for them if they would pledge that when they were returned to Parliament they would vote against the Taff Vale Judgement[1]. The miners would vote Liberal on this understanding, whether they were church or chapel, whether for disestablishment of the church or not. The important thing was that what was called the 'Judge's Law' must be repealed. The sense conveyed by the lodge chairman was that in the present state of affairs, since the Taff Vale Judgement, if we struck, the union could be robbed of its funds and that would be the end of it. We were fighting for the life of the union and we were to vote Liberal to save the union.

The union was growing in strength throughout these years and in the spring of 1912, the Miners Federation called its first national strike.

To us in the South Wales anthracite area, the question was one of principle. The main demand was for a minimum wage. But in the anthracite we had what was called in Welsh a consideration wage, by which those who could not earn the basic wage on piece-work, due to abnormal conditions, got a consideration, a percentage that went up and down with the price of coal. In the Rhondda, we knew, there was no consideration wage, and this was very bad. So we were fighting for others. It was a tremendous battle going on through March, April and May. The Co-op announced that they would give credit and since the Co-op was the big competitor, local tradesmen had to follow suit and give credit. Then it was discovered that wives and children could get relief on loan from the parish, relief which had to be paid back through wages later on. In years to come, when wages slumped again, people were taken to court to pay twopence or threepence a week.

But the strike ended with the passage of the Minimum Wages Act of 1912, and the anthracite miners had to decide whether to use the Minimum Wages Act or to use the old system. As one leader put it 'Make new friends but keep the old', and so the question was resolved in a practical way, using whatever gave the best results.

[1] In 1901 the Taff Vale Railway Co. secured damages of £23,000 from the Amalgamated Society of Railway Servants, after a strike. This 'Judgement' stimulated unions into political action.

Three years later, when I was in my twenties, I was elected pit delegate; it was thought that we should have younger men. And that year we were on strike again in South Wales, in what we called 'the six for five strike'. In 1908 the eight hour day shift system had become general, 6–2, 2–10, 10–6. There was no Saturday afternoon and no Sunday working, of course, and we only got five days' pay. We said that there should be six days' pay for five days' work. We were out for six days, as a matter of fact, and we got our six for five.

You must remember, however, that by then the country was at war. We knew the Press was against us, but the impact of the outside world on our thinking was not direct. It was not until later, with the Battle of the Somme, and the Battle of Suvla Bay when the local territorial regiment was sent to Gallipoli and one quarter of the boys were killed, that the war made its direct impact on the community.

But one thing we were aware of. Under the Defence of the Realm Act, DORA it was called, we were liable to be fined for going on strike. I had to report back to our lodge, which always met in a pub (the miners' welfare halls came later in our area) and it was impressed on me by the union that I should tell the men, explain very carefully, that while the strike lasted each man could be fined £5 a day, and that if he did not pay, he would go to jail. The unanimous decision was to go out on strike. Lloyd George himself, who was Minister of Munitions, came down to Cardiff, and made a speech about 'the black diamonds of Britain'. But we stood firm and we got our six for five and never heard any more about the £5 fine. We had been out for six days and all owed £30. The introduction of penalties failed at the first attempt, which was a measure of how deeply we felt on the question. And indeed working people will always be influenced most strongly by what affects them most directly; the threat of penalties will not stop them, any more than hardship will if they are determined to fight.

HYWEL JEFFREYS
Retired miner and mining lecturer

The miners suffered in those early days. To be on strike meant real hardship, though in our district, every miner had his garden and at least one pig, quite a number were miners and farmers, and so they were able to hold out better when they were on strike. And people would stand together. I can recall, during the 1898 strike, a few people carried on working at the Abercrave Colliery and the miners and their families turned out in their thousands and marched on the houses where those people lived. I had just started underground as a boy in that year. My earnings were 1s 8d a day for a 54 hour week. We didn't see daylight during the week at all. Many would have to get up between 4.30 and 5. am. and walk miles to reach the pit in time for work. Life was hard, but the sense of community was very strong.

We would hold socials and entertainments. People would write essays, sing or give recitations. We would all be given numbers and when your number was called, you had to speak on a subject for three minutes. Some were good musicians and developed to Eisteddfod standards. Mabon[1] who led the South Wales miners was a good singer, and on one occasion he sang 'Land of My Fathers' with Madame Patti on the stage at the Eisteddfod. She said to him 'Sir, you are a very good singer', and he replied 'Madame, so are you'. Mabon was a decent man, and so was Brace.[2] Brace looked a real gentleman, as though he had never been underground in his life. Nearly all the leaders, like Mabon and Brace, were liberals and lay preachers. Everyone was a Nonconformist and voted *en bloc* for the Liberal party. Indeed, my grandfather, who lived on a little farm on the Gwyn estate, and was a Radical, was turned off his farm during the first secret ballot, and that is why we came here to Colbren. So, when I grew up there were only Liberals and Tories. The Nonconformists were mostly Liberals and most of the Nonconformists were miners.

Mabon was in the old Welsh tradition of Liberal nonconformism, because the squire and the official church were Tory. Under people like Mabon the union and the chapel together were the conscience of the community in the valleys. Maybe they were a bit narrow-minded, but their moral influence brought South Wales together. I'll give you some idea of this religious influence. When I was a boy, when the miners paused underground to give their eyes a chance to get accustomed to the dark, the men would

[1] Bardic name of W. J. Abraham, South Wales miners' President for many years until 1912.
[2] William Brace, succeeded Abraham.

gather to discuss things. On Monday it would always be the quality of the sermon preached in chapel the night before. The old men were real biblical scholars and the young men respected their word.

The big challenge began to come to the leadership of this generation with what we called the 'Rhondda extremists', who blossomed forth around the time of the 1912 strike, men like Mainwaring[1] and later Cook.[2] Conditions in the Rhondda were much harsher than here in West Wales and the struggle was fiercer. I think the extremists were to some extent anti-religious. I remember some of the Rhondda leaders saying all churches and chapels should be closed and given over to secular use. When the 1912 strike came I had already left the pits and had gone to Cardiff college as a mining student. Later I became a mining lecturer. Glamorganshire had a very good scheme by which classes were held in the evening when the miners came home. After the Eight Hour Day Act had come into force, young boys in Seven Sisters would attend classes.

Quite a lot of miners never believed that the eight hour day would come; in fact, one old man made a bet with me it wouldn't. We had a little rhyme in Welsh, which went more or less like this:

> *Eight hours to work*
> *Eight hours to play*
> *Eight hours sleep*
> *And eight shillings a day.*

Eight shillings a day was considered a desirable goal in those days. Miners earning 30 shillings for a 54 hour week were thought to be well paid. Of course, mind you, things were cheaper. In the 1912 strike, soup kitchens were opened in the elementary school. I happened to be secretary of one and we worked out what a meal would cost per head; fourpence ha'penny – imagine that.

[1] W. H. Mainwaring, later Labour MP. He died in 1971.
[2] A. J. Cook, leader of the miners in the 1926 General Strike.

SID FINEMAN
Secretary of a branch of the National Union of Furniture Trade Operatives (retired)

Ask for a penny ha'penny an hour, get offered a ha'penny, settle for a penny; that was the way things would go in the East End furniture trade. Mind you, beer was a penny a pint and you could have a bread and cheese meal for twopence ha'penny. But hours were long, and conditions were rough. The trade was mainly small shops, three-man, five-man, eight-man, few with machinery. A lot of the workers came from abroad, Poland and Russia. When I became union branch secretary we had the minutes in English and Yiddish as well and I had to learn to speak and write it to do the job. Though there would be people who would claim I hadn't said the same in English as I said in Yiddish. The members were mainly refugees, very emotional people, but ready for a fight, sometimes with each other. Meetings were big and crowded, people would shout at the top of their voices. I remember one man shouted from the floor 'You talk like a guv'nor's man' and the chairman took his mallet, threw it and knocked him out.

When we were very small, my father was chairman of the union, and I remember one strike, where we'd been for some days without money. Then my Dad picked up the money from the branch, brought home a loaf and butter and went out for a walk with Mum. There were five of us. I was the oldest, at 12. You can imagine how hungry we were. When Dad and Mum came back, there was no loaf. Dad looked at Mum and said: 'I think we'd better go to sleep, Mother'.

I was glad to go to school on Monday. I went to the Jewish Free School, run by Rothschild. You got a crust and a glass of milk but you had to say thank you first and tell them you'd said your prayers.

Money was always tight and when there was a strike in 1905 the union had no money to pay out. My father persuaded two or three provision merchants for three or four weeks to give food in exchange for tokens, which the union redeemed after the strike, provided you traded with them.

But the hardest strike in those days was at Isaac Griew's. He was one of the bigger employers. The union rate was 10d an hour, but the best he would give was 9½d an hour for a 54½ hour week, if work was assured. The strike went on for about three months in 1909 and the shop was completely blocked. No trade union labour would go there. It was a terrible struggle. With strikers holding funeral services in the evening outside the blacklegs' houses. One man had such a hell of a time that his wife made him move out of the East End. When he moved his furniture, the wardrobe was so big it had to be lowered through the window and as it came down to the ground, the strikers seized it and smashed it up.

Strangely enough, in the 1920s, when I was a full time union officer, Isaac Griew's son would let us hold meetings inside his factory.

I. EISENSTONE
Former organiser of the Independent Cabinet Makers Union

When I came to London in 1907 the furniture trade in the East End was in a high state of disorganisation. People were working 75 hours and more a week and wages were horrible, 7d an hour for some. I became chairman of our Independent Cabinet Makers Union and would go round the shops after I finished work, stand outside and get the men together for a meeting. At first we had 70 members but soon we had 500 members and then we started to declare strikes. I told the members, 'It is futile to have more wages. You are working too long hours, you cease thinking and become slaves.' We wanted a 52½ hour week with the same wage which would be a big increase. We got this in a few shops, small ones. Then we tackled a bigger shop, with 12 men.

At the same time the Jewish masters with the help of the English masters organised an employers' federation and sent us a letter declaring a lockout of our members. We accepted the challenge. We had 600 members in the union and £70 in the funds. We called a meeting and made a levy of those working of one shilling in the pound. I went to see Alex Gossip, leader of the National Amalgamated Furnishing Trades Alliance and he agreed to call out any shop where there were Jewish members. The fight lasted six weeks, and it was quite remarkable because even people who were not members paid the levy and we covered our expenses. Eventually there was a conference of employers and the union and

I objected to signing an agreement with one of the bosses there. He was a cunning man always interfering in our affairs. He had been in jail for receiving. So they objected to one of our delegates because he had been in Siberia. But we told them 'we're proud of that'. After two conferences we signed a proper agreement for a 52½ hour week. But I objected to one man. He had done work for Maples and Maples had told him to send the men out or he would lose his contract with them. It was agreed he should be fined. He paid £5. I took that £5 and with £5 we had in the funds I went straight round to Ben Tillett and gave it to him for the dockers' strike fund.

Our people were always generous. Soon afterwards, there was a lockout in the furniture trade in High Wycombe. At one of our meetings we voted to send £50, practically the last £50 in the funds, to the members in High Wycombe.

Yes, we had plenty of battles in those days. And it wasn't until later we had a full-time working delegate. I was elected to that job with 500 votes, and the next man got 80. We had strikes all the time up to the war (when I joined the Flying Corps), and as a result our people could earn a living as a decent person.

TED ROLPH, MBE, JP
National Union of Furniture Trade Operatives (retired)

The unrest in other trades was bound to affect the furnishing industry and before 1913 a number of high-grade craftsmen, wood carvers, upholsterers, intelligent men, had moved into High Wycombe and formed a branch of the Independent Labour Party. They created all kinds of local upheavals over things like the closing of footpaths. When the Tories fought the 1910 General Election on tariff reform they organised a local exhibition of imported furniture, thinking they would stir up local feeling. But the radicals took the Tory furniture out and burnt it and the Mayor, a well-known furniture manufacturer, had to read the Riot Act.

But what sparked off the dispute was a row over the price of tip up seats in cinemas. For the cinematograph had begun to boom. There was plenty of discontent. There were no agreed times for starting and leaving off in the industry, no overtime payments, no negotiated prices, very harsh conditions. Soon three firms were stopped simultaneously over piecework prices and in October 1913, the local employers who had banded together in a federation, gave an ultimatum. Take it or leave it, they said. We realised this wasn't any ordinary dispute. I don't suppose more than one in eight of the workers were in the union and so people came in from outside to help us. Fred Bramley, who was later head of the TUC, became dispute organiser. We formed a dispute committee and presented a new schedule of wages to the employers association. The employers answered by demanding that those on strike go back to work, and offered lower rates. We demanded a 54 hour week, overtime rates and travelling allowances, because people came from miles around to High Wycombe. By the end of November 32 firms had posted lockout notices.

It went on for three months through that winter. We had a marvellous system of picketing with High Wycombe divided into four districts.

Very few blacklegs got through, though they tried to bring them in from all round. We had a Vigilance Committee that sorted them out and quite a number of people went to jail for certain things, though when they came out they were treated like heroes. The Metropolitan police were drafted in and there were some pretty rough times on the picket line. We used to throw glass marbles from the top of ginger beer bottles under the horses' hooves. These boys today who think they invented ideas like that don't know half of it.

We established kitchens in various places, pubs, church halls; shopkeepers, charitable organisations and local chapels made donations. The local Co-ops recognised chits issued by the disputes committee for hardship cases, people with so many children. All sorts of people came in from outside to give a hand, including plenty who thought the revolution was just round the corner. Herbert Morrison came in for the new *Daily Herald*. There were plenty of social activities. Wycombe Wanderers Football Club turned itself into a dispute football club to raise money. We had sports events. Squads went round with collecting boxes, walking miles; it was amazing what they collected. We had a marvellous band that went to London to play for money. And it had other uses too. It would make a noise and march one way, drawing off the police, while our pickets were going in the other direction to deal with blacklegs.

At the start of 1914 Sir George Askwith, Chief Industrial
Commissioner, began to bring both sides together and by the end
of February there was a new agreement, better prices, shop committees and shop stewards established, mutual no victimisation
clause, etc. There was so much change that the tidying up was still
going on when the war started.

RT HON. GEORGE ISAACS, JP, DL
*Former Minister of Labour, and general secretary of the National
Society of Operative Printers' Assistants*

Looking back now over those years from 1911 to the First World
War, there was no doubt at all that the industrial pot was bubbling
over. People were asking for more money, asking for two shillings,
being offered sixpence, settling for a shilling. It only eased off
when the 1914 war started. In 1911 came the first general strike in
the printing trade. We were working 54 hours and wanted 48, and
after a lot of trouble we settled for 52$\frac{1}{2}$ (when you think of the 40
hours today). The Printing and Kindred Trades Federation had
just been formed and the strike was pretty strong in London,
though very flabby outside it. I recall, just before the New Year,
one of the biggest meetings of printers, 8,000 in the Albert Hall.
After a few weeks, we got as sick of it as the employers and it
petered out. In fact there were some employers who felt we should
never have had to go on strike to get what we were after. For some
reason we wouldn't strike the newspapers, the members in Fleet
Street were reluctant to come out. Nothing definite was said, there
was just the feeling we shouldn't deprive the public of newspapers.

I had become General Secretary of the Printing Labourers
Union in 1909 (I joined it in 1901 and I've just completed 70 years
in the union) and looking back I cannot recall any big disputes
before that 1911 period. I recall the railway strike because together
with a colleague of the London compositors I had planned a
holiday. There were no trains and so we went on bikes to the South
coast. And I recall the dockers and seamen coming out at around
the same time.

If you consider it carefully, you can see that most of the strikes
were among people who had only recently begun to organise,
unlike the craft unions. I know that when the print labourers

formed their union in the 1890s (around the time when I started work) the craftsmen thought it was a damned cheek for the labourers to organise. The print labourers like a lot of similar workers had been set off by the Great Dock Strike of 1889 for the 'Docker's tanner'.

I recall that 1889 strike, though I was only six at the time. We lived in the parish of St Luke's, where today Clerkenwell, Shoreditch and Hoxton meet. Our house was about a hundred yards from the Barbican and nearby, I remember, were craftsmen's workshops, helmet-makers to the City of London.

One day, I noticed that the Carter Paterson men were standing about outside the gates of the cartage depot at the bottom of our road. I asked my father why they were standing about and he said:

'They've stopped work.'

'Why have they stopped work?'

'Because, they're not getting enough money to keep their children.'

'But, how does "stop-work" get them more money?'

'If the boss wants them to go back to work, he has to pay them more money.'

Ours was an old print trade union family. Walter Isaacs, my great grandfather, was a typefounder and one of the organisers of the protest demonstration in 1834, against the transporting of the Tolpuddle Martyrs. He was one of the two print workers whose names appeared on the appeal. And I can recall hearing my grandfather tell my father and uncles about Chartist demonstrations, when the crowd crashed through the railings into Hyde Park.

When you compare those early days of strikes and today, you can see the changes. Then men stood around looking depressed, today, they march in procession with some pride. But in those days it took a lot of guts to be a trade unionist, whereas today, it takes a lot of guts not to be a trade unionist.

JOE BYRNE
Former branch official of Transport and General Workers' Union, at Liverpool docks

In those days you had to do anything if you wanted a job, had to be prepared to take anything. There was no dole, no unemployment money. My Dad worked on the Liverpool docks, he was Foundation Member No. 34 of the Dockworkers Union, which Tom Mann and Ben Tillett founded in the Great Dock Strike of 1889.

One day he was dragging a gunny bale on a two-wheel truck. It weighs about 12 hundredweights. As he dragged it along, bent down, his coat went up at the back, and the foreman saw his union button on his belt.

'Young man', he said, 'you've gone far enough. Out you go.'

It was hire and fire who they liked, when they liked. And the pay then was sixpence an hour, just as they won it in 1889; an hour's work for sixpence and that might be your lot for a week.

Later on in the docks, you pulled your coat up and showed your button to the union man when he came down to check only union labour was employed.

In Liverpool in the 1911 strike the big point made was for recognition of the Dockworkers Union and against the Cunard Co. which had transferred all its work to Hull, where it was half a penny cheaper per man ton. The whole lot were out, dockers, carters, seamen, railwaymen; it was known as the general strike of Liverpool. Churchill said it was not a strike but a Civil War. We lived at Seaforth (it's all docks now, but then it was sands and the townies would flock down there at the weekend). Nearby was a barracks for the Scots Greys and one Sunday I saw the Scots Greys mounted with lances and flags ride past the end of the road. Some women came to my mother and asked 'Has Patrick gone down to the meeting in town?' She said he had. 'Oh God,' they said, 'I hope he won't get hurt.'

Tom Mann had come to be Number One speaker that day. There had been religious trouble and Tom Mann marched up William Brown Street with a green and an orange sash to the Plateau to symbolise Liverpool united, Protestant and Catholic. The police were waiting inside Lime Street Station, and my Dad who was on the Plateau said to Tom 'Looks as though there's going to be trouble'. There were thousands out, it was like a Sunday outing, all in their straw hats.

The mounted police sailed out of the station and drove them right off the Plateau so they ran into the troops coming up Dale Street. The fighting went on all Sunday night and the best part of Monday. Wherever people gathered they attacked them.

Years later I was asked to chair a meeting for Tom Mann, a nice tidy little boy in my best suit. I'll never forget it; the place was packed with women in shawls, sitting on the window sills. When I introduced Tom Mann, they got off their seats and hugged and kissed him. When I got home, my Dad told me all about 1911 and Bloody Sunday; that's what they called it. Those women remembered all about it and Tom Mann leading the men.

PAT MURPHY
Rank and file Seamen's leader, Cardiff

The 1911 seamen's strike started in Liverpool, on *June 14th*, when the crews of the *Teutonic* and *Empress of Ireland* refused to sign articles. The average wage for seamen then was £4 for a 30-day month. Tom Mann, in a fighting speech, declared 'strike for justice and strike hard', and later he told the newspapers, 'The men, by their action today, have only precipitated matters and you can say that the strike has begun and will be continued until the men have won'.

No ships signed on at North Shields, where the seamen held a mass meeting and pledged themselves to stand firm. Rotterdam and Amsterdam reported that the British seamen had refused work, though the crews of three steamers in Amsterdam were dismissed through this. In Cardiff, Mr Chambers, treasurer of the National Union of Sailors and Firemen impressed on a large meeting that success depended on them working together. The Great White Star liner *Olympic* sailed from Southampton after the owners agreed to pay an increase of 10s a month to ships of the *Olympic* type. But crews of the *Union Castle* and Royal Mail Co. refused to sign on.

June 15 In Cardiff there were seven ships needing crews but there was no response from the unemployed seamen crowding the street at the Merchant Shipping Office, most of whom were coloured. Captain Tupper, one of the leaders of the union made a fighting speech appealing for determination, but he made some very nasty remarks about Chinese and Arabs, who had really stood firm with British seafarers. By now Swansea and Barry ships were held up and the police had been reinforced.

June 19 A number of strikers were charged with violently assaulting strike-breakers at Cardiff. They were fined. A meeting of the Riggers' section of the National Labourers Union resolved that they would not do any work normally done by seamen. A German and a Welshman were fined 40s and costs for smashing the windows of boarding houses which recruited scabs. The type of crimps who ran these boarding houses used to harbour cheap labour for any vessels. Men were given board, etc and provided with employment through shady agents. When the men secured work the boarding-house keepers applied to have an excessive amount deducted from the wages which they had not yet earned. Some of the Shipping Office personnel connived at this.

Tupper's racialist speech inflamed some men and caused bitter quarrels among the seamen, and agents spread rumours to inflame disunity. Two hundred and fifty of the Devonshire Regiment were drafted to Newport from Tidworth. A French Socialist, Madame Sorgue, gave valuable assistance at Aberdare and sent appeals to the Continent for help.

Glasgow dock labourers and 1,000 Tyne dockers struck in sympathy. Tonypandy coal-miners came out on strike and Keir Hardie predicted a national coal strike if the miners did not receive a living wage.

Havelock Wilson, union leader, offered the owners a truce for the ships carrying passengers from Belfast for the King's coronation. The seamen rejected this and the excursions were abandoned.

June 22 Two thousand transport workers downed tools at Goole. Glasgow Anchor line settled for a £1 increase. The Press tried to scare the strikers with stories of no strike pay, but they received 21 shillings a week. Havelock Wilson issued a manifesto declaring that if the shipowners recognised the union he was prepared to concede more favourable terms, and threatened his members with fines for questioning his actions.

Shipowner Mr Radcliffe promised to recognise the union and the SS *Windsor* and the *Clarissa Radcliffe* signed crews on £5 10s a month, the union terms. In Liverpool, carters and dock labourers boycotted coal cargoes; 400 struck for recognition of their union and abolition of non-union labour. They joined the seamen in a demonstration round the Liverpool docks, completely holding up work. Hull, Barry and Swansea railwaymen and dockers refused to handle coal cargoes.

The Scots Greys, the Staffordshire Regiment and 500 police were sent from London to Liverpool, while 500 police were drafted to Hull. There were baton charges in Hull and Manchester; in Manchester women were also involved. The Lancashire Fusiliers had been drafted into Monmouthshire. In Cardiff, police interfered with pickets and riggers, and coal tippers refused to work scab ships. Cardiff patent fuel workers, coal trimmers and many others joined the seafarers and the city was now practically at a standstill, with foundrymen, wagon workers and women in the bottling firms on strike, as well as 15,000 miners. 40,000 people met in Cathays Park and pledged to stay out till all grievances were settled. A joint committee of seamen, dockers and coal trimmers was formed and it was resolved not to settle the strike till the armed forces had been removed.

July 28 The strike was settled with recognition of the union, after 20 years resistance by the Shipping Federation. Sailors and firemen were given £5 a month standard rate. Previously companies paid various rates from £3 15s to £4 5s.

The strike was unique in that all other unions gave the seamen support, financially and otherwise. Havelock Wilson was the only one of the group who took over leadership of the Seamens Union who had any experience of marine life. There were many good militant seamen in the ports, like 'Honest' Jim Hinson of Cardiff, McVey of Liverpool and others who led the struggle for the betterment of the abject conditions which prevailed on British ships. Tom Mann, Keir Hardie, James Connolly, Jim Larkin and others inspired and gave unstinted help to the men.

It may be asked why the seamen did not demand a lowering of working hours as did the miners and blast-furnacemen at the time. We must understand the era and the nature of their mode of life which was a handicap to organisation. 'Wooden ships and iron men' was the boast. Firemen (stokers) toiled four hours on and eight off all the week round. Their job was too exhausting to work the eight hours straight through. When men were exhausted with illness, the others had to share their work, minus overtime, so the sick men would be considered 'dead-wood' by some elements. Deck hands endured duty for 12 hours a day, with extra hours thrown in for 'sanitary duties', 'safety of the ship', which could mean anything. Catering department, stewards and cooks were at the beck and call of the officers and passengers at all times.

When we advocated reforms in hours of work, even some crew members argued it was impossible. 'Where would the extra men live, who would pay them', and, 'we would have to go short', were some of the arguments put forward.

Years after the 1911 strike, Havelock Wilson threw cold water and ridicule on those who agitated for working improvements, better food, decent living accommodation, extra payment for bank-holidays, etc. Victimisation was the order of the day for those who had the temerity to protest too loudly.

ALBERT ARNISON
Rank and file foundry workers' leader, Lancashire

When the dockers and carters came out in Manchester, someone was trying to move loads of fish from Market Street when the strikers stopped them. They unhitched the waggons and turned them over. The fish was flying around Market Street, with lumps of pig iron which were pulled off trucks. The lads rushed the police, tipping them out of their saddles. My father, who was a biggish bloke, snatched a baton off a policeman and in a minute there were so many policemen on top of him you couldn't see him. There were police brought in from all over. The strikers were mostly unorganised but they were fighting for their lives. Dockers were getting three shillings a shift, and on the railways a married man was getting 16s a week. And there were so many unemployed they were squatting on waste ground, putting up huts and tents. The Press called them 'land grabbers'. There was no dole, only parish relief and that meant going to 'task work' in the municipal workhouse. If you were on relief, the parish official, a big overfed swine, would walk in while you were having breakfast. Anything on the table that hadn't been allocated and you'd be in trouble. You weren't paid money on relief but given vouchers for certain foodstuffs. And you had to take what you were given. And if you refused to go to do the task work, no relief. No wonder people were desperate.

ALBERT IRONS, BEM
Retired secretary of National Union of Railwaymen, Paddington

The 1911 railway strike was something of an uprising. It was a terrifically hot year and a series of spasmodic strikes broke out, starting in Liverpool and spreading throughout the country. I believe it started there with a demand for a shilling rise, but for many of us there were no specific demands. We took advantage of the opportunity to do something about our rotten conditions – fourpence an hour for a 10 hour day, 60 hour week, no annual holidays, getting time off only when things were slack. And railway workers were considered privileged because, though the pay was rotten, it was 'regular'.

I was working in Paddington Station, though I hadn't been long in the depot before the strike started. I was asked to join the Amalgamated Society of Railway Servants and so I did (I'd been a member of the London Car-men's Trade Union before). There were 1,000 men working in the depot and I doubt if more than a handful were in the union. We didn't seem to have any leaders, though we all stuck together. There were marches to Tower Hill and we went back all together with no victimisation. I think maybe we got a shilling a week rise.

We were damn glad to get back, but cock-a-hoop all the same and there was a big canvass for the union with 50 per cent joining the ASRS. We formed Paddington Branch and it grew so strong it was split into two branches – No. 1 for traffic, No. 2 for goods and shopmen. Of course, the ASRS was only one of five unions on the railways then. There was the General Railway Workers Union, the loco-men, the clerks union and one for points and signalmen.

In 1913, the ASRS, the General Union and the points and signalmen joined together to form the National Union of Railwaymen but the clerks and loco-men stayed outside. That year we had a go on our own in Paddington. Three drivers were dismissed for delivering flour to the wrong place, so we started the 'slow march' or go-slow, or work-to-rule as it's now called. I think we may have been the first to do it. We had no other means, there wasn't any strike pay. Anyway the men were re-instated.

ISAAC ANGELL
Former chairman of the Independent Ladies' Tailors Union

There was a general strike of the ladies' tailors in London, at around the same time as the dockers were out. We wanted the hours to come down from 56 to 52. Officially the hours were 56, but people would work up to 80 hours a week. There was no limit. Men would be called from their homes and work through the day and night. When Edward VII was buried it was called the 'schwarze busy', because all the tailors' shops were making black mourning clothes. The trade had never been so busy as it was then.

Some broke away from the Amalgamated Society of Tailors and formed the Independent Ladies' Tailors Union to fight for the shorter working week. But the 1912 was a very rush affair, not fully organised. The people in the industry weren't fully organised, though they had plenty of spirit. Lots of them came from abroad as refugees, Socialists and Bundists.[1]

The *Daily Herald*, which had just been started, came out morning and evening with special editions. Our people had a revolutionary outlook and the Independent Ladies' Tailors Union used always to stop work on May Day. We would take a band from the union office and march round the workshops, pulling them out like hot cakes.

JACK CLEMENTS 'JACK MELVILLE'
Retired music hall artiste

I was a sketch artiste with Fred Karno in those days and there were a lot of anomalies in the variety business. Agents would go round the Liberal and Radical clubs, get hold of budding comics and sign them up for £5 or £6 a week, then trade them like cattle to proprietors of music halls for £15 or £16 a week. It was called 'farming'. So there was a lot of discontent.

Music hall was in its heyday. Fred Karno had started with knockabout sketches in 1896, and by 1906 he was doing very well. He had six sketches on the road. He had a horse bus and a lovely

[1] Jewish Socialist organisation in Tsarist Russia.

47

pair of horses and we would be taken from one theatre to another. People would shout 'There goes Karnos.' They'd laugh at us even before we got in the theatre. There were 200 of us going to all the halls in London. I was appearing as Nick Sharp the detective in *The Hydro* and as the deceitful husband in *The Slavey*. Sometimes they were both in the same bill and with two houses a night it was hard work. We all got wet in the first sketch and had to dry off for the second. We thought we were being badly paid. But Karno was doing very nicely. He might take a lump sum for a sketch, say £300. With 30 people, the highest he would pay would be £4, and many of us were getting between £1 and 30s; it would pay him to keep the salaries tight.

As I said, music hall was booming; people were flocking to the theatre and it was difficult to get a seat. The Stoll and Moss Empires began about this time. There was a music hall on every corner.

One of the songs about the top comedians' pay went:

> '*Two hundred a week so they say,*
> *Two songs, a red nose,*
> *A suit of old clothes.*'

There was such enormous business being done, the guvnors driving about in huge cars, we felt we should have some share in it. And we could see that other people all around were going on strike. So we went on strike. A lot of the topnotchers, people like R. G. Knowles and George Robey, came out with us, because they disagreed with the whole business of farming. Marie Lloyd joined in. She didn't have much to complain about but she supported us. We met outside the Empress Music Hall in Brixton and marched to Fred Karno's office in Camberwell, where our leader spoke to him. Marie Lloyd sang to the tune of *Oh Mr Porter*:

> *Oh Mr Karno, what are you trying to do,*
> *Make more money from the sketches, if what they say is true,*
> *All your lads are winners, not one's an also-ran,*
> *Oh, Mr Karno, don't be a silly man.*

The upshot of it all was Karno gave us all another five shillings a week.

1. Trades Union officials (to the Boy-Who-Would-Grow-Up) 'Here, I say, think of us. This growth has got to stop.' Dedicated to the officials at Unity House and their pathetic efforts to check this modern tendency on the part of the Rank and File to outgrow institutions.

Will Dyson cartoon in the *Daily Herald*, 1911

2. Liverpool Dock strike, 1911. A docker argues with troops brought into the city

G. MAURICE HANN, CBE
Former general secretary of National Union of Shop Assistants

Men like Ben Tillett, the dockers' leader were no respecters of formalities or demarcation lines when it came to giving help where it was needed in a dispute. In December 1913, I was asked by the general secretary of the shop assistants' union to go and help with a strike against the 'living-in' system at two firms in Swansea. At the time the union was making a big drive against the system, which was then common. Conditions varied, some good, some bad. But there was little privacy, the food was often inferior and when you lost your job, you lost your lodgings. The strike had started well. At a blast on a whistle, the living-in staff brought their boxes and walked out. But the local staff who lived out carried on working. The local secretary had been organising friends and supporters to come and crowd the shop without buying anything. But the firm was sticking out and we felt that if it survived over Christmas, then our people would be defeated.

Then I heard that Ben Tillett, the dockers' leader was spending Christmas at the Ship Hotel on the Mumbles. I went to see him and ask his help. 'Well, what do you want, you saucy bugger?', was his greeting. I asked him if he'd speak at a rally in support of the strikers, and he agreed. We held the meeting at 2 p.m. on Boxing Day of all days, and it was packed, floor, gallery and all, and then the dockers rolled up. Ben was in his usual form. He referred to some police interference with pickets and declared, 'I warn the police constable and his subordinates that if there is any hankey-pankey, the dockers will take a hand'. He told the dockers 'Arm yourselves with cudgels and if need be, use them'. He struck absolute terror into the hearts of the locals and the following day I had a phone call from the firm. They were only too glad to settle.

R. E. SCOULLER
Former official of the National Union of Clerks, Glasgow

It seemed in those days that everyone was striking; the seamen had a big strike, and the railwaymen, and in the shipyards where my father worked there was one strike after another. The discontent was great and rising. I can remember going down to the river in Glasgow at the weekends, watching thousands going away; they were emigrating. There was a big upsurge in the trade union movement, though two groups remained very difficult to organise, the domestic servants and my own group the clerks. I searched for a clerk's union in Glasgow for two years before I found it in a dirty wee close off Buchanan Street, though in those days it was chiefly a propaganda body. There was not just indifference but actual hatred of trade unionism among clerks. That is one thing that has changed.

When the great Dublin strike came in 1913, we were out on the streets with barrel organs collecting money to support the Dublin workers. The CWS organised a whole shipload of food for the children. Jim Larkin, or Big Jim as he was called, was the moving figure, and I can recall a big meeting at the St Andrews Hall, where Larkin and Cunningham Grahame spoke.

What a contrast between Cunningham Grahame, the intellectual, and Big Jim. Cunningham Grahame talked about the poor proletariat of Dublin, but the audience had never heard of 'proletariat'.

We knew even then that Larkin's men were buying guns for the Citizen Army. After all the 1916 uprising came only three years later. Altogether there was an enormous intellectual ferment before the 1914–18 war, with all kinds of Socialist notions around.

The political ferment reflected the ferment in industry. Opinion among Socialists was swinging from one extreme to another. One day it was all for a general strike, the next day for voting them out.

But I feel sure that in the months leading up to the outbreak of war things were building up for a general strike. After the war, the battle which had only been interrupted broke out afresh, only by 1918 the trade union movement had doubled its strength.

CHAPTER TWO

1914-1925

Heroes and Brothers

The strike wave of 1911–14 died down with the onset of war, but did not die out. After a short lull, industrial disputes multiplied as the craft union members fought against 'dilution' of trade skills as war production swelled the labour force and new techniques cut across old work divisions.

The rising tempo of work, war-time conditions and long hours aggravated antagonisms in the factories. Trade union officials, accepting increasing government control of the labour force as 'industrial conscription', became more isolated from their members. More and more disputes were fought to a finish under the leadership of men chosen in the workshop and the works committee, bringing together all trades; shop stewards made their first appearance.

The return of men from the front to the 'Land Fit for Heroes', battle-hardened and unwilling to wait patiently for the uncertain fulfilment of promises of better times, brought the trade union membership to 8 million. This was double the 1914 level and was never to be reached again until the end of the 1939–45 war. Radical demands for a new deal, backed by instant industrial action doubled and trebled the number of strikes, reaching a peak in 1920. Increased militancy was reflected in politics, with a new programme and Constitution for the growing Labour Party (including Clause 4)[1] and the amalgamation of Left-wing groups into the Communist Party.

Amalgamation in the unions, impelled by pressure of new techniques, and rank and file syndicalism gave birth to new giants, the engineers, transport and general, and municipal workers'

[1] The clause which advocates public ownership to 'win for the workers by hand or brain the full fruits of their labour'.

51

unions. An idea first mooted in 1914 of mutual aid in industrial disputes between a triple alliance of miners, transport and railway workers came into being.

The failure of Lloyd George to keep his pledge of public ownership and better conditions in the mines, and coalowners' demands for lower wages, put the new alliance to the test. It fell at the first hurdle,[1] and defeat for the miners in a 13-week lockout followed in 1921. This marked the first phase of a counter-attack by employers and the end of the post-war boom in the unions. The 1922 lockout of the newly amalgamated engineering union also struck the unions a heavy blow.

From 1921–25 the number of strikes was halved. Trade union membership fell rapidly from 8 million to just over 5 million. As the crucial year of 1926 approached, unemployment was above the million mark, and rising.

FRANK JACKSON
Rank and file building worker (retired)

Just the weekend before war broke out, the militants in the building unions formed the Building Workers Industrial Union. I was on the EC for a while and George Hicks, who had been leading the amalgamation movement, was to have been General Secretary, but he opted out at the last moment. (After the war he became General Secretary of the Amalgamated Union of Building Trade Workers.) Well, those breakaway unions were a tragic bloomer, but you have to understand that the rank and file were fed up with the way the officials had run the lockout in the building in 1913–14. The full time officials in the various unions were standing in the way of amalgamation; they all wanted to hang on to their jobs. So we went ahead and organised the BWIU and on some jobs men held two cards, one for the BWIU and one for their own craft union. But it was the technical changes which came during the war that brought about the amalgamations. Concrete, for example, became the big thing during the war as it was the only thing that would stand up to Zeppelin raids. Technical

[1] A general transport and railway strike was called for Friday April 15, 1921, to support the miners, but called off by transport and railway union leaders – hence 'Black Friday'.

3. The Cripple Alliance. Since Black Friday, Messrs Thomas, Bevin and Hodges play nightly to enthusiastic audiences of coal-owners.

Espoir cartoon in *The Communist*, 1921

changes, and the shop stewards movement, that's what brought about the merging of the old unions.

When war broke out, I had a job in Chancery Lane, where the master builder was a man called Evans. The bugger used to walk around in soft shoes and if anyone stood with a straight back he wanted to know why. Come November he was invited to the Lord Mayor's banquet; he had on a frock coat, a canary waistcoat and a top hat.

But he couldn't resist sneaking round the site for a quick look to catch somebody idling. Word got round that he was coming and a couple of navvies waited with cement sacks, one each side of the door and when he came through they flapped them over him, and then poured on water. You never saw such a sight. He offered £60 if someone would say who did it but he was wasting his time. It cured him of creeping round the job though.

I got a job in the aircraft industry soon after. There were eight of us making the first military aeroplane for the British Army; the rest had been imported from France. We were working up at Colindale, and later on moved down to Merton. We had to rout out the spars and glue everything up by hand. But it was a big cumbersome job and by the middle of 1915 the firm was beginning to feel the pinch from Sopwith who was producing a plane called the Camel. I had the job organised, Amalgamated Society of Joiners and Carpenters, cabinet makers, the lot. We opened up the Amalgamated Society of Carpenters and Joiners so anyone could join it and keep their own union ticket.

This boss, who was losing orders to Sopwith, called me up to the office one day, explained the position to me and offered me a job as secretary of what he called the 'Aircraft Workers Union'. His solicitors had drawn up documents and I was to get £6 a week. The idea was to start trouble for Sopwith up in Kingston. Well, I told him where to stick his £6 a week and got the sack. But I soon got a job with Broadwoods, who were on war production, using an old factory at Whitechapel. The top floor which had been used for silk-making was isolated from the main building.

When we had a joint committee of the trades organised on the job I went to the boss and told him we wanted threepence an hour increase, and I hinted he ought to get it settled up before the army colonel came down on inspection. 'Oh, I can't afford threepence an hour,' he said, 'it puts me out of gear with everyone else.'

'Suppose,' I said, 'I explain to the colonel what's going on on that top floor. There's all parts of pianos you're not supposed to be producing.'

He was so surprised that before he thought, he said: 'Oh, and how do we get them out then?'

'You use the lift and take them out at night when no one's looking. Now if I explain to the colonel. . . .'

'Go on you bugger, have your threepence an hour,' he said.

But he managed to get me out of there and I went down to Romford skating rink, which was being used for war production, where I was elected chief steward. They were using all kinds of prisoners-of-war, Spaniards and others, to do the work and there was a major-general appointed by the military in charge of production. The skating rink was open and we used to make up the planes under the verandah that went round the sides. We were short of tools and for milling we were using old files, that used to snap off when you struck a knot, hollowing out the spars. One day, one of the files snapped off, flew across the rink, just missed a fellow and buried itself in a wooden pillar. He went out screaming and holding his fingers. We had a meeting and decided that we would have no more prisoners-of-war on the job unless they were employed on the same wages and conditions.

We went up to see the major-general and knocked on his office door. But he wouldn't come out to see us, so we nailed up his door and he was there until 11 o'clock at night. Well, there was a big bust up about that, a full inquiry and the fellow got bumped. The POWs were moved out and proper woodcutting machinists moved in.

I went down to Lebus, the furniture people, who were building big bombing planes for De Havilland. I was working on fuselages and there were a lot of non-union men there. I formed a branch of the Building Workers' Industrial Union. Some of the other men were in the ASCJ and they threatened to strike the job over us. We dug our heels in, they struck, and the military came down and threatened to put them all in the Army. So they went back to work. The BWIU doubled and trebled its membership and got increases in wages, while the ASCJ was doing nothing. We formed a shop council in Lebus, covering all the trades.

One day in the middle of all this I fell ill; they took me out and rushed me into the Prince of Wales Hospital. They sent for my wife and told her if she wanted to see me alive, she'd better get down there quickly (it was a perforated ulcer). When I got out of there the war was nearly over . . . .

GEORGE HODGKINSON
Former Labour leader of Coventry City Council, and shop steward

I came to Coventry just after the war started. It was well known for motor cars and motor lorries and its organisation, tooling and know-how were easily grafted onto aeroplane work. I was machining engine cases, solid rings of metal like cheeses, for a plane called the BE2C; it was something of a challenge, working to fine limits, 100th of a millimetre. That plane had a synchronised machine gun, an idea pinched from Fokkers. Finesse was the thing, with no Brummagem jobs wanted. That was our idea of a joke in those days, picturing the Brummie as a dim bloke with a big hammer. I was in Daimler, which with Humbers, and the Coventry Ordnance (making naval guns) was probably among the biggest, while the others were ten a penny factories. Daimler was pretty well organised but all under different craft unions, Amalgamated Society of Engineers (my union), Steam Engine makers, toolmakers, brassworkers, blacksmiths, blacksmiths' strikers, sheet-metal workers and so on. It was only as the war went on and their craft interests began to be affected that some of them began to realise that there was another war going on, here on the home front. The employers had no conscience at all about war aims and the workers were only pawns in their game.

At first war fever was at high pitch. In 1916 they introduced attestation for military service. Under this a worker could opt to be called up as a soldier if ever he were needed. Some of the men went mad, wheeling their mates up in wheelbarrows to the attesting officer. But I refused – my Quaker background. I was the only one. I felt that the attested man was in the Government's grip, as good as conscripted. I was just dimly then trying to work out what the war was about, and that there might be a battle between classes just as pressing as the war abroad. As the war went on and the manpower problem got more acute, they began what

56

they called a 'comb out',[1] which was typical of their attitude, treating working class people as though they were lice. And as time went on anti-war arguments began to have their effect.

But the big change came with the dilutees, the infiltration into the work of the butcher, the baker and the candlestick-maker. It became clear that the employers were determined to bring in the dilutees for their own aims, to bring down the rates and undermine union organisation.

The union members on the shop floor began to doubt the ability of the full-time officials to pull the chestnuts out of the fire when they were so far away from the heat themselves. The officials did not feel the pace of the job and the urgency of the problem. So in 1916 and 1917 you began to get the shop steward movement growing, underground as it were, unrecognised, but thrusting for power. You would mix with men from other factories in your trade union branch and if Humbers made a shop floor bargain it would soon come to the ears of Daimler and so on. The shop stewards' movement grew underground, fertilised by all the delays in settling matters through the full-time officials. Under such conditions there was nothing to do but put tools down.

In one case there was a foreman, notorious for effing and blinding, bullying the men. We decided we weren't going to have it and so we just stood by our machines. We kept this 'non-cooperation' up for two days and three nights. We took books into the factory to read, while the employers were playing cat and mouse with the full-time officials. But we stuck it out and the foreman was shifted. This was the occasion for face to face talks with the management. Someone had to do the talking for the men on the shop floor and this meant I came out from underground. A shop stewards' convener was needed and they chose me. We elected a shop stewards' committee right throughout the factory, all trades without discrimination. Funnily enough, I think that my awkwardness over attestation proved decisive here. I suppose the men reckoned that if I'd defy the authorities over attestation and go in the face of my fellow workers' opinion as well, then I was the man to choose.

Towards the end of 1917 the shop stewards' movement was given its first real test in Coventry. We had been leading a growing anti-

[1] Finding more men for the Forces by a more stringent approach to each worker's claim to be exempt from military service.

profiteering movement; the cost of living was rising rapidly and modifications in the district rate didn't keep pace. We held meetings of shop stewards. I knew the lads from the various factories personally, Coventry Ordnance, Humbers, White and Poppes (they had the first strike against dilutees). There was Tom Dingley, who later became a Communist, who organised the Hotchkiss factory, making a French machine gun. There the organisation was a mushroom growth, all new workers, led by aggressive shop stewards. It was known locally as The Mint because of the rates they paid. Daimler was a different kettle of fish; the men were craftsmen, the 'steady' type, with no notions of revolution. It was only the stupidity of management that set them off. Here and there men popped up as leaders, and you would meet them casually at union branches.

In November 1917, we called a town strike against profiteering, stopped the whole town for half a day and marched to Gosford Green. It was a great day, we improvised banners. I took the sheets off my own bed, and a local artist, Herbert Wells, damn good artist, drew cartoons showing rich men with watch chains, the contrast between rich and poor, calling for cheaper food and more equal distribution.

By 1918 the 'comb-out' had gone to the limit and they wanted to stop the movement of workers from one factory to another. The cost-plus system of production not only meant huge profits. It meant wages varied enormously from one factory to another and district rates fell miles behind. So they put an embargo on this movement to stop workers exploiting the situation.

You had to be a month out of your job before you could transfer, but if you were a month away from your job you could be called up. The strike went on for about a month and everyone was involved, the skilled man and the dilutee were part and parcel of the whole situation. The townsfolk were a bit hostile against us, saying we were compromising the soldier's chances of defending himself. Havelock Wilson, the leader of the seamen's union brought seamen to the city and marched them round, declaring we were betraying the fighting men. The Government were in a panic, worried about the way the war was going; ministers were sent down to talk to the men and eventually their resolve weakened and we went back.

With the end of the war the employers, without any notice, tried to bring back the pre-war job prices. But here the shop stewards

58

came into their own. The men grasped that they should leave the talking to the stewards, instead of letting the employers play on them like the keys of a piano. The men voted rather than go back on pre-war rates, they would go on day work and ignore the bonus system the management wanted. And they kept it up for eight weeks. Production dropped from 26 lorries a week to six and in the end the management agreed to negotiate new rates.

The strange thing was that during the dispute, a man discovered that during the war, a 12½ per cent increase had been awarded. They took the management to the Munitions Tribunal and won the award, the only time I've ever heard of anyone winning an increase during a dispute.

JIM GARDNER
Former secretary of the Foundry Workers' Union

The 12½ per cent increase was known as the Churchill Award (Churchill was in the Munitions Ministry at the time) and was a bonus for all engineers. But I think I'm right in saying that it was won by the foundry workers in Scotland in late 1917.

In the Scottish iron-moulders union we already had shop organisation by tradition and during the war we formed what we called 'Emergency Committees'. We linked up with the Clyde Shop Stewards' Committee and I used to attend the shop stewards meetings on Saturday afternoons. We had found that the foundry wage was lagging far behind other industries. The cost of living was soaring. Before the war the practice was to concede increases of a farthing an hour on the rate, but the war put a stop to that. The leadership of the union was doing nothing about the situation and so the unofficial emergency committees took over.

We went all over Scotland organising committees in the different towns, and in September 1917 the foundries struck throughout Scotland. This is the only time I can recall an unofficial national strike in any trade. A deputation went to London to see Churchill and after a three week strike came this Churchill 12½ per cent award. He must have recognised that you can't fight a war without castings.

The employers were very quick to recognise the chance the war gave them to make money. The workers were a good deal slower

59

to respond, but in the end they had to realise that the war hadn't put a stop to the industrial battle. Their eyes were opened when the labour shortage brought all kinds of unskilled workers into the factories. Weirs of Cathcart nearly came to a dispute when the employers brought in Chinese labour, around 1916 or 17. A deputation made it clear that whoever came into the factory, skilled or unskilled, should get the rate for the job and no less. So they decided to withdraw the Chinese. There was a lot of bluffing. The foreman tried to threaten us with the army and I was summoned to the recruiting office, where I had to show my papers (I'd been discharged on health grounds at the start of the war).

If the shop stewards' movement had not developed then I'm convinced that conditions after the war would have been as bad as before the war. The full-time officials of the unions had in many cases just abandoned any attempt to protect their members.

It was in the Clyde Shop Stewards' Committee that I got to know Willie Gallacher.[1] I well remember the day the Armistice was announced; I was travelling with Gallacher on the top of a bus when the factory hooters began to blare and the gates opened and people poured out into the streets cheering. Gallacher turned to me and said, 'Ah well, cheers today, tears tomorrow'.

Soon the men began to come back from the war, and the munitions workers began to be discharged; by the winter of 1918–19 there were 30,000 unemployed in and around Glasgow. Officially during the war, working hours had been 51 to 54 a week, though often people had been working longer. It was clear that hours worked would have to come down or there would be even more out of work. So the shop stewards on the Clyde put forward the demand for a 40 hour week. A joint committee was formed with the shop stewards, the Glasgow Trades Council, the Scottish TUC and the EC of our union, who had learnt a lesson from the 1917 strike. In the New Year of 1919 the shop stewards decided on a strike and at the end of January 100,000 came out – shipyards, steel workers, builders, dockers, everybody. There were marches through the city and big mass meetings.

I was there on what was called 'Bloody Friday'. The police attacked the marchers who were massed outside the Municipal Buildings. I was standing several yards away from Gallacher and saw him running forward to try and stop them hitting David

[1] Later Communist MP for West Fife.

60

Kirkwood.[1] Both of them were batoned. I saw Gallacher go down. Jock McBain, from my union, got a beating as well and Kirkwood must have taken it badly. I went into the Municipal Buildings and saw Kirkwood lying flat out and groaning. Gallacher was sitting up with bandages round his head, smoking his pipe.

Outside, the workers had blocked the street with a lorry, seized empty bottles from it and were pelting the police. Some of the marchers later on got through to Glasgow Green where the police attacked them and there was another riot. That weekend, I saw the troops move in.

COUNCILLOR FINLAY HART
Shop steward of the Clyde Shipyards (retired)

I marched with the Clydebank contingent eight miles to George Square on 'Bloody Friday'. We walked on the tram lines and never let a tram-car pass us. When we reached George Square, the baton charge had taken place, and we marched through the Square on to Glasgow Green. The tram-cars were halted in the centre of the city, because the marchers pulled down the arms that linked the trams to the electric cable and bent them. There was a lorry which had been carrying lemonade bottles lying across the road and people grabbing bottles and stones to throw at the police The police would charge, the crowd would scatter, then reform and the police would charge again. I was 17 at the time, an apprentice, and vividly remember the whole business, above all the fact that we hadn't eaten since the morning and were starving.

The 40 hour week demand was raised by the Socialists among the shop stewards. Throughout the war, the workers had really worked excessive hours. Talk about overtime, they worked till 9.15 at night. When I think of what we did as apprentices, 54 hour week, then overtime on top! As a first year apprentice on eight shillings a week, working on a submarine getting ready for test, I worked all night Friday and all day Sunday, I remember. Now it's questionable whether that 40 hour strike would have taken place at all but for a rather particular circumstance.

The re-organisation of working hours which accompanied the cutting of hours to 47 a week in November 1918 did something

[1] Later elected to Parliament as a Labour MP.

drastic. It abolished the breakfast break. In the past we started work at six o'clock and then stopped for a three-quarter hour breakfast break at 9.15, worked on till dinner break 1.15 to 2 and then finished at 5.15 in the evening. There were two breaks of three-quarters of an hour. With the new hours, you started at 7.30 and worked straight through to 12, then had an hour for lunch and worked to 5.30. Men had been accustomed to going to work on just a cup of tea and a roll, knowing they would stop for a proper breakfast at 9.15. If you didn't live near enough to go home, you had your can and sandwiches, your 'piece'. Under the new hours this went, but around nine o'clock men, following the habit of years, would begin to make tea surreptitiously.

A violent struggle began with management trying to stop unofficial tea-making. At the end of the day, the effect of the new hours on tempers was remarkable, at 5.30 they were nearly breaking down the gate, a surge of men, young lads to the front. On one occasion I recall the gates almost broke, men were diving through the gate-house trying to get through quickly. Few people cottoned-on to the damage done because the 47 hour week was introduced. If they had managed a meal break, they would have avoided much of the trouble. Mind you, the battle over a tea break in shipbuilding was still going on up to the 1960s. For forty years they have been trying to wipe out tea-making.

The battle started, though, in 1919 and basically I suppose both management and men were trying to re-establish their positions after the war. But the shop stewards had become very strong during the war, and the men coming back from army service were not ready to knuckle under.

ALF GARRARD
Former rank and file building worker

In our unit at the Battle of the Somme was an old soldier, an Irish chap; we called him Porky Flynn. He used to sing the Red Flag and lay down the law about the effing capitalist class. You could hear him all over the trenches. He was my first introduction to trade unionism. I'd served my apprenticeship but it had been broken when I went into the army in France.

When demob came I joined what they called the Ivy Leaf

Movement, Discharged, Demobilised and Disabled Soldiers' and Sailors' Federation. In 1919 we had a big march on Parliament and the police went for us. I recall them drawing their truncheons and putting on their bicycle clips, to order. There was a shower of missiles, and then the mounted police – Cossacks we called them – charged. Later the same day I went to a rally in Hyde Park, where one speaker told us, 'If you chaps want to get on, you'll get into a trade union.' Well, what we got was the British Legion, the bosses' union.

I joined the Amalgamated Society of Woodworkers in Lambeth the following year. It had just been formed by various unions coming together. Almost at once we were involved in a lockout in the shipping industry, paying a levy of six shillings a week. Then came the movement for 44 hours, '44 and no more'. We were working 52 hours in the building trade. Every morning we would send out pickets to building sites all over the area to see that 44 hours were worked and no more. On one job, the foreman said 'At half past five I shall blow my whistle', and we told him 'At half past five you can blow your bloody brains out and there'll be nobody to hear you.' Every day at 5 o'clock somebody would strike a girder and that would be a signal for every bit of metal on the job to be banged. So much so, in fact, that the local hospital sent a deputation to the shop stewards to ask them to lay off. In the end the firm gave in and the whistle went at five o'clock.

But what drew me was the Minority Movement, which was formed around this time by Tom Mann and Harry Pollitt. I joined it right at the start; there was a meeting at the Elephant and Castle, with workers of 30 different trades present. I was at Waygood Otis at the time, and I used to sell the Minority Movement weekly there, until one day the foreman said to me 'Garrard, you'll be leaving us tonight.'

Really the Minority Movement was carrying on the work that was started before the First World War. It was pushing for amalgamations between the unions, getting all the militants together whatever their trade to have one industry, one union. Soon after the war, the bosses were going all out to cut wages. In the building trade in 1921 there were wage cuts in May, August and September and there were more cuts in 1922. The full-time officials didn't like the rank and file movement, but if it had been left to them there would have been no fight back at all.

ALF DRURY
Former engineer and regular soldier

No, the lads who'd been in the Army weren't going to put up with anything. I was stationed in Biggleswade in 1918; I'd had to stop in for 12 months extra, had malaria and been in hospital. I was in civvy lodgings and I'd got a side of bacon for the landlady, so I was cock lodger, you see. But the young lads in camp only had biscuits for breakfast. They came to me as an old soldier to ask me what to do, they were fed up with it.

Well this sort of thing was nothing new to me. I'd joined up in the Royal Berkshire Regiment and was sent to Dublin when I was 16. We were just a bunch of errand boys and when the captain saw us, he said 'They're worse than the last lot, if that's possible.' The next year the dockers in Belfast came out on strike, led by Jim Larkin. He was the sort they'd call a Communist these days. Our lot were sent to Belfast and the colonel, who was a funny bloke, told us, 'Now we're not here to get involved. I don't know what these blokes are fighting for. Probably for more money, and if I know anything, they probably deserve it.'

As I say, these lads at Biggleswade came to me and asked what they should do. So I said 'Tomorrow morning, when the whistle blows, don't fall in.'

Sure enough, when the whistle blew, not a man moved. The NCOs rushed round but no one would fall in. The colonel, he was a Territorial, didn't know what to do, but he said, 'Right, two men each company come to HQ and tell me all about it.' He saw I was the old soldier so he asked me, 'What complaints?' I said 'I've got no complaints. I'm the cock lodger, bacon and egg for breakfast. But these lads only had biscuits. I bet you didn't have biscuits for breakfast, sir.' Well, he had to admit that was true and the upshot of it all was we were sent down to the local library to list our complaints. We drew up a list as long as your arm and the colonel said, on the quiet, 'If it goes no further, I'll forget what happened,' and I told the lads they couldn't have it fairer than that.

When I got home that night, my landlord, who was a railway ganger, a National Union of Railwaymen member, was laughing

4. Telegram sent out by Ernest Bevin, leader of the Transport and General Workers' Union, on the eve of the General Strike, May 1, 1926

5. Three blacklegs escorted by police at Garw, South Wales, in 1929

6. Lancashire cotton workers on strike leaving a mill in August 1932

his head off. 'It's all over Biggleswade, my lodger's been leading a strike.'

I had all sorts of jobs after the war, but the going began to be rough. First there was the moulders' strike, and the unions were practically skint, and then in 1922 came the big engineers' lockout. And they were starting the speed-up in the factories, too. I got a job in Rolls Royce, Derby, with my mate. One day, my mate looked round, and saw this character with a top hat and a gold watch and said to him, 'What's your job?' And the gent replied, 'I'm timing you, my man.' So my mate said, 'Well, go and collect your cards. You've lost your job, for I'm off.' And I went with him.

That year (1921) was the year of the Triple Alliance when the railwaymen and the transport workers were supposed to come out in support of the miners. Churchill, for reasons best known to himself decided to mobilise the whole of the Regular Army. I was called up with the Reserve. We didn't know what we were doing but we were put to guarding the installations here and there. I was sent to Edinburgh, where we got out of the train and were marched to the goods yards and put in charge of the coal stacks. Along came a little kid saying, 'Can I have some coal, mister?'; so we flogged it to the kids at a tanner a time. With our wages who could blame us? And as I say we didn't know half of what it was about. I did hear one chap, a reservist in the Black Watch who'd been a miner, making a speech about the iniquity of turning out the army against strikers. But most of the Black Watch were crofters and hadn't a clue what he was on about.

They put me on guard outside the wireless station in Edinburgh. One night I was on duty and there was a crowd round us. A woman was selling a paper called *The Communist*. For a lark I bought six copies and put them in the library at the Castle. In came the sergeant and when his eye lit on them his moustache literally curled. Bolsheviks on the station! When they found out where the papers came from they wouldn't allow me near the station and asked me to give my word that I wouldn't interfere with anything in the station.

However, the Triple Alliance collapsed. I heard they called it the Cripple Alliance. I remember seeing one cartoon, the funeral of the miner, with J. H. Thomas, the railwaymen's leader, saying 'I claim the right to lay the first wreath. After all I killed him.' That's as may be, but in the trade unions you get stupidity as well

E   65 as solidarity and I like efficiency. If you're going in for a fight, then make sure you're going to win.

ALBERT IRONS, BEM
Retired secretary of the National Union of Railwaymen, Paddington

In 1919, J. H. Thomas had negotiated a settlement of railwaymen's conditions because, they said, of our wonderful service during the war. It included a week's holiday. In fact, with the holidays I was getting with my service, it meant one day more a year for me. But a row blew up over the terms of the agreement, which was interpreted differently all over the country according to which company you were working for. It varied from depot to depot even. They agreed an eight hour day, but wanted to exclude meal times and wash-times. And other interpretations of the agreement would have meant an actual reduction in wages.

By the time the autumn came, things were boiling up all over the place. Paddington Goods, where I worked, was almost 100 per cent organised, which, when you consider that eight years before in the 1911 strike there were only a handful in the union, was quite remarkable. We were feeling our strength then, because we had the Triple Alliance, and knew we had the miners and transport workers on our side. But in 1919 we were ready to come out on our own. The union had promised strike pay to all, even those who weren't in the union and so when we were called out there was a very willing response. It was completely solid. No trains ran at all, because the loco-men's union supported us.

The only annoyances were the attempt by private contractors to move goods by road, and that they brought students in from the hospitals to shift goods in the station. After we'd been out a while the boss of our depot wanted to come to a branch meeting to plead with the men to feed the 700–800 horses there were in Paddington. One of our chaps, a very militant trade unionist, but a great lover of horses, wanted to give in .

While the boss was waiting outside, he made a great plea not to let the dumb animals suffer. He made such a great impression, in fact, that we nearly busted up for the day. It took me and one or two others a hell of a time to bring the members round to see he was wrong. I used this argument: 'They're making a great plea

66

about not letting dumb animals suffer, but they've brought students into the depot, so let the students feed the horses. We're not feeding horses while the students break the strike'.

Well, we won that one. We got what we wanted with that strike. And, though J. H. Thomas has his critics, in my opinion he proved himself a great trade union leader in those post-war years, when the small railway companies were being merged into the five big ones and he was negotiating new conditions. In those days we were feeling our strength.

MRS H. E. LEWIS
Farmer's wife of Iddesleigh, Devon

That year, the railway strike brought everything to a standstill, for road transport wasn't all that plentiful. I remember the village shops running out of supplies, as they were shops for drapery, boots and all sorts of things. It was the custom to send us back to school with new dresses and aprons and boots to last us through the winter, but the materials for dressmaking, etc, were held up on the railway; they could not be sent from the mills. In those days our mums used to wear yards of material in their dresses and they were lined with silk. Mum made a brown dress with pink silk cuffs and collars for each of my sisters and myself and, as she could not get any white calico to make us aprons, she made us some out of bed valances. My brother of 12 was made a suit out of a dressing gown. It had to be new boots for us, so we had to pick blackberries and mushrooms to sell; between us we picked enough for a pair of boots each. We girls wore nailed boots as we had to go three miles to school.

Where we were living (Devon) at that time, there were huge orchards, and the trees were looked after; there was always a good crop of apples. In one orchard there were two large trees and I can remember them say that these two trees brought in nearly £90. I think they were called the Somerset apple; they were very soft and yellow and I believe they were sold for something special. Because of the railway strike, it was said, the apples could not be sent away. Some were taken by horse and wagon to a cider factory and the remainder were made into cider at the farm just below the house where we lived; puncheons were used as well as hogsheads. One

67

day one of the puncheons burst and all the cider ran down the yard into a trough and all the pigs, geese and turkeys drank it and of course got tipsy; when we came upon them we were frightened and thought they were dead.

Strangely enough, every unfortunate incident was always put down as due to the strike, I suppose because generally no one was educated enough to understand the meaning of strikes, though things were hard enough for people on the farms. My father and mother looked after a dairy and milked 20 cows by hand and did all the other jobs attached to it. My father got 12 shillings a day, two pints of milk a day and free housing, but that had to keep himself, my mother and six children. Wages were only paid once in three months and then sometimes my mother had to ask the employer for it as in many cases it was overdue by two or three weeks.

J. F. HOWELL
Branch secretary of National Union of Agricultural Workers, Walsingham

In East Anglia, because of the war, the farm labourers had pushed the wages up to 45s a week, but after the war the farmers kept applying to the wages boards and lowering the wages five bob a time. There were some hard-faced old farmers who still lived in the days of the Tolpuddle Martyrs and thought the farm labourers had had it too soft. With the lads coming out of the army, jobs were getting scarce. I was sacked and had been doing casual work around threshing time, when an old boy told me to see the District Surveyor, who gave me a job as roadman. But I was still active in the union.

Well, they kept cutting the wages until they were down to 25 bob a week and the farmworkers thought it was time something was done about it. The farmers wanted another five bob off. Now the union was fairly well organised in this part of Norfolk, in fact there'd been a strike for several weeks in 1911 led by George Hewitt who was still very active. And Walsingham was a pretty good centre, so we called a meeting. There must have been 150 there from all over the district. The meeting hall was full. A railwayman came over to address us and he said, 'Well, I know what I would do if I were you lads.' And so they decided to call a strike. First one farm came out, and then another, and soon it spread to other parts of the country. In Walsingham we were all out. The Lord of the Manor, Sir Eustace Gurney, got a surprise. He never thought his men were coming out. Anyway he and his son had to work the farm themselves.

The farmers were led up the garden path. They never expected a strike, because a chap called Sam Peel, who had been on the executive committee of the union and had big ideas, formed his own union. Lord Leicester at the time financed it to get it started, and he kidded the farmers that the men wouldn't strike. Anyway he misled them, and after the strike it was his union that faded away.

We picked March 23 for the strike, round about sowing time, to make it a bit inconvenient for the farmers. The strikers would get together at night round a farm where there were blacklegs, and when it was early morning, over the fields they'd go, twenty or thirty men, unharness the horses and turn them loose. There were police patrolling and they saw it all, but they only laughed because they were sympathetic. In the next village to us some people worked, and they used to sneak off home through the Abbey woods so that we wouldn't see them. For years after that there was always a bit more feeling to the annual cricket match.

Most of the farmers were tarred with the same brush. If you offended one you offended the lot. If one sacked you, the others wouldn't take you on, and if you were a prominent union man they'd want to shoot you. In fact one farmer did threaten to shoot some of the strikers. Another farmer tried to ride them down, but they turned his horse round and tipped him out of the saddle.

Things got to such a pitch that they brought in police from all the counties and cities around to keep law and order. They started prosecutions for intimidation. One old boy in his sixties had 60 summonses against him for intimidation. Finally everybody was brought up in court at Walsingham. Sir Eustace Gurney, Lord of the Manor, was on the bench, but it seems in those days a JP could sit on a bench even outside his own town, so George Hewitt and George Edwards (later Sir George) came over and sat on the bench. They were active in the union. In the end nobody went to prison, but quite a lot had to pay costs. The square outside the court was full of farmworkers, big strong blokes, and there were

20 policemen guarding the entrance. When Sam Peel came out of the court, the blokes made a rush for him and if it hadn't been for George Hewitt, cars would have been turned over. But in the end we won and the county boards ruled that there should be no wage cuts.

In 1924, the first Labour government did away with the county boards and set up the national wages board, the first step to improving conditions; you couldn't do anything with the die-hard farmers on the county boards. If farmworkers hadn't been organised they'd never have got any benefits.

ERNIE POUNTNEY
Former shop assistants' union organiser

The railwaymen and the miners and their victories in 1919 and 20 set off the shop assistants as well. After the war, hundreds joined in Harrods alone, where I had been working before I joined up. I discovered then that my fellow shop assistant, Randall, had been a union member all the time, but had never wanted to tell me. Soon there were 2,000 union members in the West End stores and I was invited to become a union organiser, and gladly accepted. I was deeply offended when one of the union leaders said to me, 'I don't understand why you're applying for this post. You're getting more in your own job.' Harrods, Selfridges, Army and Navy stores, all were organised; even the supervisors were joining. There was plenty of feeling among ordinary shop assistants. Few of them had been exempted from war service and when they came back they were only offered the 1914 rate. In the silver department of Harrods where I worked they didn't begin to offer any more until the union began to organise. There were two or three big rallies of shop assistants which I helped to organise in the Albert Hall; feeling was rising.

Then the Army and Navy stores struck. They came out like one man, inspired by the example of strikes in the Paris stores. The Army and Navy stores were run by military men on military lines keeping the wage rates down and refusing to budge when the union called on them to pay the union rate. One of the ways in which the Army and Navy stores assistants were organised was by putting an advertisement in *The Times*. Apparently the Army and Navy had always refused to advertise in *The Times* and so the union's advert was accepted. The Army and Navy assistants not only came out then, they came out to a man during the General Strike.

But in the other stores the employers had taken the hint. Harrods joined an Employers' Association, headed by a Mr Kay, a very astute man. He helped them draw up a scale better in some ways than the rates called for by the union. Harrods operated it and with the aid of their Staff Council won many of their staff away from the union's side.

But the real blow to union organisation in the West End stores was Black Friday[1] in 1921 and the collapse of the Triple Alliance. Originally it was the show put up by the railwaymen and the miners that brought the shop assistants into the unions, but after Black Friday they streamed out of the unions faster than they had streamed in. Our 2,000 members in the West End dwindled to about 400 and, behind our backs, even some of our own union leaders were saying privately that wages would have to come down.

DR JOHN LEWIS
Former lecturer and Presbyterian minister in Gravesend and Birmingham

I was on holiday that year (1920) when I had a telegram calling me back to Gravesend urgently. I was chairman of the Trades and Labour Council and was highly involved. There was a grave danger that Britain would start a war against Russia, and the movement against a war built up to immense proportions. In Gravesend we had formed a Council of Action, and on May Day we had an open air meeting the like of which I have never seen. All the trade union banners were there. I carried the pole of the Dock Wharf and Riverside Workers banner, and considered it to be a great honour. After all, ten days later, members of my union struck and stopped the *Jolly George* from carrying munitions to Poland for the war against Russia. (I may not have been a docker, but I was certainly a general worker.)

There is no doubt at all that in May 1920 there would have been a general strike if there had been war against Russia. I was sent by

[1] See note on page 52.

our Council of Action to a great meeting in London, with delegates from all over the country. All the Right Wing leaders of the Labour movement were lined up on the platform, including Ramsay Mac-Donald, J. H. Thomas; we were all threatening riot and revolution if there were a war against Russia. It was one of those moments when the movement had reached such a level that, even if the leaders didn't want to lead, they had no choice but to line up with the rank and file – if they wanted to continue holding their positions.

It was one of those great moments in the history of the working class. Ben Tillett, who was one of the founders of the Dockworkers, was very much in evidence at the time and very politically active, and of course Tom Mann was everywhere. I recall on one May Day just after the war, Tom Mann came down to speak at our May Day demonstration in Gravesend. There had been a series of strikes in and around London and on one occasion the Albert Hall was refused to militants who wanted to hold a demonstration. The electricians promptly pulled the fuses and put the hall out of commission until permission was granted. You can imagine what a fuss was made about that. But Tom Mann got up at our May Day Rally and said. 'What's all the hullabaloo about cutting off the power at the Albert Hall? What did Moses do in the Land of Egypt, when Pharaoh refused to free the slaves? He called down a plague of darkness. He cut off the light.'

I had Tom Mann to speak in the pulpit of my church at the time. I had come over from Cambridge after the war, and had taken over the Presbyterian church in Gravesend. There was no congregation to speak of; nobody could complain that I was driving people away by my outrageous activity. So I filled the church with workers, and had people like Mann and Saklatvala[1] down to address them. We did things then which haven't been done since, for those immediate post-war years were remarkable times. All kinds of people like myself were associated with the working-class movement, and all kinds of characters were about the country preaching politics.

There was a chap with a little pointed beard called Casey, a fiddler, dressed in a black velvet coat. He had been a sweep. He was a marvellous fiddler and wherever he went the halls were

[1] Saklatvala had been elected to Parliament from St Pancras as a Communist with Labour backing.

packed; I was always coming across him. He interspersed his violin solos with quick-fire political wise-cracks (he also did a column in the Independent Labour Party journal). He was very well known and always heavily booked at Co-op halls all over the country. During the 1914–18 war, I was with him in a pacifist campaign, along with Maud Royden, who was a famous preacher, and Reg Sorensen, who in those days was a fiery young Left Wing Socialist. At one meeting I remember Casey gave solos and I made a pacifist speech. We travelled in a caravan borrowed from the Quakers and when we got to Hinckley, the word went round that we were German spies. A crowd tried to set the caravan on fire and tear us limb from limb. I was hurried through the streets between two burly coppers to the police station and hurled inside while the door was slammed in the face of the mob. A moment later, Reg Sorensen, battered, and with his coat torn, was hurled through after me.

They were days of great militancy, 1919, 1920, but what you must also remember is that unemployment was serious and growing all the time. The unemployed would march to my church each Sunday. We discovered that in Gravesend there were 300 families not getting a penny from any source at all – you can imagine their situation. We went to the Board of Guardians about them. The Board of Guardians sent us to the Corporation, who sent us back to the Board of Guardians. We discovered that the Prince of Wales had set up a distress fund during the 1914–18 war, and it occurred to us that our authority had some of this money. So they had – £3,000. We insisted that our committee should distribute this money since we knew who really needed it. So we went round to the Town Hall each week with a chit and drew on it until it was exhausted. Later we decided on other tactics.

We knew that the Board of Guardians met in an old mansion, with the workhouse behind it. We organised a massive demonstration early in the morning and suddenly marched across the lawn up to the mansion where the Board was meeting. I went in as spokesman, and it was a sight to see the Board faced with that crowd of 300–400 men, their noses pressed up against the windows. They ordered the relieving officer to grant £1 per man. They thought they were going to be surcharged for it by the Government and have to pay out of their own pocket. This was happening all over the country.

RT HON. JAMES GRIFFITHS, CH
Former South Wales miners' president

The slide down began after 1919; pits were closing down and unemployment growing, and in some areas there was a drop in wages already. The export trade in coal was never recovered after 1918 in fact. For the miners, 1919–20 was a big turning point not only economically, but politically as well.

Early in 1919 the miners had balloted for wage increases, a six hour day and for nationalisation. During the war, the Government had taken control of the mines and we did not wish to see the owners taking over again to rule in the manner of the pre-war days. We were told 'don't strike', the Sankey Commission will look into everything; Lloyd George pledged that what the Sankey Commission decided the Government would accept. So the word 'Sankey' is writ large in mining politics. There was no question of misunderstanding. We stayed at work then because the pledge was absolutely definite that whatever Sankey recommended would be accepted by the Government.

Well, that pledge was broken. We did get something; a seven hour day and funds for miners' welfare, but instead of nationalisation we got de-control. The mine-owners took over again and they were demanding that wages should come down. Before we knew it, almost, we were fighting for survival.

Most important for the miners in Wales was that the pledge was broken by Lloyd George, the people's hero, whose picture was in the parlour of every home. The following for Lloyd George, which had always been the great barrier to Labour, melted away. When anyone said 'No, we'll follow Lloyd George', the answer was 'Remember Sankey'. This was the beginning of Wales going Labour, and it was the beginning of a feeling of betrayal that was to last for many years.

For it was something to be let down by a person like Lloyd George; the deepest feelings of all come when you are let down by your own side. We had placed great hopes in our alliance with the railwaymen and transport workers, and when it came to the test it proved to be a broken reed. First came the blow of Sankey, then came 'Black Friday' and the failure of the Triple Alliance.

74

When the owners locked the miners out in 1921 we found we were on our own.

I was not in Wales at the time of the lockout, for I was then a student at the Labour college with Nye Bevan and Ness Edwards. Our job was to go and speak, to put the miners' case, at meetings all over the place, together with a miners' male voice choir. The feeling of sympathy from people up and down the country at scores of meetings was tremendous. One of the most enthusiastic I recall was at the Plumstead Radical Club which had just celebrated its half-century. We all sat down at tables with pints.

Only once did we have a hostile reception. I spoke at Tunbridge Wells; I had the building workers' banner behind me, but the audience in front seemed to consist mainly of retired generals and admirals. They listened to the singing and some even contributed to the collection, but they howled me down.

The lockout, which went on for 13 weeks, was hard and bitter but it was only a rehearsal for 1926. It was followed by cuts in wages, pit closures, growing unemployment, and then, briefly, by what I would call an 'Indian Summer', in 1923-24. The French had occupied the Ruhr, and the Ruhr coalfields closed down. With that competition eliminated wages went up for a while but, by 1925, the situation was serious again. This time, when the coal-owners wanted more wage cuts, the Trades Union Congress promised support for the miners; the Government backed down and paid a subsidy to keep up mining wages for nine months. (That was after what we called 'Red Friday'.) But the battle was only being postponed.

LORD WILL BLYTON
Former Labour MP and Durham miners' leader

The 1921 lockout was bitter though not as long as 1926, and I have known a few strikes since I went down the pit at the age of 14 before the 1914-18 war.

When I was 16½ I put my age down as 18 and served three years in the submarines, came out in 1919 and was in an unofficial strike right away, among the young men. We laid the pit idle for two days because we wanted an allowance of sixpence a day for working among water. In fact that is what most strikes have been about in mining, having to work in conditions that made it impossible for you to earn a decent wage. I've led 14 unofficial strikes myself and had both union and management against me, and had four years unemployment in the thirties. So disputes in mining have always been hard, but 1921 was a bitter one.

During the war the wages had been brought up to a decent level. Some miners could earn five or six pounds a week. The coalowners started to complain that they couldn't compete in world markets and costs would have to come down. After 1921, conditions went downhill all the way until the Second World War, and you would get unofficial strikes because men thought they might as well starve on the surface as down the pits. Talk about 'unofficial' strikes. You try meeting a thousand angry men with a grievance at a pit-head and tell them they're 'unconstitutional'. There have been more strikes in mining than anywhere else in the past, because the coal-owners were the worst and cruellest set of employers you could find.

In 1921 when they locked us out, the coal-owners got all the war awards abolished, and public opinion wasn't always on the side of the miners. Of course in the valleys the miners have never had much regard for 'public opinion'. But when the pits are on the edge of a big town, that's a different kettle of fish.

When the 1921 lockout started I had only been married 18 months. I got my furniture on the never-never. It wasn't much; chair, bed, table, sideboard, child's cot, carpet. After five weeks they came and took it all back and we had to stop with our mothers. I was in sub-let apartments because the landlord wouldn't let us a house with my political opinions.

But we managed to see that the families had food from the soup kitchens, and old Peter Lee, who was on the Durham County Council, arranged for the kids to be fed in the schools. Peter Lee was a grand old man, one of the pioneers, a Methodist preacher. He had been out in South Africa in the gold-mines, drinking and fighting, but when he came home, he became one of the greatest reformers. The New Town, Peterlee, is named after him. He was a preacher, like a good many miners' leaders.

The Established Church in Durham was regarded as being on the side of the coal-owners because of the coal royalties they received. In 1926 the miners were angry with the bishops because they tried to arrange a 'settlement' in the middle of the lockout.

The men were infuriated with the proposals because they regarded them as being in favour of the owners. Bishops have never been regarded as being particularly helpful to miners.

In 1924, the Dean of Durham, Bishop Weldon, made a vitriolic speech on the eve of the miners' gala, saying that the men were never satisfied. Then the silly man went down to the gala. The miners marched in with banners saying 'To Hell with bishops, we want a living wage.' When this man appeared (he weighed 17½ stone), the women were so infuriated, they pushed him in the weir. His hat went floating away, but he was pulled out by the police. That night he preached a sermon on the text 'Father, forgive them for they know not what they do.'

Funnily enough, last year the Bishop of Durham was one of the invited speakers at the gala, times have changed so much. But it will be a long time before anyone in the mining communities forgets those times. We were not allowed to. I had to pay back every penny of the poor relief I got for my family in 1926. In April 1926 I was on the Board of Guardians as an administrator, but I had to come off it in May because I was a recipient. I had a wife and one child then, and got a voucher for 18s worth of groceries per week. I had to pay the whole lot back, at 1s a week.

When I was elected to Parliament in 1945, I had a final demand for £7 2s of the poor relief; the first cheque I ever wrote, out of my first money as an MP, was to pay off the last of that debt.

COUNCILLOR HUGH REYNOLDS
Former miners' lodge official at Plean, Stirlingshire

I first saw the soup kitchens when I was four; I went with my mother to the kitchen in Blantyre for a can of soup in the 1894 strike. In 1904 I started at the pit head here in Plean, at 1s 8d a day. It had only been coaled[1] in 1901 and we tipped our hutches on the level, so I've seen the pit bing grow each year for seventy years. Every year the wind has carried the seeds, till now there are trees on the top of it. Everything belonged to the Thorneycroft's[2] pit, houses, roads and all. When the 1911 strike came, I was just 18 and all we young lads thought of then was getting to Falkirk for

[1] Opened for production.
[2] He was a Minister in the Tory government.

77

a couple of pints, a night with the girls and when you were short of money, you'd pawn your watch one time, and next time I'd pawn mine.

When the 1921 lockout came, I was a member of the pit strike committee and we did our level best to see there was no scabbing. Plean was solid. There were no breakaways. The soldiers were out, and the coal-owners used to sit on the coal engine taking the wagons from the colliery to the junction. By the 1921 strike I'd learnt a thing or two.

When the 1914–18 war came, I volunteered for the Gordon Highlanders. They told us all sorts of stories about the Germans boiling the weans (children) to get fat for cartridges, and I was stupid enough to believe it. Well I was wounded at Loos and discharged. When I came out conditions in the coalfield were bloody awful to say the least of it. I got a book which entitled me to 30 days before I'd to go and get a job. Thorneycroft gave instructions that such as I were to get a light job till we got our 'pit e'en' back (till our eyes got accustomed to the work underground). That was for services rendered to King and Country, for being a good laddie.

After the general strike, my wife and six weans, all born in the same bed, were flung out in the streets, because of rent arrears. That was because I'd been a bad laddie. Not that I'm making myself out to be anything special; there were thousands like me.

During the war wages had risen to £1 a day, but it was mainly war bonus; the union leadership didn't realise the need to get that bonus consolidated. It was a makeshift arrangement. Well, in the twenties, we went to bed one day with £1 a day and woke up next day with 8s a day. The coal-owners were like the other employers, except that they were ten times worse. They made up their minds after the 1914–18 war that they were going to put us down, and put us down they did.

W. H. STOKES, CBE, JP
Retired divisional organiser of the Amalgamated Engineering Union

Looking back to that period in the early twenties, on careful reflection you cannot get away from the feeling that it was a very carefully thought-out period of challenge by the employers in all industries. In the engineering industry, there was unemploymnet and short-time working, a long and exhausting dispute with the foundry workers and then, in 1922, a 13-week engineering lockout. It was carefully worked out by someone who knew his job and the Amalgamated Engineering Union, which, remember, had only recently been formed, had this thrown at it.

I was secretary of the local shop steward's committee for Coventry at the time the lockout began on March 11. Other unions in the industry joined with us for a time, but for the most part, we were on our own. Officially the dispute was over the interpretation of a clause of the procedure agreement, but the main issue was overtime. The employers claimed the right to decide when it was necessary. The men said that the work people should be consulted. There was a ballot, the union members rejected the employers' proposals, and the employers locked us out.

Well, we lost in the end, though it was a hard-fought battle. There was good weather that summer and we were enthusiastic. There was a Communist fellow in the district, his name was Leckie, a physically powerful man, a remarkable orator with the simple slogan style of an American cheer leader. He would lead people round the town, chanting 'Who's that feller with the big red nose?' He was very popular and influential then afterwards he disappeared completely.

The twenties saw a lot of such activity by active rank and file groups like the Minority Movement, developing quickly and later fading. They were run largely by the Communist Party, but they had plenty of people in them who were not Communists. Jack Tanner, later President of the Amalgamated Engineering Union, was loosely associated with it at the time, though the most prominent were men like Tom Mann, Harry Pollitt, and Wal Hannington, the unemployed workers' leader.

Today there doesn't seem to be the same preparedness for personal sacrifice in the Labour movement, with people giving unlimited time, with nothing else seeming to matter. Then, people, mainly Left wingers, would meet in each other's houses to discuss problems; today people have cars and seem to drive away from each other. The Minority Movement never reached what they hoped to achieve. It never built up a strong Left-wing trade union mass movement, but what it did through the AEU left its mark, and quite a number of the people who were then active emerged as leaders at district and national level. I think some of this has rubbed off on leaders like Scanlon today.

Well, we lost the 1922 lockout, I suspect because the other side was much better prepared for it than we were. The effect on our membership was catastrophic. I suppose in this area we went from 10,000 to 12,000 down to 2,500 members and stayed that way until around the Second World War. Brownlie, the AEU General Secretary, upset the apple-cart a bit by giving an interview to the Sunday Press, saying there was no point in holding out, best to have an orderly return to work. No doubt his intentions were good, but the effect wasn't; the 'orderly return' became a rout.

In our district the union tried to wield the big stick; every man who went back without waiting for the word was considered to be acting contrary to society interests. They were fined; some refused to pay the fines and they were excluded from the union. I lost my job altogether; when I got back I found another member had taken it.

PETER KERRIGAN
Former Glasgow engineers' leader, Minority Movement and Communist Party organiser

I was paid off just before the 1922 lockout; I'd only finished my apprenticeship six months before, but I was active in the union, and was branch chairman. I was elected to the Central Lockout Committee in Glasgow, to represent the unemployed. At the time there were almost as many unemployed as there were locked out, and it was very important that the unemployed should not be induced to take the jobs of the men locked out.

We organised marches of unemployed and locked-out members with a flute band, and in general the men were absolutely solid. When a man worked there would be chalked over the walls of his house '—— is a scab'. There was very bitter feeling when the other unions, who had come out with us for two weeks, went back to work leaving us on our own. Lockout pay, while it lasted was 15s a week. I had met Rose, now my wife, in 1921, just after I lost my job, and we decided that we couldn't afford to get married for the moment; as it happened we couldn't get married until Christmas Eve 1926.

One thing needs to be said about the 1922 lockout and other disputes. The unemployed were blackleg-proof. I cannot think of any significant action when the unemployed could be used to break a strike.

BOB LOVELL
District secretary of the Amalgamated Engineering Union (retired)

When the 1922 lockout started, I had been out of work for some little time and was active in the Unemployed Workers Movement in north-west London, together with Wal Hannington; I had palled up with him after the 1914–18 war when we were pushing to get the various engineering unions amalgamated. I was co-opted on to the local lockout committee of the AEU and my chief job on their behalf was to organise the unemployed. When the employers locked engineering workers out, they knew what they were doing because, when the lockout started, there were 90,000 members of the AEU out of work already, and many more on short time. In 1921 the union paid out over £2 million in unemployment benefit, and you mustn't forget that the AEU had only just been formed. The employers were striking when the union was weak. But despite everything, the remarkable thing was that the unemployed did not scab.

We would organise the unemployed and march them to factories where people were working to persuade them to close down, or at least not to work overtime, while other people were locked out. There was one factory, the British Ensign Co. at Willesden Green, where the men were practically unorganised. In order to reach them, we decided we would have to raid the factory. First we organised a sham football match, and a few dozen of us carrying a football set off in another direction. The idea was to draw off the police, who in those days always kept the unemployed under very close observation.

At the same time, we had arranged for Wal Hannington to address a meeting in the Willesden Green Socialist Club rooms which was more or less opposite the factory. This gathered together about fifty of us, and at 2 p.m., when the workers went back after their regular lunch-hour, we left the meeting, walked across the road with them, and through the gates. Straight inside

F

the factory we went, where we shut down the power to the machinery, and the chairman of the local AEU branch mounted a bench and announced our purpose in invading the factory. While he was speaking the manager came down and asked permission to say a few words.

This permission granted, the manager mounted the bench and explained that while he was not friendly towards our aims he was not antagonistic. His men were still at work because his was a non-federated firm and not associated with the lockout. He invited the lockout committee to send a deputation to see him. But before he got any further with his speech, two or three dozen policemen rushed into the factory, up to the speaker on the bench and grabbed him by the coat to drag him down. It took some explanation to convince them who he was, but finally the police left and the meeting closed. A deputation went to the manager's office and it was agreed that while the lockout lasted there would be no more overtime worked.

At the Rotax factory, members of our committee went into the works canteen during the lunch hour and when they had finished their meal mounted on the table and addressed the workers, explaining what the union policy was and calling on them to work for a united front, with one industry, one union. At another factory in Hendon, I was smuggled in in working clothes at eight o'clock in the morning. At 8.30 I addressed a meeting. At noon the men walked out of the factory.

We put up a good fight for 13 weeks, but we were beaten in the end, as the employers had calculated. First, as I say, there were a hell of a lot of members out of work. Even before the lockout we'd been forced to accept wage cuts of over 16s a week. Then the AEU, which had been formed out of nine different unions only two years before in 1920, was practically on its own; the other unions in the industry only backed it for a while. The employers federation had adopted a brutal policy since the war, with the full backing of the Government. The bosses were determined that they wouldn't let us 'interfere with their managerial functions', which meant in this case that they would decide about overtime, without consulting us.

After the lockout they said there would be wage cuts of fifteen shillings imposed in three monthly stages of five shillings each and that if any stoppage occurred, they would impose the whole reduction by August 1922. Altogether in about a year wages were cut by over thirty shillings a week. And this is one thing that has to be remembered about the great struggles of the twenties and the thirties. There was splendid spirit, courage and solidarity but, unlike today, they were nearly all rearguard actions, trying to stop the employers making conditions worse. And in most of the biggest battles the workers were in fact defeated and it was only towards the end of the thirties that the trade union movement began to pick up again.

Engineering workers are still suffering from the results of the 1922 lockout as a matter of fact; when we went back the bosses imposed the 'procedure' system, which frustrates attempts to settle matters at factory level. It is the cause of so many unofficial strikes.

What made matters worse for the active union member, though, was the feeling that the leadership had let us down, particularly when Brownlie, in an interview with the Press, not in a direct instruction to his members, chose to say that the men might as well go back to work. It was actions like this, coupled with the let-down by the leaders when the Triple Alliance failed the miners in 1921, that made rank and file movements like the Minority Movement so important.

Tom Mann was already putting the case for a General Strike in 1923. He argued that the miners were beaten in 1921 because of the lack of solidarity of workers in other trades. In the engineering lockout, he said that we failed because there wasn't even solidarity among the workers in the engineering industry. If workers were going to come out with any hope of changing matters, it should be one out, all out.

CHAPTER THREE

1926

General Strike and Miners' Lockout

By 1925, the mining industry, the most sensitive part of the economy, after a brief period of boom was again in trouble. Coal-owners demanded further wage cuts. This time, after three years' of rank and file criticism over the failure of 1921, the Triple Alliance held firm. The Baldwin government provided a subsidy to hold up miners' wages for nine months, nine months in which, under the enthusiastic guidance of the Chancellor of the Exchequer, Winston Churchill, the authorities prepared for a confrontation. Prime Minister Baldwin said that 'all the workers of this country have got to take reductions in wages to help put industry on its feet.' The miners replied with the slogan 'Not a penny off the pay, not an hour on the day.'

The Left wing, including rank and file bodies like the Minority Movement, had been advocating a General Strike for some time. However, the Trades Union Congress General Council, with its new key men, E. Bevin (transport) and J. H. Thomas (railways), was less eager for a battle which would line the trade unions up not only against the coal-owners but against all the employers, backed by the government.

As May 1926 and the time for battle approached, the leaders of one side became more firm and more intransigent, the leaders on the other side became more reflective and hesitant. Faced with an inevitable clash, the TUC sought powers from the unions, which some were reluctant to grant. The rank and file were eager to fight and, as George Isaac's account shows, precipitated the battle.

The withdrawal of the TUC General Council after nine days, on terms which the miners could not accept, was followed by a

THE
BRITISH WORKER
OFFICIAL STRIKE NEWS BULLETIN
Published by The General Council of the Trades Union Congress

| No. 1. | WEDNESDAY EVENING, MAY 5, 1926. | PRICE ONE PENNY |

IN LONDON AND THE SOUTH

Splendid Loyalty of Transport Workers

EVERY DOCKER OUT

"London dock workers are absolutely splendid," said an official of the Transport and General Workers' Union.

"So far as they are concerned, it is a 100 per cent. strike. There is no trouble and everything is going smoothly."

POLICE HELP REFUSED

At Swindon the railwaymen are obeying Mr. Cramp's injunction to remain steady and to preserve order. The Great Western works are, of course, closed, and no trains are running.

It was stated at a mass meeting of the N.U.R. that Mr. Collett (the

The General Council suggests that in all districts where large numbers of workers are idle sports should be organised and entertainments arranged.

This will both keep a number of people busy and provide amusement for many more.

chief mechanical engineer) had declined the oer of the police and the military to guard the railway works, saying he could rely on the strikers to preserve law and order. Railway workshops at Wolverton, Crewe, and elsewhere are closed.

CHANNEL SERVICES

At Dover the whole of the tramways staff are out. The cross-Channel boat service is greatly curtailed, and a large number of passengers are awaiting the opportunity to cross.

NOT ENOUGH!

From 2½ to 3 million workers have ceased work.

The Government announced by yesterday's wireless that 30,000 volunteers had registered, expressing willingness to take the strikers' places. It doesn't seem enough!

Published for the General Council of the Trades Union Congress by Victoria House Printing Company, 2, Carmelite-street, London, E.C.4. Telephone (8 lines): 8210 City.

WONDERFUL RESPONSE TO THE CALL

General Council's Message : Stand Firm and Keep Order

The workers' response has exceeded all expectations. The first day of the great General Strike is over. They have manifested their determination and unity to the whole world. They have resolved that the attempt of the mineowners' to starve three million men, women and children into submission shall not succeed.

. All the essential industries and all the transport services have been brought to a standstill. The only exception is that the distribution of milk and food has been permitted to continue. The Trades Union General Council is not making war on the people. It is anxious that the ordinary members of the public shall not be penalised for the unpatriotic conduct of the mineowners and the Government.

Never have the workers responded with greater enthusiasm to the call of their leaders. The only difficulty that the General Council is experiencing, in fact, is in persuading those workers in the second line of defence to continue at work until the withdrawal of their labour may be needed.

WORKERS' QUIET DIGNITY

The conduct of the trade unionists, too, constitutes a credit to the whole movement. Despite the presence of armed police and the military, the workers have preserved a quiet orderliness and dignity, which the General Council urges them to maintain, even in the face of the temptation and provocation which the Government is placing in their path.

To the unemployed, also, the General Council would address an earnest appeal. In the present fight there are two sides only—the workers on the one hand and those who are against them on the other.

Every unemployed man or woman who "blacklegs " on any job offered by employers or the authorities is merely helping to bring down the standard of living for the workers as a whole, and to create a resultant situation in which the number of unemployed must be greater than ever.

The General Council is confident that the unemployed will realise how closely their interests are involved in a successful issue to the greatest battle ever fought by the workers of the country in the defence of the right to live by work.

MESSAGE TO ALL WORKERS.

The General Council of the Trades Union Congress wishes to emphasise the fact that this is an industrial dispute. It expects every member taking part to be exemplary in his conduct and not to give any opportunity for police interference. The outbreak of any disturbances would be very damaging to the prospects of a successful termination to the dispute.

The Council asks pickets especially to avoid obstruction and to confine themselves strictly to their legitimate duties.

SOUTH WALES IS SOLID !

Not a Wheel Turning in Allied Industries

'MEN ARE SPLENDID !'

Throughout South Wales the stoppage is complete, and everywhere the men are loyally observing the orders of the T.U.C. to refrain from any conduct likely to lead to disturbance.

So unanimous has been the response to the call of the leaders, that not a wheel is turning in the industries affiliated to the T.U.C.

MONMOUTHSHIRE

Complete standstill of industries in the eastern valleys. Absolute unanimity prevails among the rank and file of the affiliated unions, and not a single wheel is turning in the allied industries.

Monmouth Education Authority—which has a majority of Labour representatives—has arranged to feed the school-children where required.

ABERDARE VALLEY

All railway and bus services are at a standstill. The miners' attitude indicates that they are absolutely loyal to the advice of their leaders to refrain from anything in the nature of riotous behaviour.

NEATH

The workers have unanimously responded to the call in support of the miners, and the stoppage is complete.

With one exception, safety men are remaining at their posts.

The behaviour of the men is splendid.

AMMAN VALLEY

Every industry and almost the entire transport services are at a standstill at Ammanford and throughout the populous Amman Valley.

GLAMORGANSHIRE

The men are obeying implicitly the instructions of their leaders not to create any disturbance. Crowded meetings of miners have registered their unanimous intention to stand by the T.U.C.

ABERTRIDWR

At the Windsor Colliery, Abertridwr, a deputation of the men and the management met and agreed to safety men being allowed to work.

A Trades Council, composed solely of branches affiliated to the T.U.C., has been formed to act as a Lock-out Committee for Abertridwr and Senghenydd.

PORT TALBOT

Perfect order is being maintained at Port Talbot, where all the industries are shut down.

7. Front page from *The British Worker*, the TUC's official newspaper for the General Strike – May 5, 1926

six months' lockout which crushed the miners and depressed the trade union movement for years to come.

It is interesting to reflect that in 1926, twice as many days' work were lost as in all of the 25 years following World War II, all to compel the miners to work longer for less pay.

RT HON. GEORGE ISAACS, JP, DL
Former Minister of Labour, and general secretary of National Society of Operative Printers' Assistants

The night we took the final decision on the General Strike the union executives met in the Memorial Hall in London. There was a roll call and every General Secretary was asked to stand up and say 'yes' or 'no', whether his union would hand over its powers to the General Council of the Trades Union Congress. I remember one who said 'no', W. J. Brown, leader of the civil service people, who later became an MP, anti-Labour Party. He hummed and ha-ed. They were willing he said, but they had special duties, and so he edged out of it. The plain fact was that he had the wind up, and he was not the only one.

That night as we were leaving the hall, I walked along with Williams, secretary of the international dockers and transport workers. He was scared stiff of the fact that we had handed over our powers to the TUC. I didn't feel very happy about it at the time and wondered where it was all going to end. I wondered whether we had bitten off more than we could chew.

But there could be no mistaking the feeling of sympathy for the miners. From all that we had been told by the miners, we knew that there was only one set of employers more bitterly detested by the trade union movement than the mine-owners and that was the dock employers; they were two gangs of powerful men grinding these two sections of workers down. So there was a strong desire to help the miners. All in all it was a great demonstration of working class solidarity and I'm not sorry to have taken part in it.

The night it happened, I was on the doorstep of the *Daily Mail*. I was going round to tell the men not to stop work till they were told to. As I reached the *Daily Mail*, out came the father of the chapel, the leader of the union organisation inside the newspaper.

'There's trouble in there, George. They've got a leading article saying we're fighting against King and country.'

The compositors had set the leading article and the stereotypers had cast it. But the machine minders wouldn't put it on. 'I'll get you a galley of it.' He got it out and gave it to me. I kept it for nearly 20 years. I gave it to Ernie Bevin after the Second World War when he moved rejection of the 1927 Trades Disputes Act which the Tories brought in after the General Strike. Yes, my galley proof came in handy in that debate. Bevin flaunted it in the face of Churchill, for he had written that editorial.

But the fact was that it wasn't the remark about King and Country that put the backs of our lads up. It was the charge that they were 'intending to bring hunger and want on their own people'. They weren't going to put up with that.

What must have happened was that when the editorial had been set up and was being read, someone upstairs, perhaps a Communist or Syndicalist or some militant or other, had spotted it and sent a copy down to the men in the machine room. When they read it, they walked out.

'Well,' I said to the father of the chapel, 'I'm not going to tell you to go back.' So I walked away from the *Daily Mail* and down into Shoe Lane, where I met the men from the *Daily Express*.

'Where are you going?' I said.

They said, 'The *Daily Mail*'s been shut down, so we're all coming out.' And from then on, there was no stopping it.

GEORGE HODGKINSON
Former Labour leader in Coventry City Council, and shop steward

It was an emergency, and it brought the old shop steward movement back into business with a quality and level of work which proved what working people can do. In those days the local trades councils embraced almost every industrial organisation in the district. They were considered as Councils of Action and though the General Strike only went on for nine days, the level of organisation was higher at the end than at the beginning. The miners had been locked out and we were going to their assistance; an injury to one was an injury to all. I had been out of the factory work for some time, in fact I was Secretary of the Labour Party.

But they seconded me to the Council of Action propaganda committee, as scribe and general master-mind for public relations.

Each morning we would have a meeting on Pool Meadow in Coventry to report the situation. Already the power of the workers showed itself, controlling the vital services such as supplying heat, power and light for hospitals, under strict trade union sanction. We sent lads out to address meetings for 30 or 40 miles around, youngsters who had never been on public platforms in their lives.

In London Winston Churchill was publishing the *British Gazette*, having it printed in Paris and brought over here. But the TUC was not responding in the same way. The TUC structure made it impossible for it to handle a national dispute. Having been given the power, it didn't know how to delegate the responsibility. It found a situation in its lap it didn't expect and wasn't really prepared to counter Churchill and his *British Gazette*.

When it began to publish the *British Worker*, we sent a runner by motor bike up to London every day to get copies. But we also invented a strike bulletin of our own, a foolscap sheet printed on both sides, punched out on a stencil by typewriter and ready every morning at six. Every morning, too, the newsagents were waiting outside. We had made a bargain with them. They did not sell the *British Gazette* and in return they were sole distributors of our news-sheet. They sold at a penny a copy, and our Gestetner made £47 and paid for itself.

This news bulletin was vital, for false information was flying all over the place. We heard that troops on Salisbury Plain had refused to be used against the strike. I was cagey about this story and asked Noel Baker to check it and he told me it wasn't true. By keeping the people well informed, we kept the situation in Coventry solid, and when the strike was called off I went down with a deputation to London to demand that it be continued, for the rank and file in our area were ready and willing to carry on.

R. E. SCOULLER
Former official of the National Union of Clerks, Glasgow

I was seconded by the Clerks' Union to the Scottish Trades Union Congress office where, together with Bill Elger, the General Secretary and Agnes Richards, the typist, I made up the staff. We did the donkey work, while the General Council sat around issuing edicts. But it was a thrilling time while it lasted.

We decided to issue our own *Scottish Worker*, and at first the TUC in London was a bit nervous and unwilling to let us have our own newspaper. But the Civic Press printed it. The Forward Press put its newsprint at our disposal and journalists and typographers fought for permission to work on it. Every day there were crowds outside the office, fighting to get copies. Joe Duncan, chairman of the Scottish TUC got a black eye from one bloke who took three bundles instead of one. No wonder, because the news boys were paying us 1d for it and selling it for 6s. One day the crowds were so thick outside the office that we had to call in our enemies, the police, to assist us by clearing a passage.

In and out of the city, not a vehicle could move without our sanction. We would have commercial travellers ringing us up, highly indignant at being waylaid on the road by gangs of miners. One day I had an anxious phone call from one of the pickets.

'What shall we do? The field's full.'

'What field?'

'We're stopping the cars on the road and turning them into a field.'

'Well, find another field,' I said.

I handled most of the requests for permits to move. Some were granted without a moment's hesitation, supplies for hospitals. But some tried to move commercial stuff, though they very quickly packed it in. If they tried to do it without a permit, they never got beyond Glasgow. It was quite an experience to have contractors come and ask permission to move stuff and be refused. Some young people thought the revolution had arrived.

There was a strategy to the general strike. The theory was that they were to be called out in three lines. The first was to be road and rail transport, the second the main factories; the third line was supposed to stay in and provide assistance, financial and otherwise, to those who were out. That was the theory. The fact was that the enthusiasm was such that many came out without waiting to be called. And remember, they came out without strike pay. But how long can you run a strike without strike pay? Some of the critics have denied it, but there were signs that after nine days the strike was beginning to crack. While it lasted though, the spirit was tremendous.

The students were out to smash the strike, supporting Churchill's OMS (Organisation for the Maintenance of Supplies). They manned the tram cars. But they only got about three out of the depot. The strikers went to the depot, paid the minimum fare and stayed on, crowding out anyone else who tried to board. There was some trouble with the police. Some boys as usual went to extremes.

PETER KERRIGAN
Former Glasgow engineers' leader, Minority Movement and Communist Party organiser

In Glasgow the majority of the strike breakers, such as they were, were recruited from the students. They tried to move lorries from the docks and manned trams, mainly in the centre. But the trams couldn't move half a mile without being smashed up and the lorries from the docks had to have military escort. It was a long time before what the students did was forgotten. There was the utmost hatred towards them for years afterwards. The trades council and trade unionists would have nothing to do with students' rags for years afterwards, even though they were then new youngsters who had had nothing to do with the General Strike. The university was anathema even though three or four years later there wasn't a student left who had blacklegged. Still it was almost the mid-thirties and the period of the war in Spain before workers could look on students with anything but a jaundiced eye.

There was a hell of a row in the central strike committee over these battles with blackleg transport and local clashes with the police. On the Left we wanted the lads picketing to carry sticks, but we were voted down on that, though in the local councils of action set up in some of the areas there was a more militant line.

ALF GARRARD
Former rank and file building worker

When the General Strike came, our local Right wing ran away and left us high and dry on our own. So, on the Lambeth Trades Council, we set up three committees, ways and means, communications and Press. The Communications Committee had 300 vehicles at its disposal, including 20 taxis, 30–40 motor-cyclists, wagons and vans, all lined up in the streets outside the Strike Committee rooms, with permits for petrol, etc, being issued to authentic drivers. We issued milk permits to the local borough council for the schools; they could get it no other way.

We produced our own news-sheet, the *Lambeth Worker*. One day, as we were in the middle of printing the paper, there came a bang on the door. The police were there. The lads were passing bundles of papers through into next door where there was a friendly news agent and away on motor-cycles. The dustbin was full of smoking, smouldering stencils by the time I managed to get the door open and admit the police.

They barged in and grabbed hold of a big box.

'What's this?' they said.

'I don't know.'

They forced it open. It was full of prayers and hymn books. They grabbed a parcel from the mantelshelf and tore it open. It was full of copies of the local Labour Party constitution. They lumbered us off to the police station and kept us there all night. But we carried on until the end and when it was called off, there were more people out than there were at the beginning. We were let down, but it taught us a lesson. It was good training in the art of running things.

ALBERT IRONS, BEM
Retired secretary of the National Union of Railwaymen, Paddington

Our committee, which brought together all the National Union of Railwaymen's branches in West London, met in a pub and one day I was asked by the publican to come down into the back room, where someone wanted to meet me. It turned out to be the divisional superintendent from the local police station and naturally I was on the defensive. To my surprise he said, 'We can avoid trouble in this area if we can co-operate.' The fact was, he said, that he had a problem. He could cope with his own men, but there were a lot of specials in the area and he was 'having some difficulty in getting them to conform to the regulations I've laid down'.

So after that, I went to see him a couple of times to sort things out. The second time came when the General Strike was over. We had to call another strike over the terms of settlement; some men had been suspended or put on other jobs. I had called a meeting outside Paddington Station when suddenly a posse of specials arrived and scattered us right and left. I'm a nervous chap, but when they set about our chaps with their truncheons, I grabbed the leader of them and insisted that we went down to the local police station, where I saw one of the under officers. Finally he took a group of regulars down and held back the specials while I finished addressing the meeting.

FRANK JACKSON
Retired rank and file building worker

Splits? They were everywhere. They even followed my missus about while she was shopping. I was organiser for the St Pancras Trades Council, and in St Pancras the strike was absolutely complete. When they tried to move the buses, we lined them all up, pulled out the distributor wires and hauled the blacklegs out of the cabs. Mounted police were escorting the trams down the Chalk Farm Road, so we staged a fight and drew off the police. Then we planted wedges between the rails with a sledge hammer and brought the trams to a halt. Every day we brought out two issues of the *St Pancras Gazette* from 67, Camden Street, our headquarters. The police raided it, but we had a tip off and removed the duplicators from the iron cases and filled them with bricks; that was what the police carted off to the station. After that they closed No. 67 down. and we opened up new offices in a fellow's house; it backed up on the police station, but they never thought of looking there.

We had a united committee with all the women on it. The Trades Council fitted up a canteen, where meals were organised for the pickets and tea fights for the kids. The women organised the lot.

As soon as the strike was over the first thing the Right Wing did was bump the trades councils. I was delegate from the St Pancras Trades Council to the Labour Party Conference and they turfed me out of that. Among the rank and file we had no faith in the trade union leadership, but we didn't have a real suspicion there would be a sell-out and never made any move to counter-act what the officials were doing. The rank and file did not have a real objective in front of them, what to do if they won the strike.

J. WITHERS
London machine branch, National Society of Operative Printers' Assistants

1926 was a real experience. A triumphant disaster if you like. The unions lost, but they frightened the Establishment all right. I was nearly 20 at the time, and working at the *Evening News*, but because of the Paper Workers set-up I could not belong to the appropriate union. So I paid into the builders' labourers' at Blackfriars Road. I did this not through any altruistic motives, but simply because my father, who had worked at the *News* all his life, had indoctrinated me with the idea, which I still retain, that anybody who aspired to a job with conditions and wages of a reasonable standard should *want* to join a union, not *have* to join. So my experience of the General Strike was unique, to say the least. Officially I was not on strike, but in my heart and by my actions, I was not only on strike because of the shut down but participating in it with all the amateur bravado of a 20 year-old.

I remember being given bundles of the Scab sheet the *News* was printing and being told to distribute them. They were dumped into the pond at Chingford. Poor Billy Horne, the inspector, didn't believe me when he asked for the money and I told him I thought they were for free distribution.

A few of the lads and myself paid a visit to a firm off Long Acre where some fellows were blacklegging and there was a scuffle. Later we found a van driver getting some newspapers out from John Tallis Street and we raided the van, cutting open the bundles and scattering them all over the street. Unfortunately in the skirmish the driver received a punctured posterior and ran up Whitefriars Street, yelling blue murder. Wrong of us, I now know but, in my opinion, 1926 was the trade union movement's finest hour, despite the abortive result.

The miners' terrible conditions following the owners' ultimatum of a wage cut, the government trying to keep the workers down, in fact the whole business of class war being waged when the poorest were weakest, all showed that if ever the unions and the workers in general were to establish some sort of dignity, 1926 was the time. Baldwin, the students and many of the smug white-collar brigade did their damndest to break the strike and I suppose they still live in the belief that they did. But did they? My experience was that Big Business received the biggest shock of its life, that such a situation could happen. The City of London itself, with its marshalling yard at Guildhall for lorries to blackleg on the docks and wharves at Upper and Lower Thames Street, was all part of their response. I remember on one occasion I was remonstrating with a crew there about to embark in convoy when a chap, obviously anti-union, got down and tried to have a go at me. Well I was handy myself in those days, and was ready for a go, too, but a policeman singled him out and told him to shut his big mouth or else. Whether it was my intervention, or the police's or the strength of the dockers' picket, that convoy at least turned back.

But I experienced police brutality in Kingsland Road. The whole area was a seething mass of frightened but nevertheless belligerent people. The roads and pavements were jammed, horse vans, lorries and 'black' transport were being man-handled; police were there in force and I suppose that for a time things could have been described as desperate. The crucial point came when a fresh force of police arrived on the outskirts and I heard an officer call out, 'Charge the bastards. Use everything you've got.'

And they did. I saw men, women and even youngsters knocked over and out like nine pins. Shades of Peterloo. If they had been armed, apart from their truncheons and boots, Kingsland Road would have gone down in history as an even greater massacre. Luckily there were two hospitals nearby, the St Leonards and the Metropolitan, although I wonder if treatment was given to those desperate people. On the whole, I am sure, the police themselves were sympathetic, remembering that only a few years previously they were on strike themselves (in 1918). But one had to remember that they also had to take orders from their hierarchy, plus those handed down from the government. So what could a policeman, with his training and background, do?

Things would be different today, I'm sure. The students are now possibly the most militant, the white collar workers, including

Whitehall are organised and the police more aware of people's problems. And the army today, would they be used in the same way?

ISOBEL BROWN
Communist organiser, rank and file leader in woollen textile industry

I saw very little of the General Strike, for I was in jail after making a speech at Castleford, urging soldiers to remember that it was their fathers and brothers who were coming out on strike. The Press reported me as a 'well spoken young woman with a marked foreign accent' (I was from North Shields). When I came out three months later, to my horror, police were picking people up all over the place. They were fining them £50 or seven days for chalking slogans on the pavements. But I was really furious to discover that all the fines were being paid, such was the solidarity. I objected to the workers being milked in this way and proposed to the Communist Party that the next leading person picked up should accept prison and not have their fine paid. Well, the next one to be arrested was me and it was three months and £50 or another three months. So I fully expected to be another three months inside. But the Bradford Trades Council collected the money and my husband met me outside Hull Prison. I was furious. He was furious. But there was nothing to do about it. They had collected the money.

I was put in Hull Prison because, apart from Strangeways, it was the only one near at hand with facilities for women. The women there, who were mostly prostitutes, used to do the laundering for the 300 men there. They wouldn't let me near the laundry and generally kept me away from the other women. On the first day I was admitted with five other women. They issued us with a cotton chemise, a petticoat, a coloured cotton skirt, bloomers with a flap that buttoned at the back, an apron, a little white bonnet that wouldn't fit a child and black woollen stockings with red rings so that they could spot you if you tried to escape.

First of all they asked me what my religion was and when I had convinced them I was an atheist, they left me locked up in my cell, but later asked me if I would like a book. I said I would and they brought me *What Katy Did at School*.

That day the new arrivals were brought before the Governor who was sitting at a long table next to a big window with the chaplain and matron. The Governor said, 'I'm extremely sorry to see a woman like you in prison. I am against the persecution of people for political views and would advise you that if you will keep to the prison rules we will try to make it as easy as possible.'

The Chaplain added, 'I am a member of the Industrial Christian Fellowship and I am very much in sympathy with what you feel about the miners, though I do not think what you said was ethical or wise.'

Dr JOHN LEWIS
Former lecturer and Presbyterian minister in Gravesend and Birmingham

During the nine days of the strike the Presbyterians held their annual synod at Liverpool. One or two Socialist parsons and myself brought the case of the miners before the synod; there was an overwhelming vote of support, and a message went to the Church leaders, the Archbishop of Canterbury, etc.

It was simply a matter of getting the facts over, for the miners had a cast-iron case, the steady degradation of their wages and conditions since the war, cuts in pay which was already at rock bottom and the betrayal of pledges made to them.

But generally speaking the professional people just listened to Baldwin, The broadcasts were very important in the absence of newspapers, which were stopped by the strike. Under this influence such people just took the view that the strike was forcing the demands of a minority on the whole country; the rights or wrongs of the miners' case never came into it.

By contrast, among the trade unions there never was such solidarity, such feeling. You could feel the tide rising beneath you. It was a time when trade union members, who had never before taken any interest, were as militant as you could find. My church was then one of 13 'Labour' churches in Birmingham, where on Sunday evenings there would be speakers, music and songs, all with a slant towards the Labour movement.

When the General Strike came we threw open our church for any kind of gathering, providing cups of tea and coffee. The strike committee sent me round to visit trade union branches; we visited every branch in Birmingham, including ones with strange names I never even knew existed before. They were all drawn in and there were huge meetings in Canon Hill Park. I remember one at which I spoke from one platform and Oswald Mosley spoke from another. I was chairman of the Ladywood Labour Party and he was our candidate in those days. There was a great air of excitement, and while it lasted a feeling that anything was possible.

BESSIE DICKENSON
Retired weaver at Burnley and Nelson

I had a bike and would ride with messages for the strike com-mittee in Barnoldswick over to the strike committee in Burnley. My brother collected money during the strike and the miners' lockout that followed, and I'd help him. In the end I raffled all the stuff I'd collected for my bottom drawer, and my umbrella as well. We kept it up all through the lockout and I can recall the miners coming down from Yorkshire with bands, and we organised concerts to help them.

I'd always been political, reading the old Socialist literature (Dad's copies of *Justice* and *Clarion*) from the time I was 12. I'd seen the big textile strikes after the 1914–18 war against the wage reductions, when we used to line up and throw sods at the knob-sticks as they went into the mill. Some of them who lived opposite us we never spoke to again. After I started work I bought a little duplicating set out of my own savings and put out my own leaflets about India and the Black and Tans in Ireland.

So when 1926 came I did all I could to help the strike com-mittee. One day I cycled over to Burnley with a message and I saw the soldiers moving into the town in big lorries. There was a Parson Joe, standing by the side of the road and I turned to him and said:

'And what do you think of that?'

And he replied, 'Oh, shut up.'

Then when it was all over and I saw the railwaymen going back, dejected, the tears rolled down my face.

RT HON. GEORGE ISAACS, JP, DL
Former Minister of Labour, and general secretary of National Society of Operative Printers' Assistants

Well, we had to go back, and the bosses were cock-a-hoop. The print union leaders went to see the President of the Federation of Master Printers, Colonel Fletcher, a great big man, colonel in the territorial army and a big man in the printing trade. Our spokesman was Charles Bowerman, retired but still president of the Printing and Kindred Trades Federation.

This Colonel Fletcher began to hector us, and after a bit of this, I whispered to my mate,

'I'm not standing for any more. I'm going.'

So Fletcher said to me, 'Have you got anything to say?'

And I stood up and said, 'You can shit on us, but you're not going to rub it in.'

And with that we all walked out. As we reached the London Society of Compositors, headquarters in Blackfriars and were standing outside, a bus-driver saw us from his cab. He stopped his bus, jumped out and shouted, 'One out, all out, mates. If you're out again, so am I.'

I explained to him that we weren't out on strike and he drove off. But that was the feeling of those who had taken part.

There was a vigorous movement running down the TUC leadership afterwards, saying that the fight would have been won if only they had been prepared to carry on. Well I was glad it had happened, for it taught us a lesson in two ways. We knew that we could rely on the working man to stand by the less fortunate and we knew that we were not organised to fight the government. It will never happen that way again because, for one thing, as soon as it was over Ernie Bevin, leader of the Transport and General Workers Union, had its rules changed to prevent the union ever again handing over its powers to any other body. If it ever happens again, it won't be with the unions handing over power to the TUC, but you can't wash out the possibility of a spontaneous outburst – say if they were to put troops in to get the men out of the UCS shipyards – there could be an explosion, for there is a streak of gunpowder running through the situation. But 1926 won't happen again.

GEORGE JAMES
*Retired executive member of National Union of Railwaymen, railway
workshop man*

The General Strike ended on the Wednesday with J. H. Thomas,
the railwaymen's leader, throwing in his hand. But on the railways
the strike went on, mainly to ensure that there was no victimisation.
In Cardiff during the strike we set up a joint committee among the
railway unions, the strike was solid, and many were confident we
had the Government on the floor. They'd have to resign.

But I argued that the General Council of the TUC had no heart
for the strike, and that we'd be sold down the river. Sure enough,
there was a picture in the local paper of J. H. Thomas in tears. My
mate said, 'See, he's in tears.'

'He can make them come any time', I said.

We held a mass meeting in Cathay's Park and there was this
bloke Cook, an inspector, on a box on top of a wagon, telling them
all to go back to work. They were shouting at him, 'Come down
you silly bugger.'

I climbed up and said that we should not go back to work until
we knew the truth from our own side. The fact was that from the
Tuesday the railway officials, led by a man called Wilkinson, had
been at the offices in Cardiff, waiting for us to come back. The
Master of the Cowbridge Hunt, even, had decided to carry on with
the hunt. When asked if it was wise, he replied, 'Oh, it'll be over
by Wednesday.' They knew what our leaders were like, even if
we didn't.

The question was, how were we to go back? Crawl back? We
sent a deputation to Wilkinson to discuss the terms of a return to
work. He wasn't interested in discussing terms. He gave us an
ultimatum. Everybody's service was terminated. The week's
wages in hand were automatically forfeit. The company would take
back who it liked, when it liked and how it liked.

Our deputation went out of the offices into Charles Street,
which was packed, one mass of faces as far as I could see. I got up
on the wall and told them the terms from the Great Western
Railway. Everything was down the drain, all past service was
cancelled, the guaranteed day and the guaranteed week were gone,
they would re-instate who they liked. It was like a graveyard.

Then I said, 'We have decided that the grass shall grow in the streets of Cardiff before we go back on those terms.'

You could have heard the cheers up in Merthyr.

The following day *The Times* editorial said that up until Wednesday the General Strike had been under control. Now it was in the hands of the mob.

On Friday night we were called in by Wilkinson who told us that all past service would count, the week's pay in hand was OK, that it would take time before the guaranteed week could operate. Everyone would start work, though, but one, the station master at Caerphilly, Tom Lewis, who had been boss of the strike committee there. Well, we refused to accept the terms until Lewis was reinstated and finally we all went back to work on three days a week. Jimmy Thomas, meanwhile, went off to the West Indies to recuperate, and in the *Reynolds News* that weekend, Charlie Cramp, another leader of the National Union of Railwaymen, wrote his famous article 'Never again'.

But we had to go back to work, knowing that for a second time the miners had been let down. In 1921, when the miners had been locked out and the railwaymen didn't come out in support, some of the lads taking trains up the valley had been stoned. Those railwaymen who came from homes in the coalfield knew that their fathers and brothers in the pits were still out. It was a terrible feeling.

RT HON. JAMES GRIFFITHS, CH
Former South Wales miners' president

There was a feeling of complete bewilderment in the valleys as the General Strike was called off. Round our way everyone had been out, nothing moved on the roads without a permit from the strike committee. There were no middle class people strike-breaking. And we were a long way from London, a long way from Cardiff even, with no newspapers and only a radio in the occasional house. All that was known was that the rest were to return to work and the miners were to stay out. By that time I was a member of the executive committee of the South Wales miners, the youngest official in the anthracite coalfield. Our executive was called to London for a special conference of the Miners' Federation of

100

Great Britain, where we were given a report by our leaders. We were also told for the first time what had been going on for the past nine days.

Roughly the story told to us by Herbert Smith, one of our leaders, was this. The miners leaders had not been kept informed of what was going on. They did hear that the Trades Union Congress had been in touch with Herbert Samuels, chairman of the Royal Commission on mining, who had offered his services. We had replied we'd had enough of Samuels and didn't want any more of him. But the TUC went ahead against our advice and in the end we were told that Samuels had been able to make some arrangements, which still involved wage reductions. But we still stuck by our demand 'Not a penny off the pay, not a minute on the day.' When we were asked at that conference if we supported the action of our leaders, we agreed unanimously; then we had to go back and report to the villages and the kitchens where the miners and their families were waiting for us.

Our first feeling of bewilderment was followed by one of let-down. We felt that the TUC was backing down on demands that they had accepted. And we knew this feeling was shared not only by the miners but by many among the other unions, especially in our area. After the feeling of let-down came the feeling that we would dig in our heels and stick it out to the end. And that we did. Other workers felt guilty about going back while we were still out. We felt guilty that so many lost their jobs on our account and in the end we were driven to our knees after six months' lockout. We fought ourselves to a standstill and this was followed by years of disillusion, widespread victimisation, increased unemployment and wage cuts. It was the greatest tragedy of that period and the echoes still remain; echoes of bitterness that the TUC and the miners had not found a way of sticking together.

Still, we were on our own and prepared to stick it out. There was no strike pay. The little money which had been in the coffers when the strike began was soon used up. We received money from the Labour Party and money came from Russia. We had to draft a scheme by which this money could be spread over, for if it had been used to pay straight strike pay, it would have gone in a week. We went round to see the local education committees to get them to operate the Act for 'feeding necessitous schoolchildren'; it wasn't mandatory but prescriptive. Then we went to the Guardians to make sure that people could get relief, on loan, for their children. Then to the Co-op to get credit, knowing that the private shop-keepers would have to follow suit.

The balance of the money was used to establish the kitchens in every village, in a miners' hall or church hall, to provide one meal a day for miners and families.

We had special permission to dig for outcrop coal to fuel the kitchens and appealed to all those who had allotments to make gifts to the kitchens so that there would be one good solid meal every day, good broth with veg and bits of meat. Now you must not think of these as charitable soup kitchens; I had seen such soup kitchens in the East End when I was at college. After the meal there would be meetings, and every official was under obligation to be present. Then there would be singing, carnival band competitions, a combination of things to develop fellowship. A spirit developed which I do not think that I have seen or experienced on any other occasion except perhaps during the Blitz in the Second World War. To continue in this way, day by day, displayed a remarkable courage and the fine thing was that this daily meal brought the women into it. They were in the kitchens, cooking in rotation, and then they attended the meetings; they were part of the strike and, as you can understand, while the women support a strike, the men cannot easily be driven back. Unless the union and the home are one, then men may easily be defeat-ed.

As it was, we went through the whole six months in our area without a single breakaway, mainly due, I think, to the fellowship engendered by that one meal a day. Indeed we were able to send our officials to lend a hand in remote areas where there were signs of weakening. I can recall the first breakaway in South Wales, in an isolated place called Heol y cyw (Chicken Road), just a little village of one street with the pit at the end of it. We held a meeting there to decide what to do about the blacklegs. A man with white hair stood up. He spoke in Welsh and I had to translate for some of the people there. He said, 'We have had battles with the police and they have had the batons out. We cannot fight them all. So let us avoid that. Let us treat it as a funeral. They cannot stop us standing by our own doors.'

And so this was done. Every afternoon when the blacklegs came down the road escorted by the police, all the people in the village stood by their doors, hats off and heads bowed. And within a week, all those blacklegs were out again.

WILL PAYNTER
Former general secretary of the National Union of Mineworkers

There was one blackleg family in our village and the police escorted him to work every morning. They were lucky they had a big wall round the back of the house, for the lads would get up the mountain and roll boulders down; the feeling was that strong, as in the 1921 lockout, and the hatred of the coal-owners so intense. Young people today are not able to personalise capitalism as we could then, as the man in the big house at the top of the hill. And the hatred for the owners was extended to those who helped them. In the Rhondda you could dig in almost anywhere and find coal, and during the lockout people were prepared to come in with lorries and take it away. There was more than one lorry tipped down the side of the mountain.

When the whole business was over and we had to accept defeat and the drift back to work began on worse conditions (a longer working day and less pay), the employers never wanted the blacklegs. The fact is that they were not good workers. It was undesirable to have them around afterwards, as the other men were so hostile to them. You have to have team work down the pit.

MEGAN MORGAN
Daughter of John Morgan, miners' leader, Ynysybwl

The colliers would turn out to watch the blacklegs at the colliery down the bottom of the road. The police told my father, who was secretary of the central strike committee, that if he didn't keep the people quiet they would arrest him. So they stood in silence with bowed heads while the blacklegs walked past. And the silence was worse than the heckling. Finally one of the fellows walked into the road, took off his hat and dusted the road in front of the blackleg as he walked. And that one never went back to work afterwards.

It was beautiful weather that summer, what we called strike weather. It never seemed to rain. Some nights there would be dancing in the streets half the night. The jazz bands would walk from the Rhondda, half starved as they were, parade the streets and then walk home again. I was 17 at the time, young enough to enjoy what was going on, but old enough to remember what I saw. The men shaved their heads to keep down the cost of having their hair cut. They dammed up the river, made a pool and there was bathing by moonlight. Everything was organised: the soup kitchen, even the boot repairing, was done co-operatively. Whoever had something extra would share it with someone else and, for all the bitterness, it was a happy time.

We were broken-hearted when the men had to go back. You can imagine the disillusionment, a chance of a lifetime and it had ended in defeat. The Ocean Coal Company put a mark on many of the men so that they never got back to the work in the pits. My father didn't have pay for a year after the strike; even at work he and his brother didn't bring home more than £2 in those days. They punished them by giving them all the worst places in the pit where they could earn very little. It was a very subtle game played to break their spirit. though it didn't work.

My father had been lodge secretary from the time the pit was started and we grew up with the union lodge. At a time when there was no village hall they hired a house and turned it into a library – a first class library, for my father had good taste in books. He'd a universal knowledge of trade union affairs, of customs and religions in this and other countries and his greatest love was to walk for miles in the country reading poetry for anyone who would listen. He founded the Labour Party in our area, he and two others walking down the road singing the 'Red Flag'; people called 'infidels' after them. Arthur Horner said that he was the perfect lodge secretary and when he retired the employers told him. 'We hated your guts, Morgan, but we knew what side of the fence we would find you.'

Well, those times were not forgotten. Only the other day local people were talking about some trouble with a girl, and one said, 'What can you expect? Her grandfather was a blackleg.' No, it isn't easy to forget. No wonder they say the Welsh have a chip on their shoulder.

HYWELL JEFFREY (JEFF CAMNANT)
Retired miner and farmer, Seven Sisters, South Wales

There was a bad part of it; the nastiness between the men who stopped out and the blacklegs, the rumours that went round – so and so has gone back to work, or they've gone back to work in Durham, and so on.

But the funny thing is that everyone speaks of the lockouts in 1921 and 1926 as the best time of their lives. You could sleep late without having your lamp stopped. There was no fear of losing a shift. Everyone was the same, there was no jealousy. Everyone was idle, only the vicar was working. But we kept busy. We knew where all the outcrops were and we would mix coal with clay to make fires. It gave good heat, though it needed fire to start it.

We had no right to dig for coal of course, but we all did it. It was done at night and it was dangerous, for the roof would cave in. Most of the homes had gardens and everybody tilled them or had a little patch, an allotment, and gave cabbages, turnips and swedes. The farmers gave vegetables and the bakers gave bread. We would fish for trout in the streams and gather blackberries and whinberries. The good weather made a big difference. There were mushrooms everwhere. We ate mushrooms until we were sick of them. We smoked tealeaves, rolled coltsfoot leaves, dried them and smoked them for tobacco.

If nothing was saved, nothing was wasted. There was a lot pinched off the railways, but nobody pinched off each other.

COUNCILLOR HUGH REYNOLDS
Former miners' lodge official at Plean, Stirlingshire

Thursdays were special days. We had mince and tatties on Thursdays. All the other days, it was bone soup. The church in Plean gave the use of the mission hall, and we used the boiler at the back to make soup. You would go up with a can and, according to the number of your children, you would have a plateful; it was fair to everybody.

Some of the farmers were very good and gave us tatties. But others weren't so good and wouldn't give us any. One landowner we asked for a couple of bags, said that if we all went back, he'd send a bag for every family. So I got the boys and we went one night and took six bags. Where they wouldn't give, we took, as necessary. Some of them were so mean. I remember one of them, in the Second World War, wouldn't even give us a penny for Red Cross bandages.

So we took tatties, and hens, and sometimes lambs out of the parks. But we were not daft, mind you. What was lifted in Stirlingshire went overnight to Fife. They sent theirs to Lanark and Lanark sent theirs to us. It wouldn't do to have the landowner come down with the police to our soup kitchen and find his potato sacks there.

In Fife, one time, they spread the word round that they were to raid a certain farm, and sent the miners tramping round there. The police went up there and stayed out all night, but never saw anyone. And when the police went back in the morning, one came to the other and said, 'Joe, my hen house was cleaned out last night.' And the other said, 'So was mine.' We never took from farmers that gave something for the kitchens though.

We remained solid as a rock until December 1926. I was then a member of the pit committee. We had a meeting one night where we decided that in order that the pit should be put in a condition to resume work, we should allow the safety men to go in. Now the manager violated that agreement which was only to get the engines running to keep the water down; he persuaded some of the silly men to dig coal. This came to our ears and we decided to go down the following day to ask them to stop producing coal. As we went up the brae, we met the fireman and there we asked him to desist. But some silly individual threw a stone at him and before you could say Jack Robinson, the woods were lined with policemen who drew their batons and attacked us.

On November 11, Armistice Day, five of us were in the dock for brutal assault. One of the five, a die-hard Tory, burnished up his war medals thinking that they would take pity on us. But he went down along with the rest, for 30 days in Barlinnie Jail.

Now, when we had been there a fortnight – the dirty rotten sods – Thorneycroft told his manager to get all the foremen together in the Masonic Bar in Bannockburn. From there they went to organise as many masons as possible to make a breakaway. In that busload of scabs that went down to the pit, 30 out of 32 were masons. Now the Catholics are another matter. The devil in hell himself wouldn't get them to scab. But the masons went in and as the pickets went up to the bus to ask them to stop they shouted to the drivers to drive on and run over the top of them.

Well, they threw me out of the house after the lockout, because I was 'no longer in employment'; with my wife and six weans I had to go into an old shack at three and sixpence a week, from 1927 to 1955, 28 years. Its all demolished now. Well I have just one regret about it all. In the thirties, my wife caught pneumonia and died. The miners' agent took pity on me, left with six weans and got me a job on the county council. All six of the kids I sent to High School, some of the time on the dole and some of the time working for the council. But they would never have me down the pits again.

The funny thing is that I saw that pit coaled 70 years ago and I have seen it closed. On the County Council we have been discussing having the tip shifted and dumped in a quarry. When it is levelled, some of the land will go back to a farmer named Martin, whose father owned the land before the pit was sunk. So those battles are all now in the past. But I've no regrets; I would do it again. And there is nothing special to my case, there were thousands like me.

ABE MOFFAT
Scottish area National Union of Mineworkers president (retired)

Great hopes, great betrayal; that was 1926. But at least the miners did stick together and went back in a body, when it was all over. While it lasted, and the miners were on their own, the Government certainly became more vicious. Hundreds of Scots miners were jailed, some for as much as 12 months. But one lesson the authorities had learnt from the 1921 lockout, and that was not to bring the troops into our area. During the 1921 lockout they brought troops into Lumphinans and the miners fraternised with them. The women invited the soldiers to their homes for meals and social evenings. So that risk was not taken in the Scots coalfield in 1926.

The women, in fact, played a vital part in the councils of action that were set up all over West Fife during the General Strike and the lockout. This was most important, because involving the women helped ensure that the strike stayed solid. And so it did. It was complete. Even the safety men were withdrawn. And to protect our men from the police we organised strong forces of miners. An ex-army man trained them and they patrolled the area. It was good to see them marching through the streets, armed with pick handles, pokers, any weapons they would get together, picketing the main points and drilling in the fields. I wonder how we got away with it.

By the 1926 lockout I had become more active in union work and was a parish councillor in Barlinnie. We granted relief not only to children, but to the men as well. The Board of Health stepped in and every member of the council was interdicted for £175. But they never got it back.

But, in the end we took a battering. Alex, my brother, and I were out of the Fife coalfield. Altogether there were five brothers, two cousins and my father who were sacked. Many years later my brothers got back to work in the Fife coalfield, but I never did.

JOHN COLLINSON
Durham miner

When the final capitulation came, we turned up in queues at the colliery office. Though it was a waste of time if you had been active during the Strike and Lockout. 'We'll send for you when you're needed', they said. The blokes must have been sick of saying those words. It was 1929 before I went back to work in that pit; they were short on the night shift and must have forgotten about us by then.

While it lasted, though, it was good; an organised way of life, based on not working. It was as good as a university course. We had speakers down, like Tommy Jackson, the Marxist lecturer, and we gave them good audiences. Harnessed audiences, in fact, for we were not going anywhere. So we used the time to learn; you can learn something even out of a defeat. And you must remember that all the great battles of those days were rearguard actions that we fought and lost – 1921, 1925, 1926.

I remember 1925 well. There were company pits along both sides of the valley, but Chopwell was the spearhead of them all.

The company agent used to stand outside his house and look across the valley and say, 'I'll bring those bloody Reds to their knees.' Before that strike Matt, the overman, who was a red-hot Methodist, was at a meeting in the chapel, (it was known as Matt's chapel). They wanted to build a new chapel and they said to Matt, how long will it take? 'Well', said Matt 'If they come out on June 25, it'll take six months.' And he was right, for when the pits stopped, they had all the craftsmen, the masons and so on at their disposal. One's loss, as they say, is another's gain.

But there was no telling in 1926, at least in May, that it would weary on until November. For nine days in May we took power and enjoyed every minute of it. The councils of action in every village were as good as Soviets. We took over the local council offices, next to the police station and the local Catholic church – very handy – and we ran it from there. We had our own printing press and sent a lad by motor-bike to buy paper on the council's account, the only time the ratepayers really got value for money. Of course we ran head on against the forces of law and order.

Between July and September they drafted over 90 policemen into the village and there were 128 prosecutions for this and that. They recruited a lot of specials and issued them with a uniform and when they marched in an old woman shouted out, 'Eh, hinny, the uniform doesn't fit.' 'Ah,' said he, 'But the money does.' The place was alive with coppers all dying to know just where we kept our printing press. But they had no idea at all. The quietest bloke in the town was picked up and questioned and got three months in Durham Jail for refusing to say where. And there were a lot more arrested. We had a roll of honour in the Council offices, with everyone's name, when they were knocked off. Even Sir William Lawther got three months.

There were one or two blacklegs; we would give them the old slow march treatment, surround them, singing hymns and keeping it up till they couldn't stand it any longer. Some of them went away to a little pit in Northumberland to work, and in fact there was no breakaway of any consequence.

DICK KELLEY
Labour MP for Don Valley and former Yorkshire miners' pit official

They hung a list of names outside the lamp cabin under the heading 'Left', and after the lockout was over you had to go through the whole rigmarole of re-signing. That was, if your face fitted.

I had stuck my neck out and was arrested at Craghead for 'interfering with the transit of goods.' A convoy had come through the village from Durham, taking a devious route to avoid pickets. We stopped them and they had agreed to go back, when the police arrived and the superintendent read the riot act. With a revolver in his hand, he jumped on the running board and forced the driver, who was shaking like a leaf, to drive through. There was a Salvation Army hut nearby with a pile of stones outside it, and within seconds those stones had vanished and were raining down on the police. The police were driven out and came back later with armoured cars and arrested the whole Council of Action, all thirteen of us. But thousands of people had come in from the neighbouring town and they couldn't get the coach with us on board through the crowd. I had a boil on my face which started to bleed, and the crowd thought I had been hit and started to get angry.

Come four o'clock the superintendent said he would release us on condition we undertook no further picketing. But I said he had no right to release us under conditions. Picketing was within the law and we weren't prepared to relinquish our rights. Eventually he told us to get out.

After the strike was over I was lodging with my wife's step-father; we had two kids. One night at 11 o'clock the police sergeant, a big fellow named Bradshaw, came down and told the wife's step-father that he'd have to get me out of there or there'd be no job for him. So I had to move out that night, bed strapped to my back, and go knocking from door to door till at last a bloke took me in. The next thing was that he was told there would be no job for him in Craghead while I was staying with him, and he began to fall out with me for no reason at all. We lived in a caravan for a while, and then one Saturday night I drew my dole money and gave it to the wife. Then, with a couple of blokes, I walked off down into Yorkshire where I'd been told there was a pit with some work.

JOHN CAMPBELL
Scottish miner

All the way through to November it was a jug of soup a day; twice we got half a crown from the money which the Russians sent, and once or twice we got eight shillings a shift for shovelling coal gum which the hospitals were allowed to have for fuel. And that was all. I was in lodgings at £2 a week and had to pay every penny back afterwards. If you were married it was worse; you had to sell your furniture; if they gave you parish relief, it was, 'You don't need that carpet; why do you want those fancy curtains?'

When I got my job back my place was a bad one, in an 18 to 22 inch seam, howking lying on my side, with a patch on my arm from wrist to shoulder like emery paper where the skin rubbed. We were digging coal for the Canadian market and every year when the St Lawrence froze up we were laid off. By 1930 the pit was worked out and I was 13 months out of work (we were married and living in rooms) cycling miles every day looking for work, until the supervisor in the Labour Exchange, who was in the same mob as I was in the 1914–18 war, sent me to the Clyde Navigation Trust as a labourer. We were shovelling road metal, building up a quay wall for loading iron ore; there were all sorts working there, out-of-work engineers, clerks. I felt sorry for some of them, for they were not used to this kind of work, and their hands were in a mess; I would give them a hand every now and then. But they had to put up with it, for in those days and for years afterwards, you had to take what work you could get.

CHAPTER FOUR

1927-1945

After the trade union defeat of 1926 came the passing of the Trades Disputes and Trade Union Act of 1927. This outlawed general strikes and sympathetic strikes. The protection of trade union funds from claims for damages over strikes (given by the Liberal Government in 1906) was removed; picketing was made more difficult. Trade unions were no longer allowed to levy political funds with objectors having to 'contract out'; from now on those wishing to pay had to 'contract in'. This struck hard at the Labour Party, and the Labour Government of 1945 was quick to repeal the Act. But it is doubtful whether the Act, stiff as its penalties were, was the main reason for the swift decline in the number of strikes, to 300–400 a year over the next five years.

The trade union movement was in retreat. Its membership was back almost to the 1915 level of 4.3 millions, while the Depression brought unemployment up to three millions. A sense of weakness, rather than the fear of prosecution, held workers back from striking. The rift between leadership and rank and file, opened by the failure of 1926, widened. Agreements between top union officials and employers to facilitate new schemes for rationalisation in the faster-growing motor and light engineering industries were regarded as betrayals by the Left. Opposition movements within the unions grew rapidly and the number of unofficial strikes rose, until by 1937 the strike total reached 1,200. Some strikes in textiles and mining in the early 1930s were protracted and bitter. In some unions the antogonism reached the stage of open breaks and the forming of breakaway unions in clothing, mining, transport and shipping; some were 'Red' unions led by the Communists, some 'non-political' unions led by the Right Wing.

By the time war broke out in 1939, these more serious breaches had been healed. By 1940, with war production slowly getting into gear, unemployment at last fell below the one million mark and trade union membership climbed to six millions. The war pro-

112

8. A mass meeting of airmen at Drigh Road, February 1946. The speaker is Arthur Attwood (see Page 170)

9. Jack Dash addresses a London dockers' strike meeting, 1960

10. The Striker's Return. Employer: 'Glad to see you back my lad. But you'll understand that in the circumstances we can't run to a fatted calf.'
(Reproduced by permission of *Punch*)

duced a complex situation, with old battles over working conditions, piecework rates, etc, continuing under the surface of national unity and the joint drive for production. Indeed, as the war progressed, the number of strikes increased, topping the 2,000 mark in 1944; these were rarely on a large scale or of long duration. The shop steward movement recovered from its decimation by unemployment in the 1930s and now achieved a higher level of organisation and influence than ever before. It often skilfully blended action to increase production with action to secure improved conditions, even to the extent of using the good offices of the Ministry of War Production to get rid of laggard managers.

Part I REBELLION AND BREAKAWAY

PETER KERRIGAN
Former Glasgow engineers' leader, and Minority Movement and Communist Party organiser

In the summer of 1926, Rose and I decided we would go out to mining villages in Stirlingshire. We went on our bikes and put the money we'd saved on fares into buying food which we took with us for the miners' families. It was a lovely August day and we cycled some 20 miles from Glasgow. In Plean the whole village was solid, though the lockout was on into its third month. We had a marvellous meeting there, and at the finish two-thirds of the population, men and women, enrolled in the Minority Movement.

I had been active in the Minority Movement since the beginning in 1924, when Tom Mann and Harry Pollitt set it going. Even before this I had been involved in the Red International of Labour Unions. In fact that year when I was convenor of shop stewards in M Shop at the Parkhead Forge, I was delegate to an RILU conference in Moscow. At the same time I was active in junior football and recall having to leave for Moscow just after our team won the Scottish Juvenile Cup. Althogether the Minority Movement was active both nationally and through different groups of workers, miners, engineers and building workers. However, the

114

railwaymen's minority movements had a much better programme worked out for the whole of the trade union movement, very different from the rank and file committees of today which come together on specific issues.

The Minority Movement was very active in the 20s and was very important in the resistance put up by the rank and file after the defeat in 1926. And it was not only opposition to the Government and employers, but opposition to the official leadership of the trade union movement.

We were influenced by a tremendous sense of betrayal, not only by the TUC leadership but also by the Lefts on the General Council. The effect on myself and on others was to turn against them, and this made it easier for the tendency to be against the whole 'official movement'. 'They're all the bloody same' began to be applied to some who had been regarded as Lefts; it helped to make stronger sectarian tendencies among Communists – our hand against everyone, everyone's against our's.

Still the idea that the trade union movement should be united was never lost sight of. Tom Mann, who was always a syndicalist at heart, never took it to the stage of the IWW in America. He always associated with the trade union movement even when he was free-lancing in South Africa and Australia, and he threw himself into the work of amalgamating the engineering unions. Harry Pollitt always had this concept of working within the trade union movement. In 1927, before the leadership managed to force Communists out, I was delegate to the Labour Party from the AEU, Pollitt from the boilermakers and Arthur Horner from the miners. Pollitt's idea was that of transforming the whole movement by working within it, and he certainly had a great ability to co-operate, to work and be accepted by the Right Wing, even when they hated his guts on other matters.

Even at the height of that period of disillusion which followed the General Strike, there was a great reluctance, whatever the leadership's attitude, to agree to any organised break. The very phrase 'Minority Movement' indicates the reluctance to set up rival organisations. When the United Mineworkers of Scotland was formed, for example, I took part in miners' strikes in 1931 and 1932, speaking to miners' meetings for the Minority Movement, though I was not a miner. The other side had broken the rules and the majority of miners supported the UMS. Still there always was the strong feeling in this country that the trade union movement should be united, not split. In the thirties you had the growth of rank and file movements within each union, sometimes tolerated by the official leaders, more accepted and integrated within the whole movement.

E. MOFSHOVITZ
Former organiser of the United Clothing Workers Union

The United Clothing Workers started out in 1929 because of what the rank and file in London regarded as sabotage by the top officials of the Tailors and Garment Workers Union of the Rego strike in 1928. What stuck in the throats of the London membership was that the Rego strike was for trade union principles; there were 600 workers, mainly young girls, out for 13 weeks; they put up a terrific fight for the union. But in the end the union leadership let them down.

Rego Clothiers of Shoreditch was a big firm with a modern line of development, cutting out the middleman by having their own chain of stores. In 1927 those workers were making £70,000 a year for Rego's and the shareholders got 63 per cent dividend. In the 1920s the trade was in a state of chaos, with big firms introducing machinery and rationalisation on a bigger scale, but still lots of smaller shops in operation. There would be one dispute after another, particularly in London and the organisers would settle them only to come back a week or two later to find some crafty employer trying to bluff the workers out of what they had.

It seemed to us that the national leadership, based in Leeds, was too interested in negotiating rationalisation agreements and hoping to get good treatment from the big employers, rather than protecting the members' interests. London seemed to have had more than its share of local disputes and relations between London officials and Head Office were getting more and more strained.

I was a convener at Rego in 1928 and things had been brewing up there over a period. The women were working a 49 hour week and adult piece workers were getting anything between 22 shillings and 40 shillings, with 16 year olds on something like 11 to 13 shillings. With fares of up to 4s 6d a week, dinners 2s 11d and teas 10d, you

116

can imagine what some of the young girls were taking home. And bear in mind in those days, a girl might be the only one earning in her family, with fathers and brothers on the dole. There were other grievances too, about working conditions. Girls would come in at 8 am on a Saturday, and be laid off after only quarter or half an hour's work, earning less than it took them to reach the factory. Then the making of trousers was rationalised, by a new system in which instead of three sections being made by three girls, the whole would be made by one. The girls found it impossible to get their old earnings on the new system and there was a stay-in strike in the trouser department. A London official negotiated a small increase in rates, and lots of the girls joined the union.

Quite suddenly, one girl on one floor which was 100 per cent union refused to pay her subs. She'd been paying them for years. After the management interviewed her she became even more stubborn. Then, strangely enough, the management became very stubborn and wouldn't meet the London organiser. They'd been happy enough to recognise the union when it was a matter of rationalisation agreements, but this was something different.

So the 600, mainly girls remember, came out on strike. We had been led to believe that it would be recognised by the union within a week, and though the girls picketing the factory and shops were given the usual Press treatment, they confidently expected the strike to be made official. But that official recognition never came, and we fought on without it.

The girls caused a tremendous stir with their picketing and marching through London, singing their own special songs. There was one to the tune 'How long's this been going on.'

> 'We've never had decent wages,
> And always done our work well,
> How long must this keep going on?
> Our work they've made it harder,
> We've had to travel farther,
> How long must this keep going on.
> More work – less pay,
> But every dog will have its day,
> We'll stick, by gum, by golly,
> The bosses they'll be sorry.
> We'll show them how they're in the wrong,

117

> *We'll never drift back one by one,*
> *We'll always stick together,*
> *In every kind of weather,*
> *Until the fight is won.'*

The official trade union movement was little help, but the rank and file were generous with their help. I remember old Tom Mann as head of the National Minority Movement coming down to speak to the girls. The management used every weapon it could. It issued leaflets attacking Sam Elsbury, the London organiser of the union; it tried to get an injunction against picketing and boycotting the shops. This was the first such attempt after the 1927 Trades Disputes Act. But the magistrate said he could see nothing illegal.

At first the union leadership tried to negotiate a settlement, leaving out recognition of the London officials, but the strikers wouldn't have that. It was three days before Christmas Day when the strike ended with recognition and no victimisation.

But the feeling in London was that the Rego strike had been won – for union recognition – against the union leadership, and in the Spring of 1929 a mass meeting of London members formed the United Clothing Workers' Union. It included all the London officials, though Sullivan, the Secretary, finally decided not to come in. Right away came the counter-attack from the old union. They took the UCW to court to restrain us from using their money, but since we had no intention of doing so, the judge said we were a bona fide trade union and entitled to collect contributions.

Next came a threat from Bevin of the Transport and General Workers' Union that they would see that bus and transport companies did not place orders with firms that recognised the new union. When the workers at Polikoff's factory came over en bloc, the firm recognised the new union and then suddenly withdrew. The Polikoff workers came out on strike in May 1929 and the firm issued a poster saying,

'Strikers, what do you hope to get from this strike except applause from the Red International? The strike is a Communist attempt to destroy the recognised British trade union movement.'

And the Polikoff workers answered with a song:

> *'The TUC loves Mr P,*
> *So Mr P loves the TUC;*

> *Both combined love the T & G and*
> *The whole damn lot love skinning me.'*

And they marched with the slogan 'Make old Poli cough, cough, cough.'

It went on for 12 weeks, and at the same time UCW members in Glasgow were locked out. We could have settled that strike for recognition on equal terms with other unions, but the other side wanted to fight it out to the finish.

Well, the UCW lasted until 1935, when the members went back into the Tailors and Garment Workers Union. The fact was that the forces were too little to make it effective, but it shook the union leadership and I think made them realise the feeling among the rank and file.

SARAH WESKER
Former official of the Ladies' Tailors Union

At the time the Red Union was formed, and at the Rego strike, I used to go around Fleet Street and collect from the printing lads there. Whenever they were flush, they always gave generously. It was a good fight and the girls stuck it out well. But it led to splits among the union officials, Sam Elsbury versus Bernard Sullivan. Elsbury fought to the bitter end against the union leadership.

But looking back now I feel the breakaway union was a mistake. It was mainly among the Jewish workers in London, very courageous but very emotional people, the people who came over here at the beginning of the century and their children. There were already so many divisions, so many sections. of the trade, each with their own union. I became an organiser of the Ladies Tailors' Union and right from the start I had to fight the old gang who wanted to use it as a sort of club. J. L. Fine, the leader of that union told me, 'I was told that when you became an official I'd have to fight you all the way. They said you'd have them out on strike every day.'

Well, it turned out the exact opposite. I was just as likely to advise against having a strike as calling one. You have to be realistic as well as militant, even though there were people in the

119

union who would say that as soon as you became an official you were no good. Very often though, the employers would leave you with no option. Some of them were terrible.

The first strike I remember, in the 1920s, was at a firm where the employer was so bad he wouldn't even let me go out of the shop to get a doctor for a girl who was having a fit. When we were working on dark material he would turn out the light to save electricity, and when I said we couldn't see he'd answer, 'Take your eyes out and wash them.' We had this strike for a farthing on the price of a pair of trousers and he never forgave me for that, even though he won, not us. I used to stand outside the factory and collect the girl's contributions. He would call me all the names under the sun and call the police to me, but the policeman would say, 'She isn't doing anything wrong.' I wasn't even on the gate, I was outside on the pavement. And I wouldn't budge from there. But it was difficult, and eventually the girls decided they didn't want to be in the union any more. After the strike he wouldn't take me back, or my sisters.

A lot of strikes would happen in the slack time, when the bosses were trying to cut wages by 5 per cent, 10 per cent. Then you had to stand between the workers and the employers and say, 'There'll be no cuts.' The trade was seasonal and when they had no orders they would sack you. In one shop, with less than 10 workers, the employer wanted to cut 10 per cent.

'What do the workers say?' I asked him.

'I didn't ask them. They ought to be grateful for what they've got.'

So I asked the workers and of course, they weren't willing to take a cut in pay. We called a strike. Then I found out that he had got this work from a union shop where they were on short time. He was doing it for less money than they would take.

'Do you think that's fair?' I asked him, and I told him, 'I'll stand outside in the street and let everyone know you're under-cutting by four and six.'

'If you promise not to make it public.' he said. 'I'll only cut two and six pence. I've got to eat, after all.'

'So have these people got to eat.'

Well, he wouldn't hear of it. So I went out, got a platform and set it up in the Whitechapel Road, to make the whole thing public. A man called Williams from the employers' organisation came up and said, 'They ought to be grateful he got them work at any price. You ought to be ashamed of yourself.'

Well we had a terrible row on the spot and I don't suppose I've spoken to him from that time on. But we won that strike.

ISOBEL BROWN
Communist organiser, and rank and file strike leader in woollen textile industry

All wages would have to come down, that's what they said, and in the textile industry in 1930, they had a $12\frac{1}{2}$ per cent cut. The textile unions proposed to negotiate a slightly smaller cut, but among the rank and file the resistance was building up, as they started to apply the cuts throughout the industry. Apart from the men in key sections like woolcombing and dyeing, the factories weren't highly organised, the unions were amorphous, with no branch meetings. In Shipley, where I was living, there was just one full-time official at the Weavers' Hall.

We decided in the Communist Party to try and bring the woollen workers out on strike against the cuts. It wasn't only against the bosses, but against the unions nationally. It was an unofficial strike led by the Party, though there couldn't have been more than five Party members in the whole of the industry. I was not a textile worker, but when the strike got going I was chosen chairman of the strike Committee in Shipley and my husband, Ernie, was chairman of the strike committee in Bradford. We knew the people in the mills. They knew us and that was good enough for them. We were very thin on the ground, but we aimed to bring out the mills one by one. We knew that if we could bring out the men, the woolcombers, industry couldn't run without them. And that was how it came about, though in fact the women came out by their thousands and fought well.

At first though, it was hard. In Howarth, of the Brontes, there was a little non-Federated shop. The main body of the workers who lived in Keighley, had come out, but the workers who lived in Howarth and knew the boss personally, wouldn't strike. We decided I should go up and try and talk to them, and so I set out up the hill with a picket. We met the non-strikers, a crowd on each side, in a little lane near the Bronte parsonage. Me and my

121

battalions stood here, the non-strikers there, and in between stood the only bobby in the place.

'What have you come here for?' he said to me.

'I just want to talk to these people,' I said.

'Right,' said he. He went over to the non-strikers. 'That's your line. Stop there.' Then he went to the strikers. 'That's your line, stop there.' And he left a no-man's land for me to speak in. But they still didn't strike.

But some of the mills began to strike. We were so few we couldn't picket them all. I went on my own to Saltair, the biggest mill next to Listers, where they owned the mill and the houses as well. There were 2,000 in the mill, but not more than 50 of them would listen when I spoke at the factory gate. I was out in all weathers and was nearly exhausted. Each night as I walked home along the canal I wondered 'Is it worth it?' One day as I walked along the canal, a window in the mill opened and a red-haired girl popped her head out. She was waving one of our leaflets, which ended 'Down with imperialism.' We were at our most sectarian in those days. She shouted across the canal at me, 'Up with the lavatory seat. Down with the lavatory chain.' You can imagine how I felt.

Three days later, I stood outside that factory as the girls went in, selling the *Daily Worker*, with a poster tied to my little boy's pram. It was the morning of the pay-out with the new, lower wages. I stood there calling out, 'Weavers, don't go in.' And a little group gathered round me saying 'What shall we do? We want our pay.' So I said, 'Pick two or three to go in and negotiate to get the wages for all of you.' The funny thing was the brightest spark among them was that girl with the red hair. We stopped the weaving shed that day and the girls stood all around me. 'What do we do now?' So we marched to the next mill and they came out. So it snowballed. As soon as we got some stopped, we took them to another mill. After three or four days the whole lot were stopped. Some of the women did not want to come out, but my brother-in-law, who was a woolcomber, got the men to strike and that stopped the lot.

A number of the girls had been recruited from the coalfield in the south of the county. They lived in hostels belonging to the factory and of course were getting no food. Our first effort was to raise money for them to go home, or get food and lodgings if they wanted to stay. Lots of them volunteered to stay. Being miners' daughters they knew what strikes were about. Some of them travelled round the country raising money and did a magnificent job.

Many strikers could get no relief, so we decided on simultaneous demonstrations in all major towns to demand relief for the families. In Shipley there was a big bell belonging to the Socialist movement, from the year dot. This we took with us and went around from street to street calling all the people out.

We shouted out, 'Do you know how much Charlie gave Mrs So and So?' (Charlie Clapham was the Relieving Officer.) Then we told them 'Let's all go back with her to the office and make them give more.' The crowd grew and grew, street by street. The police reckoned we were 5,000. We carried a stool with us and held meetings here and there, electing a deputation. When we got to the office the Shipley police force, all six of them, were barring the way. A fat sergeant said to me, 'You can't go in there.' 'Take your choice,' said I, 'either 12 of us go in or the whole bloody lot does.' Which, since I'd been a teacher and was considered quite lady-like, rather surprised them.

We wanted to get at those people in the Labour movement who were serving on the Board of Guards. So we marched next to the house of a Labour railwayman, named Gray. He was out and when his wife saw us, she fainted. Next we marched to the weavers' Hall and here the police stopped us again. We protested; the hall belonged to the strikers anyway. As each speaker got up, they arrested them, but they avoided arresting me, until I managed to irritate them so much they took me off to jail. They took me off to Bradford because there was no proper jail in Shipley and one of the detectives offered to walk round the streets with me so that I could get fresh air. He told me that in the pubs people were taking bets on how much I would get. The lowest was three months, the highest six months.

Outside the court a terrific crowd gathered. I defended myself and one of the warders went to the witnesses and said, 'I don't know how long you'll have to wait. She's started a speech.' Well the crowd were waiting there, ready to protest when I was imprisoned. When I got out of the court and told my husband I'd only been fined two pounds, he told me, 'You'd better get out of sight.' But we got the relief. The authorities overspent, illegally, by £57,000, but nothing was done about that.

We still had to feed the strikers though. The Co-op society gave us the Co-op hall as a centre, installed a gas cooker and instructed the butchers' department to give what meat they could, while extended credit was given to strikers' families. Every day a hot meal was given, in two sittings of 400 each. Someone gave us a donkey, we called him Textile Billy, and he went round the town with a cart, collecting plates spoons, knives, forks and anything people could give. He earned his keep ten times over.

The strike went on for over two months and holiday time was coming. Usually everyone saved up their Co-op divi, which was then four and sixpence in the pound, until holiday week, and then went to Blackpool. Well this year they were spent up, and so it was decided to run a big picnic excursion up to Ilkley Moor, by coach and bus. It was a sight for the gods, those people streaming up the hill; there was one little girl carrying her baby brother still in his nightshirt. Later on when we were rounding up everything, we found that little lad, asleep, still in his nightshirt.

The tragedy came in the tenth or eleventh week. A group of women had been picketing one mill, trying to argue some other women out of going in, when the police moved in and picked up eight women at random. By this time the police force had been reinforced by men from all over Lancashire as well as Yorkshire. The night before the trial we held a meeting and asked everyone to turn up the following day. A little fellow pushed his way to the front of the crowd and said his wife was one of the women arrested. His two children had pneumonia and he appealed to everyone to be there the next day.

Then someone who shall be nameless, got excited, and shouted 'Why wait. Let's go and get them out now.'

This was just what the police had been waiting for. They sailed into that crowd with all their strength. One man was almost killed, there were many arrests and that helped to break the strike.

BESSIE AND HAROLD DICKENSON
Weavers of Lancashire

In the Lancashire cotton mills in the thirties they brought in the 'more looms' system in one or two places, which was another way of getting more work for less pay. It was tried on at Spencers in

Burnley and later they wanted to extend it to other mills. We weren't working there at the time; we were unemployed like a lot of other people, but we took part in the strike from outside. There was a certain amount of friction between the unemployed and some who were working and wouldn't come out. Naturally the unemployed were more against the system, which meant fewer people doing more work. The union wanted to put formal pickets on the mills in dispute. But we wanted mass pickets. We used to march round the streets, with comb and paper bands, the only way we had of making a noise. One mill was being kept going by 30 people who had been expelled from the union. Mass pickets from all over Burnley, mainly unemployed, would assemble outside the factories at night, when the people were coming out, booing as the knobsticks came out. It was all the police could do to get them away.

We heard that there was to be a meeting between Spencers and the union, and rallied 200–300 people and marched them up the hill to Spencers' house. We passed the Town Hall on the way and didn't know that the meeting was going on inside. When we got to Spencers' house, it was surrounded by police hidden in the garden. Someone shouted, 'Let's get in there', but someone else, a bit saner, shouted, 'No, keep back.' Eventually, they served a summons on us two for 'watching and besetting' knobsticks. They waited until we were on our own in a quiet back street, then slipped up and served it on us. We got three months apiece in Strangeways. The agitation later obliged the union to call a town strike, which spread through the towns around Burnley and for a while the 'more looms' movement was stopped until new agreements were negotiated in 1935.

But when we came out of jail (eleven weeks with remission) in January 1933, the strike was over.

JACK R. LONGWORTH
Retired divisional organiser of the Amalgamated Engineering Union

Early in 1933, things blew up at Fords. The company had set up its plant on the marshes at Dagenham and obviously intended to run it as they tried to run their plants in the United States. Work in the whole motor industry was seasonal. There used to be an 'examination of personnel' every three months, which involved lay-off, which is how they maintained discipline.

It was the habit at Dagenham to send men home again if there were not work for an hour or two. A worker in the machine shop might get up at four in the morning to start work at six, then be asked to hang about for hours till work was available. On the assembly line men would be sent outside perhaps twice a day if work was short. A man could be in the factory up to 12 hours a day to get 8½ hours work. This 'temporary' lay-off was still going on when I left Fords later in the thirties.

I transferred to Dagenham in 1932 from Trafford Park, where I'd been active in the union and I intended to carry on the good work at Dagenham. Now at Dagenham it was a big building with open shops, no walls round, only wire netting cages for tools, and white lines on the floor to mark the extent of departments. So it was possible to get around if you were careful. Fords of course, did not recognise the union and didn't intend to. Matt Smith, a friend of mine, who had emigrated to the United States and helped organise auto workers there, told us something of the bitter struggle in Detroit against Fords, and so we had to be careful not to start the fight for recognition on a false issue.

As it happened the management, in 1933, presented just the issue, by imposing wage cuts. And I mean imposing. They started with the weakest links, the line workers on the assembly line, then the machine shop, engine assembly and so on. During this time there was considerable resentment in the works. This was growing. So when the notices of wage cuts went up in the toolroom everybody was up in arms. We held a short meeting there and then and decided to call a mass meeting in Barking Park that Sunday. I went on my motor bike to Hammersmith to see Jack Tanner, who was London divisional organiser of the AEU and arranged for him to be there on Sunday to take the chair. We expected about 500–600 workers (there were about 400 men to a shift in the tool room). We didn't expect more because there had been widespread sackings at other London factories.

To our surprise, thousands turned out, including a big proportion of the production workers, most of whom weren't in any union. We decided there and then to strike and block the works to stop anyone getting in or out from 5.30 am on Monday.

On Monday morning the strikers massed on the bridge which

carries the private road down to the factory, asking all who arrived to turn back. When cars tried to drive through, the workers lifted the back wheels and turned them round; if the engine was running and the gears in, they went backwards. Very soon the road was blocked off and no one was getting in or out. I contacted Rigg the chief labour officer to ask the management to receive a deputation, but the word came back – no hope of any interview. So the strike went on. The police tried to get buses through but failed. The London dockers agreed to block Ford materials that were being transported to Ireland. After four days, despite everything in the Press plus the attempts by local religious bodies to interfere, the strike was becoming more solid. So they agreed to meet a deputation, but not one with Jack Tanner. We laid our plans carefully, to stop the management from sowing confusion by picking on the members of the deputation one after another, and it was agreed that I should be sole spokesman.

At the Ford gates, Mr Rigg met us and immediately chose six workers and said they would come in with us. After an argument I convinced our deputation of the folly of cross-talk and we withdrew, to the cheers of the strikers waiting down the road. But it was not long afterwards that the management capitulated and met us. They had a shock when they saw how we stood up to them in the talks.

They agreed to restore the cuts, that there would be no further cuts that they would look into shift and overtime conditions and recognise a works committee. The tragedy was that they would not recognise the union, for all even the TUC could do, until the end of the war.

Our strike committee stayed in existence as a Ford Workers Committee, which issued its own bulletin. That strike was a bit of a turning point. Afterwards, hundreds joined the union. Later on, Ford workers who went to work at other places carried on the good work. The Pressed Steel strike at Oxford, and at Briggs Bodies in Dagenham, in a way were an outcome of that 1933 battle at Fords. From that time on, the rank and file committee at Fords was ready to give help to other people in and around the car industry who needed it. In fact, one of the first issues of the Ford Workers bulletin the following month asked for help for workers out on strike against the Bedaux system at Hopes in Smethwick.

JIM CRUMP
Former Amalgamated Engineering Union shop steward, Birmingham

I knew men working at Hopes in Smethwick and other factories, who experienced all the refinements of the Bedaux system. Crudely speaking you were timed on a job and the formula was supposed to represent the necessary production and leisure time. There were two charts on the wall, those who achieved the time and those who did not. Those who didn't were weeded out. The new formula then worked out was based on the quickest and so the time was reduced yet again. It was based on maximum output, 80–90 per cent per machine. In fact it was the survival of the fittest in the crudest way; it was bloody cruel and it drove men and women mad. There were men working at Hopes whose hands were battered to pieces, chipping off castings, their nails destroyed. You know how when hot metal strip is run out, it has to be taken down the shop, and stretched out; then you walk back for the next. Under the Bedaux system you ran down and then ran back.

Birmingham and around was full of places like Hopes, where speed-up rationalisation imposed on a semi-skilled or unskilled and unorganised work force was coining it for the bosses.

I'll give you an idea of what conditions were like at the time. In the mid-thirties the Birmingham Information Bureau Publicity Department issued a brochure which said, 'Birmingham's labour is good, plentiful and cheap; lower wages are paid here as compared with London, as much as 16 per cent in printing, 17 per cent in cabinet making, 7–5 per cent in building and 8 per cent among engineering fitters. . . . Labour unrest is practically unknown. Birmingham is an ideal centre for speeded up production.'

There was a good deal of truth in it. Birmingham was low on organisation. The influence of old Joe Chamberlain's ideas had got into the trade union movement, branch after branch had Tory chairman or secretary, and the workers in the factories would have nothing to do with it. The fact that they were unorganised though, did not mean they weren't militant. A lot of them, like the Hope workers in 1933, were ready to have a go if they could get support from anywhere. Tom Roberts, the Communist Party organiser in Birmingham helped them to run the strike. They got a lot of support from local retailers, the local chapel and cinema and tea rooms

11. Seamen on strike demonstrate outside 10 Downing Street in the summer, 1966

12. Harry Hitchings, GKN shop steward, makes his tower-squatting
protest, May 1971

and, in the end, through Tom, the trades council was involved. They succeeded in getting the Bedaux system modified there and afterwards the factory became organised. When the strike was settled there was a big meeting with the local trade union organiser, and Harry Pollitt spoke.

Tom was working nights, at the Russian Oil Products, and leading strikes during the day. He wore himself out in the end. We would hold factory gate meetings outside every factory where the Bedaux system was introduced, putting out leaflets and, if the workers were ready to come out on strike, we had no inhibitions about leading.

There was more than a grain of truth in the myth about Communist agitators. But in the strike in the early thirties at the Kynocks factory, an arms firm, the strikers came to us. There were a lot of spontaneous strikes against the speed-up and the workers would come down to the Communist Party office for help and advice.

One big argument which we had to resolve was, should workers be advised to join the 'reformist' trade unions whose leaders we were quite opposed to, or not? The Minority Movement, for all the mistakes it made, played a vital part here; it organised workers who wouldn't go near the trade union movement and whom the trade union officials often ignored. We resolved the question by the early thirties, agreeing that the best thing was that the trade union movement must be changed from within. But there was a lot of misunderstanding, a lot of contradictions, employed versus unemployed, and a lot of sheer sectarianism, alongside a lot of devoted and absolutely self-less work on behalf of unorganised people.

For me the problem was to some extent personal. My father was a full time official of the Transport and General Workers Union. His aim was to avoid strikes. He'd be trying to put them back while I was pulling them out. He and I were at odds a good deal, though looking back I can see the contribution he made to the trade union movement, organising the tram and bus drivers, meeting them for talks at midnight, walking home in the small hours. It was tough going.

It had its comic moments. I can recall being up before the magistrates, picked up for distributing leaflets. I had to be shifted to another court, because my Dad was on the bench that day.

On that occasion, I'd been handing out leaflets outside Lucas's. Most of the workers there were girls who came in from the Black Country, in droves, young girls whose fathers and brothers couldn't get a job. They were the breadwinners and you can understand they needed some nerve to come out on strike. But they did, and it was remarkable to see how much more highly the skilled workers regarded them afterwards. Thanks to that strike the Bedaux system was withdrawn and a new, modified system introduced. I was directly involved, speaking at meetings of the girls. I was working at Cadbury's at the time and I'd leave my work in the evening and rush down to meet the strike committee. For me there was nothing new or strange in this kind of life; it was union work, and I'd helped my dad with union work as a kid. (The funny thing is, that when I was 15, and apprenticed at Cadbury's, we went on strike. I went home excited and told my Dad. I thought he'd be pleased, but he gave me a roasting and told me to go back to work.)

We were certainly working from the outside, but you can imagine that workers like the Lucas girls came out on strike not because we told them to. It was because their conditions had become intolerable.

JESSIE MCCULLOUGH
Former Lucas factory worker

My mother remembered the Lucas brothers when they made bicycle lamps in a back house and went round selling them door to door. When the firm grew like it did, she was amazed They made money fast and they intended to make it a lot faster. The men who were doing the heavier work and the women the lighter work, if that's what you can call it. We were filing shock absorbers, weighing three or four pounds, standing up at a bench. It's rough work even when nobody's pushing you around.

One day I turned round and saw someone standing behind me while I was working. I asked them what they were doing and they said they were timing me. Why me and not her, I said, pointing to another woman. The fact was I've always worked quickly, and we were getting so much per gross, so that if you wanted to earn anything, you had to get a move on. You were lucky if you got

130

25 or 30 shillings. They obviously wanted to set the time by me and the others would have to keep up with it. Well, I had a talk with the girls about it and in the end they had us all in the office, offering us cups of tea and cigarettes. But the other girls just watched what I did and we all refused.

I decided to go to the union. The AEU wouldn't take in women, so I went to the Transport and General Workers, and got forms for the girls to join. Now unions were something new for them and they wouldn't go to the branch meeting unless I was with them. And when they went they found it very dull. The union officials were very lax and they used to look at me amazed when I brought in the application forms filled up. They just didn't believe women would join the union. But every week I took down more forms, and eventually we had a big meeting outside the gates and most of the girls joined. When the strike came, all the girls walked out.

Lucas's got me out, though, and the TGWU paid me victimisation pay. Several hundred joined the unions and Ernie Bevin presented me with a medal at the union conference. After I left Lucas's I tried to keep quiet for a while, but they had me marked and I was pursued from factory to factory. One time I got a job on a capstan lathe and I'd just been there long enough for the fitter to say 'You're doing fine', when they sent for me to the office and had me escorted off the works.

ALF GARRARD
Former rank and file building worker

When a militant wasn't being kicked out by the boss he was probably being kicked out by the union leadership, which made matters doubly difficult. Throughout the late twenties and thirties, the building trade had 25 per cent unemployed, and we were highly dissatisfied with the way the unions ignored the unemployed men. We in the Builders Minority Movement used to organise the out-of-work members who would come to a building trade labour exchange just opposite the Strand Palace Hotel in Tavistock Street. We used to call it the Tavistock Hotel. Thirteen of us, including Frank Jackson[1] and myself, were expelled for sending out a circular calling for more contact between the branches. We

[1] See pages 27 and 52.

got back in the union again, but then we organised a Minority Movement conference for building workers and were expelled again.

I got a job in Edmonton, north London, and they elected me shop steward. I told them I was expelled from the union. Never mind, said the men, your our rep, not theirs. When the union official came down to get me out, the men saw him off. And a little while later, the firm saw me off.

But eventually through the ramifications of the minority movement, I was able to get together with my old mates again and I got a job at Exeter House, building private homes in Putney. Most of us were back in the union by now and we organised the job thoroughly. There was a progressive film organisation which loaned me a camera and we made a complete film of how union organisation works on a building site, which was shown at meetings all over the place. Unfortunately it was lost as some stage or other.

Altogether that 15 months at Exeter House was an education. I used to sell literature to the men, dozens of copies of Grassic Gibbon's *Sunset Song* and *Ragged Trousered Philanthropists* (200 copies of that we sold). Frank Jackson was the foreman carpenter, and our unofficial lecturer; he once surprised all the lads by giving a talk on evolution. We sent teams of men with their tools to help build the Unity Theatre, transforming an old chapel into a theatre by tearing the guts out. They left their jobs at 6.30 at night, and went and worked until 11 pm; it took six weeks. It would have taken an ordinary building firm six months. I remember the first show there, called 'The Aristocrats', about the man who built the canals.

We had a nine day strike, to make them take back the chief shop steward they'd sacked. We used a local pub for HQ and sent lads round to the various building sites with collecting tins.

All the time, though, we kept up our work with the unemployed. It was that work, together with the shop stewards movement, that made the trade union movement come out of the Second World War so strong. Some people criticised me for it but I used to sit on committees like the unemployed assistance boards. I always reckoned that if you couldn't win the case for the worker, you could always vote against the ruling and that would mean the man could appeal. And often enough we won.

I remember one lad up before the Court of Referees, for leaving his job without good reason; his benefit had been cut. The chairman asked him why he'd left the job; wasn't £2 a week, live in and all found good enough for him? The young man took a matchbox out of his pocket and tipped it out on the table. It was full of bugs. The chairman and the other member of the committee left the room immediately, and while they were out I found the lad's case justified 'on the evidence provided'.

When the war came, I sat on the Essential Works Order Committee and then, often enough, I would see two employers literally fighting to get one man directed to their work. What could they do? Like Solomon, we couldn't cut him in half. I had to pinch myself to believe it could happen so soon after the thirties.

SID FINEMAN
Retired secretary of a branch of the National Union of Furniture Operatives

One of the best things about that period was the way the unemployed, far from strike-breaking, would actually turn out to give a hand in a strike. They would turn up outside a factory with their own crude, hand-made posters and it did our members who still had jobs good to see them.

There was one wonderful strike in the thirties at an East End furniture factory. A fully organised shop it was. In fact the owner was a member of the Workers' Circle Friendly Society. He was one of our best chess players and had been known to give talks about the struggles of people in Poland and Russia. Now any employer who wanted to remain a member of the Workers' Circle most definitely had to run a trade union shop.

We discovered however, that there were two lads who would come in by the back entrance, lock the front door, and work overtime, without sanction from the union, which was very bad at a time of mass unemployment. They were fined five pounds apiece by the union and they refused to pay; the employer wouldn't do anything about them. So we decided to strike the shop.

The strike went on for three or four months and we had the full backing of the unemployed, they would turn out to mass

133

meetings outside the factory, with banners and a band. It was marvellous. Then, one day, as the meeting was going on and the band was playing, the boss walks out of his office, turns his back on us and drops his trousers down. You can imagine the shock. We decided to put a complete block on the shop.

But in the end, he phoned Alex Gossip, general secretary of the union and said, 'Tell that silly sod Fineman to come and see me.' So I did. Then he called in the two men and said to them, 'Look you idiots. Why not pay up now?'

There were many sacrifices in the years between the wars, but I don't recall our members, employed or unemployed, grumbling about them. In the twenties we had a strike at Harris Lebus, over labourer's pay. The skilled men came out, on principle, but the labourers didn't. Lebus himself said to me 'You'll never win, these are my men, not yours.' He was right. Mind you, it paid dividends, for by the 1930s, that factory was 100 per cent trade union organised and we never had that kind of trouble again. We kept that strike up for nine months, on the question of principle, supported by a levy of the members and not one of them left.

During the miners' lockout of 1926, we had a levy of six shillings a member, and it went on for six months. Now and then one would say 'This is hard; my kid wants a new pair of shoes.' They would moan, but we didn't lose a single member over that. In fact I think we made members.

JOE BYRNE
Former branch official of the Transport and General Workers' Union, at Liverpool docks

After the General Strike, things went from bad to worse. People seemed to lose faith in the union and it became an awful job to get men to come to meetings. It certainly shook me as a young man, and it became a real effort to stick to and stick up for union principles. On the docks where it was casual labour, conditions were horrible. I've seen men sent off the ship just for looking sideways. And you had only to walk to the gate to see another man taking your place. Being young and a bit cheeky, answer back and you were off. I've seen the fellow for my job, coming up the gangway as I've been going down.

I became unemployed in the early 1930s. I was working at Huskisson Dock, Liverpool, on a German ship. I was foreman and there was only one gang of men. We'd started Friday morning and we were to finish Saturday noon. Just after we'd started a German ship's officer, who spoke English, took me to his cabin where he produced a cable from Hamburg, from his union, informing them that they would be on strike as from 12 midnight. Apparently they were fighting against wage reductions much in the same way as we were in Britain.

He asked me if I would keep the men away from the ship. If the cargo was moved, then the company would put another crew on board and the strikers would go to jail if the ship sailed. I asked him if there was steam up on the ship. He said no. So I told him I saw no reason why we should work it.

I was down at the docks at 7.30 the next morning. I didn't call a meeting; you had to be careful about that in those days. I said casually to the lads, 'Look, it's only half a day, don't go in the gate, just book on.' But one fellow, a nasty piece of work, an Orange Lodger, said 'We're going on. Why should we lose the work for the sake of a bunch of bloody Germans.'

'I don't care,' I said, 'they're trade unionists.' So I dodged through an alley-way and up to the ship, which was surrounded by police now. I went up the gangway to look for the officer who spoke English, but two detectives said, 'You've looked far enough' and marched me down the gangplank again and back to the gate where the men were waiting. By this time the English-speaking officer had arrived and he addressed the men, but they didn't seem interested enough to take any notice. I jumped up on a wagon and shouted out that the war was over a long time ago and these men were our brothers. That was as far as I got, because the police picked me up bodily and dumped me in the street where they told me to eff off.

I thought the men would go in and work then. But they didn't. All of them, six or seven hundred of them, stood and watched me as I was carried across the road. I jumped up on a junction box and said, 'Look, we'd expect them to do the same for us.'

After a bit the majority of them accepted this and went to sign on. Later that day, the German officer told me he'd had another cable. The employers' had withdrawn the wages reductions and the strike was off.

But when I went in to work on Monday morning at 7.45 there was another bloke there; 'I'm taking this gang over', he said.

'Oh, and what happens to me?' I said.

'You report to the town office. Mr Moorland's waiting for you.'

Well', said Mr Moorland. 'You've let me down. But you can still keep your job. But on one condition. You keep your trade union and your politics away from the job.'

'I'm sorry . . .' I said.

And that was that. I was black-booked all over the bloody docks.

ALEX ROBSON
Rank and file seamen's leader, Middlesborough

I was barred from work for years between the wars. But that was the union's doing. The National Union of Seamen broke off from the TUC after the General Strike, and we organised the Seamen's Minority Movement; 2,000 joined on the north-east coast. Plenty of seamen had already begun to refuse to pay contributions to the union earlier on; even before the General Strike Havelock Wilson, leader of the NUS, to everyone's surprise, had spoken up at a meeting of the National Maritime Board, and offered a voluntary wage reduction of one pound in the seamen's wages, which were then £8 2s 6d a month. And that, he said was only a start, a drop in the bucket. Well, there were strikes all over the place; Australia, South Africa, men were walking off the ships. And I must say the trade unions in those countries were very good to the seamen. I was on a ship in the Straits of Magellan and by the time I was in port again, the strike was off. But the following year when I had shipped on the Southern King, a whaling fleet factory ship, I led the boys off the ship on a demonstration up the quay in Montevideo, against the wage cuts.

We struck the Southern King, too, that year, at Easter. It was Good Friday and we were in port so that the tanks could be scraped clean of oil. We were all forward and we were issued with one and a half sardines a man. I was missing a sardine and I raised hell with the steward. 'That's your Board of Trade Ration', he said. So I went down to the tanks where the local labour were working and shouted down to them, 'English rules. Holiday today. No work.'

136

So they all turned it in. Then I went to the skipper and said, 'We're all out on strike.' He sent for the steward and said, 'For God's sake give them their sardines.'

Now there was a rule that no man could sign on a ship without a form PC5, and that you could only get from the union. The result was that in the late '20s some of the best seamen were on the beach. That was one of the main jobs in the Minority Movement, to fight the PC5. They got me barred from sea, for forming ships' committees, and they kept the bar up on me for years.

Not that it stopped me from going to sea, and in the thirties I was aboard the Linaria, with my brother. We were carrying anthracite from the Black Sea to Portland in Maine. Now in mid-Atlantic we ran into bad weather and didn't have enough bunkers. So the watertight doors were lifted and for three or four days till we put into Bermuda we burned the anthracite, which is very poor steaming coal. In Portland, however, we discharged part of the cargo and they wanted to load a cargo of nitrate for Seville. Well, we got the map out and had a look. Seville was Franco's HQ. We decided, my brother and I, we'd call a meeting; the upshot was that we refused to carry the cargo. I let the skipper know that if there was trouble I'd let it out that we'd broached the cargo at sea. When we got to Boston I slipped ashore and told the local paper and when the headlines appeared the skipper was flabbergasted. So were the crew, for that matter.

Well, we were three weeks on strike in Boston, with American seamen and a defence committee with three local parsons on it picketing the ship. We decided we should stay on board because I'd just read in the papers about the Woolworths girls in America, who'd just had a stay-in strike. We decided that we would only go on shore two or three at a time. The British consul wanted to split us up and send us home dbs (distressed British seamen) but we told him, all together or not at all. The consul told our crew that he wanted to warn them their leader was an active Communist as he had been informed by Scotland Yard. Well we won and they sent us to Liverpool in a liner from New York.

When we arrived in Liverpool, the police were waiting with a hurry-up wagon and we were in the calaboose before we knew it. The Shipping Federation took us to court. Sidney Silverman[1] defended the crew and I defended myself. There were 85 charges

[1] The late Sidney Silverman, Labour MP for Nelson and Colne.

137

under the Merchant Shipping Act; disobeying a lawful command, wilfully and continually disobeying a lawful command, impeding navigation, wilfully and continually impeding navigation, and so on. With three months on each if I'd been found guilty I'd still be in jail. But they were all washed out except for a £2 fine on the impeding navigation charge. Silverman advised me to appeal against that and I did with money donated by local miners' branches and the Co-op; not a penny was from the National Union of Seamen. The skipper said he hoped we'd win the case, for we were the best crew he'd had in 35 years. It went to the Kings Bench Division before we were through with it.

Later in the thirties the NUS came back into the trade union movement; Havelock Wilson did some kind of a deal with Ernie Bevin. In the seamen's minority movement we decided to carry on our fight within the union. But even when war came I was still barred. There were thousands of good seamen on the beach when the war started.

J. W. (BILL) JONES
Former London busmen's leader; on Executive Committee of Transport and General Workers' Union

I suppose the one group of workers that successfully fought off a wage cut was the London busmen. In 1932 the London General Omnibus Company wanted to operate speed-up and wage cuts, and though the Press made out that the reduction was 'only' one shilling or one and sixpence a week, the altered working system meant we were losing a lot more. As it happened, the threat of a strike was sufficient to get the cuts cancelled. In those days when a strike was on in a garage, the garage doors were closed and the officials made no attempt to get blacklegs. Today the officials will stand outside the doors trying to persuade the men to come back.

In the thirties there was one strike after another, and the hall-mark was militancy and a high level of organisation. On one occasion we demanded double time for working after one o'clock on Saturday. They wouldn't give it, so we turned every bus back into the garage at 1 pm. It required tremendous organisation to ensure it, but it was a marvellous sight to see those buses rolling into the garage dead on one o'clock. They had an immediate inquiry and awarded us time and a half.

There really were no inhibitions about strike action in those days. I recall one strike at Dalston, shortly after the First World War, when they stopped the buses on Armistice Day. When they were asked, 'Is it right?' they replied, The better the day, the better the deed.' Indeed, that's why they chose May 1937 for the big battle, because they knew that with the Coronation there would be millions on the streets and the strike would have the biggest effect. The men were so militant in fact that their leaders had to ask them not to strike for sectional demands but to reserve their power for the big fight in 1937.

The key to the strength of union organisation on the London buses was the London busmen's rank and file movement. We really had a tremendous organisation. Our representatives would go round the branch meetings and one of Ernie Bevin's full time Transport and General Workers' Union officials would be following us round. But in all that time he never succeeded in getting one branch to disaffiliate from the rank and file movement. The London bus section of the TGWU in fact carried over the democratic procedures of the old vehicle workers union which had been amalgamated into the TGWU. Bevin was always trying to curtail their power. The rank and file leaders do their own negotiating. Officials may be present, but it is the busmen's own elected leaders that do the bargaining.

I can recall many a meeting with Lord Ashfield in later days when he was head of the London Passenger Transport Board. He never used to know quite what to make of us.

One day he said to me, 'I'd like you to see my portrait Mr Jones.' So we all went down to have a look at it. 'It's by Sir William Orpen.' 'Ah,' I said, 'My favourite painter.' We looked at it and I said, 'It's wonderful.' He looked at me, not knowing if I were serious or not and said, 'Do you really mean that?' I said, 'Yes. Just look at the expression – "not a penny more".'

The power that the rank and file had was jealously guarded. For as well as militancy and high organisation, the London busmen were blessed, or cursed, with rank and file leaders of exceptionally strong personality, powerful debaters. I'd hazard a guess that the London bus leadership of that time was the strongest bunch of rank and file leaders the Labour movement has seen.

139

There were about 20 of them, able organisers, strong platform personalities and this unfortunately was a bar to complete unity between the bus and tram sections. Each thought that they ought to be in the lead and tended to look after their own houses. Ernie Bevin played this division for all he was worth. He knew all about these clashes.

His moment came during the 1937 Coronation strike when we were out for the 7½ hour day to counter the effects of the growing traffic and speed-up in working between the wars. The busmen voted for a strike and demanded that the tram section be authorised to strike in sympathy. The union EC granted full powers for strike action, but refused to call out the trams. The tram section had indicated to the union that they were ready to come out if called, but they decided not to come out in support of us without union sanction. That didn't come. We went ahead. In fact a good many argued that Bevin only made the bus strike official in 1937 to give the rank and file enough rope to hang themselves. History indicates there's a good deal of truth in this.

After just over three weeks Bevin called off the strike without consulting the busmen's committee. After he'd done that he proceeded to discipline the leaders. He expelled Bert Papworth and myself, and a number of others were debarred from holding office. After the expulsions a number of the rank and file leaders, led by Bill Payne and Frank Snelling of Merton, both powerful men, set up the National Passenger Workers' Union. It was a strong breakaway, and I'd estimate at the height of it, there were between 20 and 25 per cent of the busmen in it, with some paying to both unions. Those of us who stayed in the Transport and General Workers' Union and rejected the idea of a breakaway were admitted back to membership shortly afterwards. But those who remained outside burned their boats. The breakaway lasted right through the Second World War, which in fact prevented us from tackling it in the way we might have tackled it. It wasn't until after the war that the split was healed, and by that time a good deal of damage had been done.

Part II   THE MINERS RECOVER

ABE MOFFAT
Retired president of Scottish area National Union of Mineworkers

The miners took a battering all over the place and took time to recover. In the Fife coalfield the owners were ruthless, victimising people and trying to follow this up by evicting them from their houses. My father was victimised along with my brothers and myself. He had seven months' arrears of rent by the end of 1926, and he was getting solicitors' letters. It had a terrible effect on him. I had the house transferred to my name and went to see the manager. I told him, 'You'll get the arrears when you take me back.' Well, he never took me back and he never got his arrears.

With the effects of the 1926 defeat, union membership had gone down. But worse was to come. In those days the union was organised by county, and in 1929 came a split in the Fife organisation. The Right wing had been defeated in the vote for the executive committee, which they had previously controlled. But they would not accept the verdict of the vote, and so set up a separate union. Eventually the Lefts formed the United Mineworkers of Scotland, with its main base in Fife with a bit of Lanarkshire. When I took over the leadership of it in 1930, it was thought to be a sinking ship. It had a short independent life but in that time it attempted to work for miners whether they were members or not, on the question of wages and safety. It did establish the principle of working inspectors in the pits, and government inspectors paid tribute to the work of these men.

The work of the Red Union meant I was soon involved in strikes beyond the Fife coalfield, where I had worked all my life. We brought out the men from ten pits in the Shotts coalfields over piece rates. Here we had to bring together a strong Catholic population and active Protestants, including Orangemen, and we had to cope with a situation where the Right Wing leaders had let their members down. No one had been getting relief, not even the children. We organised soup kitchens and demonstrations to the parish council. They argued they were not legally entitled to give relief, but I persuaded them to phone the Board of Health and

141

tell them we would occupy the place, and finally they agreed to pay ten shillings to each wife and three shillings for a child.

In 1931, with the second Labour Government in, an act was passed for a $7\frac{1}{2}$ hour working day, to partly restore the position lost in 1926. The Miners' Federation of Great Britain decided that $7\frac{1}{2}$ hours only should be worked. But against this and the Government's intention, the officials of the old union in Fife co-operated with the coal-owners in enforcing an eight-hour day. This time we brought out some 15,000 miners and after three weeks not only won the strike but for the first time got unemployment benefit for those who were laid off during the strike. The next year in the same coalfield, every pit came out against a threat to cut the wages by a shilling a day, a threat withdrawn after a week.

An important strike came in 1935 at Valleyfield pit, where the owners were trying to impose a greater amount of dirt and a reduction in the weight of the coal, thus cutting the pay the men would get. They were out for 13 weeks, and during this 13 weeks the General Election took place. Willie Gallacher stood as Communist candidate for West Fife and in Valleyfield the women walked for miles to the schools to vote. We organised babysitters and even ran dances in the playgrounds of the schools where the voting was taking place. I don't know how we got away with it.

Gallacher got into Parliament and the first thing he did was to get the Ministry of Labour to send someone down to deal with the Valleyfield strike. The claim for 13 weeks benefit for everyone laid off, except for those directly on the coalface who had withdrawn their labour, was established and on the eve of the New Year there was more money in that village than there had been for many a year.

Gallacher's election and the election of myself and my brother Alex as councillors I think shows the extent of our support among the population, and I think I would acquit us of any charge of political sectarianism in those days. I would say, too, that we did our best in various ways to promote unity among the miners. But looking back I feel that for the Left to form the United Mineworkers of Scotland was a mistake. I sensed that after I had become its leader and did what I could to foster unity.

I was a personal friend of Ebby Edwards, general secretary of the Miners' Federation of Great Britain; he tried to use his influence to bring the UMS and the old union together, but they rejected the idea. Eventually we decided to liquidate the UMS, against the wishes of some of its members I might say, and arrange for our members to go into the old union. Well, they would not take back Alex and myself nor another active member, Alex Campbell. For a while I found myself out of the union I'd been in all my life.

In the end, though, we regained our membership and later, shortly after the war started, I became President of the old Scottish Miners Federation. You can guess the extent of the weakness in the trade union movement by the fact that the total funds were £2,000, and the potential membership was 80,000. But I persuaded the leadership of the Federation to ballot among the county unions to form one Scottish union. When that was formed we were not long in achieving 100 per cent membership.

But, as I say, it was a mistake for the miners to be divided in the 1930s. I'm not under-estimating what the UMS achieved, but on reflection I think it would have been better to have suffered the Right Wing leaders and preserved the one union. The split weakened the miners and played into the hands of the coal-owners at a time when they were on the offensive everywhere.

WILL PAYNTER
Former general secretary of the National Union of Mineworkers

It was a desperate period, after 1926, with the miners' lodges dropping to 50 per cent of their membership. I remember after the passing of the 1927 Trades Dispute Act having to stop people at the pit top to get them to 'contract in' and pay their political levy to union funds, instead of 'contracting out' as they had before, if they didn't want to pay. It wasn't so easy.

Next came the round of wage cuts, and in South Wales we came out on strike for three weeks, Now at that time the Minority Movement was fading away, but in every valley there was a rank and file committee. The South Wales union leadership were going to call off the strike and the big question among the Communists was whether the Party should assume independent leadership and carry on the strike. At a mass meeting of about 2,000, a very noisy meeting, the vote went 50–50 on whether the strike should be called off. The chairman decided that it was a vote to go back. In those days I didn't like to get up on the platform and speak; I was bloody mesmerised up there, though I could always say a few words from the body of the hall.

Next day, the rank and file committee in the valley met, under the chairmanship of Arthur Horner, and it was decided we should call the men out again. So on Monday, there was I standing on a stone outside the gates of the colliery, telling the men why they shouldn't go in. I'm no speaker, but I managed to get a hearing, when along came the colliery manager with his deputies. Now I was a checkweighman, and there is a Checkweighman's Act of 1860 which says that checkweighmen are not allowed to interfere with management. They yanked me down off that stone and the manager pointed with his finger to the crowd. 'In or out', he shouted and they trickled away. 'What about me?' I asked. 'Go back to your place,' he said. A bit later I was stopped in Porth by a man who said, 'Have you seen the paper?' And there were the headlines 'Colliery seeks injunction'.

So I was unemployed, but still active in the union, paying a special sub of one penny a week, and trying to organise the people out of work; I was chiefly trying to get better benefits, allowances, milk, boots, coal. Imagine, living on a mountain of coal and couldn't afford to buy it. Families were being broken up, for if you had a son working his wage would be taken into consideration. There would be a kind of grapevine operating. When the investigator came round, the lad would have to run out of his home the back way and into the house where he was nominally 'lodging'. There was a lot of argument about the means test administration. The Labour Party argued it could be administered more humanely. We argued co-operating disarmed the fight against it. And a lot of prominent local Labour people were involved as investigators.

While I was still unemployed I was elected to the executive committee of the South Wales Miners. A drive had begun to build the union up again.

I can remember, even before the war came, stopping men at the pithead and sending them back if they didn't have a union card; this was strictly against the law, under the 1927 Trades Dispute Act. The fact is that laws don't stop people going on strike. We would pick a pit where membership was low, concentrate all the union leadership on it for a week, not stopping until we had most of the men back in the union. Then we'd strike the pit until the rest were joined up. How the hell were they going to proceed against 500 men? The only thing that could stop them would be their own weakness, and as the thirties went on, that was gradually overcome.

DAI DAN EVANS
Retired general secretary of the South Wales area, National Union of Mineworkers

At first we were driven back, till morale in the valleys was very low. At that time we were down to less than 40,000 members out of a possible membership of between 140,000 and 180,000. And in that period of extreme weakness, the Spencer Union got a toehold in South Wales at Parc and Dare Pit, Nine Mile Point. Taff Merthyr and Bedwas pits. This breakaway, so called 'non-political', union was started by Spencer, leader of the Nottingham coalfield and he was trying to spread it, with the connivance of the coal-owners, into South Wales. The Bedwas Pit, a militant pit with better conditions of labour than the surrounding area, in a pocket of mass unemployment, was one of their targets. In the middle of a strike, the management challenged the men, by recruiting non-union labour. There were plenty of nons in and around Bedwas who fell for the bait and in that way the pit was lost to the union.

At this time the executive committee of the union was mainly full-time officers and very weak. Week in, week out, membership was flowing out of the union. From the stronger sections, like Maesteg and the West, arose a demand for the union to be reorganised. Out of this came a semi-centralised system of organisation with a rank and file executive. No one who held full time office at pit level or EC level could be elected to the EC. So this brought the breath of the pit to the executive decisions, and the first thing to be tackled was the problem of non-union recognition. The rules were changed to allow lodges to combine together in opposition to the powerful and growing company combines. These combine committees of the union were the spearhead of the drive against the Spencer union. After a determined campaign, Spencerism was

K   145 wiped out in all the places where it had secured a hold, except for two, Taff Merthyr and Bedwas.

Into these collieries had been recruited a nucleus of the real non-union, or anti-union, man. The local officials were in league with the employers and any person who brought a real grievance to the branch committee would be dismissed immediately. Price lists and conditions of piece-work were imposed on the men, the tempo of work increased tremendously. But the effects were wider, they spread outside the pit into the community. Not only did the man at the coalface mistrust the man working next to him, but no one trusted his neighbour on the surface, and people in the locality would not dare to talk to any of the old union members who were now laid idle.

I came from the anthracite coalfield in the West, one of the places where the union was still strong. It was a place where, by tradition, the seniority rule as, it was called, had such sway that it was impossible for the management to sack a man simply because he was an agitator. The last employed was the first one out, and this rule was so strict, (there was a hard fought strike in 1924 to enforce it) that in the anthracite area the meekest lamb would roar like a lion.

There was not such a difference between leadership and rank and file as in the other areas, where the leadership stood out. To get to an agitator the management might have to sack 50 or 100 men, and who would want to bring the whole district to a standstill over one man? This seniority rule, which worked like a religion and was as keenly observed by the women as the men, knitted the anthracite miners together and gave extra strength in the difficult days. It meant we could help other areas where the union was weak.

So I found myself in Bedwas along with Jack Davies, an old friend from Ebbw Vale, trying to make contact with the old union members. We called in a pub one morning, thinking we might see some. We gave one man 'Good morning', and one by one the five or six men who were there left. After this happened, the landlord, who was in fact sympathetic to the old union, asked us if we would mind keeping away. The men, he said, were not averse to talking to us, but dared not.

Outside of Bedwas about two miles away over the country lanes was another pub. We would go there at night and meet the Bedwas men and they would talk to us, but outside, not in the bar. There were men coming into Bedwas from other villages and if you went there they would talk to you. But in Bedwas no. And even outside they would only talk to you individually, never in groups. They were leading a double life, an open one, a very trivial life of work, home, a few pints and a dance, and another secret one in which the real social or economic problems might be discussed. It was not easy for these men, for the lodge had been militant. Yet in the local council elections, these men had been returned as councillors. We knew there was a core of men waiting to be returned to the union.

There were two entrances to the colliery. One for the men who came in and out by bus, the other for men who came by train. On the station side, hundreds of men would wait for the trains and we could talk to them over the fence, which gave you a chance to state a case, to speak for 20 minutes. You could feel the men responding to you. On the other side, the men would race across the road as the bus came up and you had no more than three minutes to talk. I called this the 'oyster end' because the men would not open up. An added reason was that the Spencer union had a bunch of men hanging around with rubber truncheons under their jackets.

After months of work, Ness Edwards, Jack Davies and I made up a list of contacts, men known only to us, and not to each other, as supporters of the old union. We asked each one separately and got their agreement to a meeting at a pub in Bargoed. You may imagine their surprise when they came together, asking each other 'Are you a contact? I'd never have known.' Now they would not split on each other, they were sworn to secrecy and gave us other names. We had 50 men still loyal to the union.

The day came when we said we would have a stay-down strike at the beginning of the morning shift and the end of the night shift. A man from Abertillery was chosen to head it. I went down that morning and saw the winder working. 'My God', I thought, 'It's been a flop.' He came out and told me, 'I couldn't do it.' But the others stayed down. A little chap had taken over the leadership, one of the group with the truncheons who had stood over the other side of the road, a die-hard scab, he led it. Later the chap who found he hadn't the nerve to lead the stay-down, fought in the defence of Madrid; he had courage of a different kind.

This was the beginning of the end for the Spencer union. In

147

Bedwas Pit were the best part of 1,800 men. Only about a dozen men stayed down, but that was enough. For no man would go down the pit to work, while they were there. We called a meeting. The hall was packed. We had a ballot and the coal owners realised the Spencer union days were numbered.

EDGAR EVANS
Unofficial strike leader, South Wales

Bedlinog, where the Taff Merthyr stay-down was fought, was famous for its militancy, It sits up in the mountains in a valley between Merthyr and Rhymney, the way out at the top was a narrow road over the mountain. The Bedlinog pits had closed in 1923, worked out, and this put the village in a desperate situation. But the Ocean and Powell Dyffryn Combine decided to sink a new shaft between Trelewis and Bedlinog, which was to be known as the Taff Merthyr. Powell Dyffryn Combine was notorious; it was called 'P & D' or 'Poverty and Death'. The colliery only became operational in the backwash to the 1926 defeat and so Gregory, who had been in the South Wales Federation in Monmouth but now was a big man in the Spencer union, saw it as a good place to get a foothold. The manager of Taff Merthyr, a man called Dai Hughes was a very useful person from Gregory's point of view and he accepted an agreement that anyone coming into the colliery should be a member of the Spencer union and sign a card that he would not join the Federation.

The company built a village up on the hill, which became known as Storm Town, a disreputable name in later years. It was to accommodate the main core of people to be employed. Dai Hughes raked up a few hundred of the worst cronies in the Rhymney Valley and ran them by special train into the sidings at Taff Merthyr (this was company property and so barred to anyone else). The weaker elements recruited locally were housed in Storm Town. To get work in Taff Merthyr, you had to have a letter of introduction from the local doctor, local police or local squire. Dai Hughes being a new man was taking no chances.

There was a natural reluctance to take work under such conditions and we had to make a decision, was the pit to be filled with such elements or should we tell the chaps to get into Taff Merthyr even if this meant signing the card? For years men paid to both unions.

From 1927 to 1934 we had an unusually trying period. The average person was almost afraid to stop and talk. They couldn't get at me, because I was not in the pit, but ran a little ironmonger's shop in the village where people would meet. One of the cronies used to spend hours outside my shop; if we had a meeting there and a miner was spotted, the next day there would be a ticket on his lamp and he would be out. At this time there was a public debate in the Bargoed Judges Hall between Morris, a local Tory, and John Wilson, candidate of the Trades and Labour Council. On the theme of liberty, John Wilson told Morris that he would take him an hour's walk across the hills to a village called Bedlinog and show him intimidation comparable to that of Mussolini's Italy.

The Communist Party ran a series of meetings outside the pit, and Gregory and his crowd brought a huge van with a terrific loudspeaker playing one record after another until one couldn't hear a word. The company fixed a special siren like an air raid warning but the police had to stop it for it interfered with what little traffic there was in Bedlinog. I remember one meeting where Arthur Horner spoke in 1934, where he said that conditions were so bad a fight must be made. It was around dusk, and you could see people sneaking along the wall to listen, until there were around 70 people listening just out of sight in the darkness.

During this time I had been helping in the union's recruiting campaign, using my van. Some of the officials just wanted to use the van and loudspeaker, but others were not averse to telling me, 'You seem to know more about this than us, so you have a go with the mike.' Now when the Ocean Colliery Combine Committee decided to have a campaign against non-unionism, it was thought to leave out Taff Merthyr because Gregory was entrenched. But I told the NUM boys that Taff Merthyr ought to be included and the officials finally agreed. Arthur Horner was deputed to take charge of the campaign and it went on for months, with union officials being put up in my house, even sleeping on the floor. Some were astonished when they came to the area and asked for the local union HQ, to be directed up the hill to the ironmonger's.

We had our ears close to the ground, and we knew that more and more people were secretly signing up for the Federation and we felt it was time to come out into the open. We had a portable shed which we assembled on the railway embankment. People would come up there and sign on for the Federation. A couple of times it was bowled down the hill at night, so for months we dismantled it every night. And day by day a couple of blokes would come in and sign up. Things hotted up and soon I told Ness Edwards that I thought the men would be ready in a week to strike.

That Friday night a score of strangers, obvious thugs, a real collection of broken noses and cauliflower ears, appeared and began to parade around near the shed. Ianto Evans, a huge man, stood at the door with a big spanner up his sleeve keeping his eye on them. Then came a rumour that two brothers who had signed up had been sacked, and the night shift had refused to go down. At first I didn't know whether to believe it, but as we stood by the shed, I heard the strains of the Red Flag coming up from the baths, sung like I've never heard it before. And the next thing the whole afternoon shift marched up to the shed to sign on. The gang of thugs had melted away.

That night sitting in my front room on the hill, we saw a platoon of the Glamorgan police march up with a few scabs while the people lined up on either side, hats off and heads bowed. A car came up the road, but not down again. We decided we were ready for bed, when we heard a car engine coming down the road. Next minute my plate glass window was smashed to splinters. We got dressed and rushed to the police station, where the sergeant took 20 minutes to get ready. We went down in my car to the next station and asked the sergeant there if he'd seen a car. Of course he hadn't. But a friend said he'd seen a car with no back lights being driven hell for leather down into the colliery.

The strike at Taff Merthyr went on for months. By now Jim Griffiths, who had been South Wales miners' president was in Parliament, and Arthur Horner was president. I put it to him that Taff Merthyr was ready for a ballot. Arthur pointed out that there was still a hard core of three or four hundred diehard Spencer men. But I felt we could win, and I had my way. We lost by two bloody votes. But a compromise was reached and the management recognised the Federation. But for one year the officials in the pit were to be Spencer officials. After that there would be a ballot for the positions. There followed a big battle for the funds, particularly money for a workman's hall dating from the 1914–18 war, around 2,000 pounds. S. O. Davies, a miners' agent, forced the issue and the Spencer men had to give in. The whole business was cleared up and soon one of the nicest little workers' halls anywhere was being built.

But in the Taff Merthyr pit one of our chaps, a bit of an adventurist, pushed through a stay-down strike on the grounds that some Federation people had been victimised. A few of the lads got into a section of the colliery, but two or three were pounced on by the officials and came out, one with his arm in a sling, another with his nose bleeding. Within hours, thousands of men marched down and surrounded the colliery; they were held off by the police. The manager inside the pit had sacks of stone dust dumped outside the working where the men were, and then turned on the pipes to blast the dust in. The men used mufflers like respirators to keep the dust out, soaking them with water. After 12 hours the management turned off the water at all points and concentrated the pressure. They rigged up a hose and directed the water onto the roof above the working at a point where it was giving way, and forced them out.

By this time there were hundreds of police at the colliery and they drove us back down the hill. From the Bedlinog end a crowd went round the back to try and outflank the police. Some reached the railway bridge at the Trelewis end and pushed a coping stone off the bridge which just missed a train going down the valley; 83 of us were arrested and tried for organising a riot, which included the incident on the bridge, though most of us were nowhere near it. Some 33 were sentenced to between 3 months and 15 months. The judge is said to have underlined certain names in red and I got nine months.

When I came out, the workman's hall was up, and my name was engraved on one of the corner stones.

HYWEL JEFFREYS (JEFF CAMNANT)
Retired miner and farmer, Seven Sisters, South Wales

There were two stay-down strikes in our area at the Banwen colliery. Conditions in the locality were bad and D. J. Thomas, the manager, was a tyrant. He was known locally as 'Dai Baw' ('Dai Dirt').

I took part in one of the stay-down strikes; it was over conditions in one district of the pit, known as the *Cwtch* (cubby hole, space under the stairs), because it was small, confined and stuffy. The atmosphere was so dank down there that the fungus grew white as snow on the floor, and the props would snap so that you wouldn't think it was seasoned wood.

I suppose you could credit Dai Baw with getting the strike going, because one of the men who wanted to get it started put the word around the institute that Dai Baw had been saying he had 1,000 men at Banwen he could twist round his little finger. That was enough to provoke anyone. and it started the men off. I joined in the stay-down because one of the lads asked me, though I noticed that in the end he wasn't there when we stayed down. There were youngsters with us, boys of 14–15 working with men who weren't their fathers. They wanted to stay down with us, but I didn't want them, so finally it was about twelve of us. We made up our minds quite suddenly that we would stop in, and found a little place tucked away where we could get in, but they couldn't reach us so easily to get us out.

It was middling warm and the men brought food down to us in tin baths, searched very carefully to make sure that we had no matches. They brought us tins of sardines and one bloke looked his mate's sardines over and said, 'Your sardines are redder than mine.' He looked down at them and said, 'All right you have both of them.' We curled ourselves up between the sleepers and the rails and tried to sleep. But there was one man who wanted to talk. Now he had twelve of us who had to listen and he kept it up for two days, driving us mad. When we finally went up, there were only eleven of us. He'd finally dropped off. When we went back and woke him up, he was mad.

They tried all sorts to get us to come up before we were ready. The local official came down and tried to coax us out, by telling us stories about things going wrong at home, 'Your wife is sick; there are ashes from your grate to your front door.' The manager even wanted to rip the top down.

BEN DAVIES
Former lodge official, Banwen pit, Seven Sisters, South Wales

He was a terrible man, D. J. Thomas. He had a habit of picking up a chair when he was arguing with you, as though he were going to throw it at you. I told him 'Two can do that', so I tipped the table up. Show him you were afraid and he was even worse. There was one man kept saying, 'Yes, Mr Thomas, sir,' so Thomas gave him a kick in the backside and said 'Stand up and be a man.'

The story goes that when the *Thetis* sank with the men trapped on board Thomas said he couldn't understand how they suffocated so quickly, when we had hundreds working in the *Cwtch* every day.

I remember, when they introduced the mechanical cutter in Banwen, around 1938, Thomas was in his element. He had been to Germany to see how they were managed and when he came back he was busy lecturing all his cronies about it. When they installed the conveyor belt and cutter in the 'Grey' seam, a very low one, the engineer who supervised the installation, said to me, 'I hear you are a bit of a poet. Could you express your view of the new machinery in verse for me?'

I said that I could:

> *'Endless hub of moving rubber – the drone*
> *Of the drill and cutter;*
> *A current-driven carrier,*
> *A model of hell is here.'*

The engineer had to agree that the description fitted.

With the conveyor introduced and the demand for coal built up with the onset of the war, the owners introduced as a kind of incentive, a standard wage of 14 shillings a day and a list of prices, so much per yard above the minimum. Thomas tried to revert back to the minimum and we fought a series of strikes; I was vice-chairman of the lodge at the time. At one point there was not a week without a strike. People were coming to work from Merthyr and Dowlais to find pit-head meetings and no work. I was sorry for them.

The war was on and the Germans were in the Channel Islands. It was a dangerous practice to strike, but it was all due to the stubbornness of D. J. Thomas. Eventually Horner himself came

153

down to meet the coal-owners at Neath. The dispute was settled, and it opened the eyes of top management. They couldn't allow him to go on putting a spanner into the wheels of the war effort, and so Thomas was finally slapped down.

Part III 'THERE'S A WAR ON'

DICK ETHERIDGE
Shop stewards' leader at Austin Motors

As the war approached the employment situation began to get a little better. Earlier on, in the midst of the Depression when I'd been at Handsworth Tech, out of a form of 30 pupils, perhaps one would get a job. I worked for a while in a laboratory, making up prescriptions, formulas for industry, but I got browned off with that. Then our family started a business, an all night cafe, where I started to meet people active in the trade union movement. I joined the Transport and General Workers' Union and worked in a garage until war broke out, and our place was bombed. I wanted to join the Air Force, but I was turned down for my eyesight, and I went into Austins, starting on nights on a capstan machine in the machine shop.

Government orders were coming in for aeroplane parts, tank controls, shafts for aero engines, parts for ambulances, and the change over to war production was going on. But in other senses things were going on as before. The factory was mainly un-organised. I was in a shop where the AEU had a bit of organisation, but there were no shop stewards on the night shift; they were all frightened to take the job, since the failure of the 1929 strike, which had more or less broken up the organisation which had built up after the First World War. The break up of the shop stewards plus the seasonal form of employment meant that no one could get established. Unemployment was used deliberately to undermine union organisation and it used to be said Austins couldn't be organised. In the early war days, I doubt if more than one in ten were in a union.

In my shop the day shift was pretty well organised but the night

154

shift was poor. The foreman on that shift was a terror. He used to come poking round at night with a torch, shaking it at you. Much to his annoyance, after I'd been there for about six months, they couldn't get a shop steward for the shop, so I took the job on. A fortnight later I put in for an increase in rate, and later on we had a number of small strikes over people refusing to join the union. By then the emergency powers order was in force, and you weren't even supposed to put out leaflets. If two or three were gathered together they called it a meeting. When we put leaflets out for a wages strike, a copper would come round to the house.

But in fact this emergency legislation didn't make a lot of difference to the men. The effect the war had on them was to make them feel freer. With war production and the owners on a cost plus basis, the blokes knew that they had great power to disrupt. By the time the war ended the shop steward's authority was very strong. I could call the men out at the wave of a hand (couldn't do that now), but with the shop stewards' movement backing war production, I would get up on many occasions and talk the lads out of it; I was very unwilling to call a strike unless the issues were very important.

We had Stalin, Roosevelt and Churchill's pictures up in the shop and were determined to aid the war effort, although this was mixed with a determination not to put up with any nonsense. And we didn't.

The foreman used to say 'Wait till the war's over. We'll deal with you lot.' But it was him who got done in the end. We got him the sack. Never been known before or since. There were all sorts of underhand things going on, and towards the end of the war we all went on strike for his removal. The employers tried all the ruses under the sun to get him back, but he had to go. They couldn't afford to have the place stopped. All the petty corruption came out and they had no choice.

Today, of course, the employers would sack a bloke like that as soon as they found out about him, without waiting for us to do it. But before the war they had encouraged this sort of bloke to push the men round. Before the war, whether you were in the right or the wrong, you could say nothing. But the shop stewards movement, as the war went on and it got stronger, gave the bloke on the shop floor some dignity and a sense of his own power.

GEORGE WYLIE
Official of the National Union of Woodworkers, Newcastle

October 1941 there was a flare-up in the shipyards up and down the Tyne, both sides of the river. It was the first big strike in ship-building for many a long year, and you could tell that the blokes were feeling their oats after the pre-war years.

Before the war it was one of those industries where it was heads down and arses up. Some sections, the iron trades particularly, when they went in the gate had to assemble in what was known as 'the market'. They had to stand round in a ring, while the gaffer detailed them off. He was always looking up to see if there was any rain coming. If so, he'd a dry spot for a chosen few. The rest were out. He would stretch out his hand and point if he wanted a man, and that man had to step forward like a sheep.

But it was a different story when the war got going. The ship-building bosses were getting open contract, time and materials. The more workers they had on the payroll the more profit they made. So there was a terrific upsurge in the industry and men came flooding in, the number doubled and trebled. The trouble started over making up the pay. The whole business of making up the fellow's time sheets was being done by rule of thumb. Some trades still marked up their jobs on a board with chalk. It would be thrown in a basket at finishing time and next day, they'd draw it out, spit on it and cover it with chalk again.

At that time, Tuesday was the chosen day for calculating the wages, allowing the clerical staff to make it up between Tuesday and Friday. The employers reckoned it was a physical impossibility to make up the wages in the time. So they said that Sunday would be the day, which would have meant two days short that week, and those two days would have been missing until a man left.

So it flared up and it was spreading from yard to yard down both sides of the river. Now the local Press, owned by Kemsley, which never to my knowledge offered any sympathy to anyone on strike, came out in full support of the dispute, which we put down to the general Kemsley sympathy for Hitler. The Communists were against it; Harry Pollitt came up and worked in the back-ground. It was argued that the strike could do more damage than all the bombs that Hitler could drop. I tried to impress on the 600 joiners and shipwrights I was working with the dangerous consequences the strike would have; whether it was because of my arguments or not, they decided not to come out.

The strike was settled when the employers gave the men a sub to make up the two missing days, and it was over after about two or three weeks.

DICK NETTLETON
Former apprentices' leader

Six of us, apprentices at Metro Vickers and other factories in Manchester, were dragged into court in 1941, probably one of the first prosecutions under the new regulations which Ernie Bevin had introduced at the Ministry of Labour during the war. You were supposed to give 21 days' notice of disputes, but we were only kids, between 16 and 20 and we didn't know about niceties like that.

The apprentice strike was part of a series of strikes in different parts of the country, starting in 1937, when the apprentices in Scotland, mainly on the Clyde, came out. Some Manchester factories came out then, and Metro Vickers apprentices were out and in again on the same day. Scots apprentice conditions anyway were a good deal worse than in England. In 1941 the whole thing blew up again, mainly a matter of pay. There were no national apprenticeship rates, no form of recognition; the unions were not allowed to negotiate for apprentices, who were supposed to be under a private binding contract between employers and parents. The agreement that was reached did produce national rates and it gave the trade union movement the first foot in the door. But the settlement was mainly to placate Scotland and had a number of odd results; some of the rates in England were a ha'penny less, which got England very annoyed.

It sparked off a wave of strikes, with something like 10,000 apprentices out, with the MV lads in the lead. The Metro Vickers apprentice committee was a peculiar one. It had been set up by the company and it was mainly made up of the blue-eyed boys with an eye to promotion. In 1937 this committee had been against the strike, but by 1941 the blue-eyed boys were off the committee

which was now led by more militant apprentices. We came out at
Metro Vickers (there were some 1,500 lads altogether) and marched
to a common in Openshaw, where we waited to see whether any
of the other Manchester factories would join us. Around 12 o'clock,
when only one or two had arrived from another factory, we began
to talk about going back and treating it as a one day protest strike.
But slowly lads began to roll up from other places, from Bolton,
Rochdale, even from Liverpool. As more and more arrived, it
turned into a one day strike meeting and we began to set up something of an organisation.

We rented an office at the Conway Hall run by the printing
unions and we had lads dashing in and out all day long, rushing
out bulletins, getting in contact with other factories, raising money,
asking shop stewards for support. The police began to follow us
around, but there was no confrontation. There was one detective
who used to meet me every day. He'd wait for me and we became
quite matey – 'Where are we going today?' like.

So when they decided to prosecute us it came almost as a bolt
from the blue. I suppose we thought they wouldn't start on a bunch
of kids. But they did, they picked six of us; myself as chairman,
a lad called Warburton, secretary of the Manchester committee
and one or two lads apparently chosen quite at random, people we
didn't even know.

The strike had been going for about eight days when they got us
into court. We had Platts Mills, KC, to defend us, and eventually
they found us guilty and bound us over not to do it again. Platts
Mills in court tried to hold things up by trying to get them to
make Ernie Bevin come up from London and give evidence that
he hadn't been notified of the strike. And there were hilarious
scenes in court when they tried to prove that we were out on strike.
They had the foreman in the box giving evidence that I, for
example, hadn't been in the factory. To establish it, they had to
produce the clock cards which hadn't been punched, and the old
magistrate had to have it explained to him very laboriously what
these cards were for. Then there was an argument about whether
the fact that the cards hadn't been punched proved we hadn't
been in the factory.

Generally speaking it was good clean fun and public opinion
wasn't against us. I suppose apprentices were not considered
crucial to the war effort, which in any case didn't get going until

the following year with joint production committees and so on. We were still not long out of the phoney war period.

There was also a general tradition of frivolity about apprentices' strikes. In Manchester there was a habit among apprentices of leaving the factory on Shrove Tuesday each year to go home. It was regarded more or less as a lark. The management tried to stop it but not seriously, though, and the older workers egged us on. During the 1937 strike, the manager at MV was a shrewd character called George Bailey. He met a great bunch of apprentices coming down the shop and asked them where they were off to. 'On strike.' Where were they going to next? Down G. Aisle. 'OK', said Bailey, 'Let's all go and get them as well.' When the lads got there the foreman tried to stop them, but the manager said to him 'Get out of the way, you fool.' He led the whole bunch up to the canteen, had refreshments served, let them play the piano, and then when three o'clock came, he said, 'OK, lads, off you go home, and if you feel like striking tomorrow, just stay home.' Of course, nobody did.

In 1941 it was a different matter. A different manager met the lads and when they told him they were going on strike he said 'Get out, then.'

The union officially gave us no support, at top level, though there was a good deal of sympathy from the shop stewards. But the union was obliged to negotiate for us. In 1937 there were very few lads in the union, but in 1941 many had joined and the unions were that much stronger. It helped to change the attitude of the men. The settlement gave us some increase, a penny or penny ha'penny an hour. The pay was related to the men's rate by a percentage. It meant we were now covered by the normal pay negotiations and it was written into the AEU constitution that from now on there should be junior workers' committees.

All in all we were pretty well pleased with what came out of it. I don't think we really took the prosecution seriously. We felt coming out on strike was the only way to get things done, and that was it.

JIM CRUMP
Former shop steward, Amalgamated Engineering Union, Birmingham

Life has its ironies. Rover's got rid of me at the height of the war, when I was doing everything I could to raise production. In fact just at that point the shop stewards had begun to put the skids under the management because of its failure to meet the needs of the war effort. There had been all sorts of production drives and the feeling was growing that, 'the gaffer can't do the job.' The fact was that the management were not too happy about joint production efforts, because they didn't want us to know the production plans.

They were quite prepared to say 'There's a war on' when it was a matter of making inroads into trade union rights or particular conditions we'd established. But we kept an eye on the rates and working conditions during the production drive. It was a logical thing that if we made a drive on war production there would be more money in it for the workers. The management accused me of urging members to go out on strike. That was a laugh; we had just been running a 'Tanks for Joe' week. The fact was that there had been lightning strikes in various sections, because people were fed up to the teeth with the management's attitude, a strike in the polishing section, one in the assembly section, possible strike in the milling section. They claimed that I had walked into one section and said 'Right, all out.' The row went on for six weeks. When it went to the local appeal court after I was dismissed, they could only find one person out of 400 who was prepared to say that I had called a strike.

So I was sacked at 5.30. That night there was a meeting of 300–400 AEU shop stewards in Birmingham, and a bloke moved that if I was not reinstated in 24 hours, then they should call a town strike. It would have been carried, if I hadn't spoken out against it. The biggest disappointment of my life. Imagine to have the whole of Birmingham's factories out on strike, and having to speak against it.

160

ABE MOFFAT
Retired president of the Scottish area National Union of Mineworkers

While we were urging men to dig more coal for the Second Front, the manager at one pit tried to bring down the piece rates, and the men came out on strike. He refused to let the men go back, after we had urged them to return, unless they accepted the lower rates. We reported his action and the manager was fined £50 under Emergency Regulations, Order 1305. It is the only time I've ever known such regulations to be used against management, and the pit was taken out of the hands of the company and put under government control.

In another case, men at Cardowan Colliery came out because they thought a man was being unfairly transferred to another job. Some 34 miners were taken to court and fined £5 or 30 days in jail. Nine miners refused to pay and the authorities were so stupid, they arrested them and put them in prison. Before they knew what they were at every man in the Lanarkshire coalfield was out. Because of the Second Front and the need for coal, I arranged meetings at every colliery, but the loyalty of the men to those arrested was so great, despite the war, that we had a job getting them to go back. I phoned the Secretary of State for Scotland and told him I'd like to meet the lads in jail. He replied that it was impossible, and I told him that if he didn't agree he'd have the whole of Scotland out.

He got in touch with the Governor of Barlinnie Jail, and a meeting was arranged in the prison chapel. The lads appointed their own chairman and I addressed them, told them that I thought they should agree for the fines to be paid in this particular situation, of the Second Front and the importance of the war effort. They voted 8 to 1 to come out of jail, I suppose the only time prisoners have ever done such a thing. But I had to admire the lad who put his hand up against.

JOE BYRNE
Former branch official, Transport and General Workers Union, at Liverpool docks

All the Liverpool docks came to a standstill in 1943 over a dispute on an Irish coaster. I was working nowhere near the area, but I got the blow there was a strike on and went up to where they worked the coastwise trade. No one could tell me exactly what was going on, but they were out and meeting the next day. Next day the strike spread to two other ships and it began to look as though it would involve other areas. I held a meeting outside the gates and told them if the strike wasn't settled we would all be involved.

The docks had been taken over in 1940 by the Ministry of War Transport, and the men were expected to work wherever required. But the principle in dockland is that you do not work where there is a dispute. Still the employers persisted in requisitioning labour. When the men didn't turn up, they would send to the Ministry's officer for more gangs. When the men arrived, they found a dispute going on, and so the thing would spread.

So the following day, we were involved. A requisition came down from coastwise to Gladstone No. 1 for men for three ships. When they got up there, they found the coastwise men outside the gate. When they got back to the control point, they were told their pay had been stopped. 'OK,' I said to our lads, 'Just tell the foreman, we're coming up.' We marched off down the road to North Park, had a meeting, elected a committee, of which I happened to be chosen chairman. I realised that now we were out we couldn't get the backing of the union for what had happened on the coastwise boats, which was just pure cussedness.

So I put forward a programme. There should be lay members on all committees that affect our work, along with the full time officials, and a wage increase of a pound a day. There hadn't been an increase in the basic pay since 1924, and remember that in 1932 the Labour Government had taken back two shillings a day from us to save the country.

It was agreed that the committee members should put this to all the control points and report back faithfully what the men said. The union area secretary got on to me because the stoppage was now complete. He pointed out that the Government would bring troops in.

The next day Jack Donovan, the national docks secretary of the union, arrived, and his attitude was 'It's unofficial.' I put it to him that if we could get a meeting of all the registered dockers and get the programme I'd outlined adopted, then we might be able to get them back to work. 'Where can you hold a meeting of 12,000 men?'

As it happened I knew Shand who ran the White City Park, and he said that we could use it provided we were out of the place at six before the people came in for the dogs. It was agreed that if the men adopted the charter of demands, the union would give its answer within a month. It was a noisy meeting. I put the demands to the men and reminded them 'There's a war on'; (the battle of the Kursk Salient was going on right then); 'This is a difficult time. The Press is putting the heat on and we can't allow anyone to say this strike is being used to disrupt the war effort.' One bloke rushed on to the platform, shouting that I'd let the men down, but for all that a lot of the men went back to work that night.

But at 7.30 the next morning there were still a lot out and our lads were all looking at one another, unwilling to go in. A bloke rushes up on a bike, falls off it and says, 'No. 2 and 3 haven't gone in.' We marched off down the docks picking up men as we went till we got to a derelict railway yard. There must have been about 9,000 men in a blitzed space. There was no noise this time. I could hear my voice coming back at me from a warehouse wall. I asked them to stand by the decision of the meeting. I pulled out the programme. 'We want our place in the machinery', I said. And next day everybody was back at work.

In those days, dockland operated on rumour. If we had had shop stewards to let you know what was happening then, instead of all the power being in the hands of the full time officials, that strike need not have happened.

CHAPTER FIVE

1945-1960

Influence and Affluence

The end of the war saw the trade union movement stabilised at a membership of around 8 million, roughly equal to its post-1918 peak. There all resemblance between the two post-war situations ends.

The lessons of the inter-war years had been learnt; consolidation was not only of trade union organisation but of the financial gains of the war, and resulted in more solidly high peacetime wage rates. In face of the post-war economic crisis, instead of retreating, a more powerful trade union movement devoted itself to maintaining and increasing these rates, providing a basis for what is loosely referred to as the 'affluence' of the 1950s and 1960s. The different situation expressed itself immediately in the votes of the armed forces which helped bring in the first Labour Government with a real majority, the servicemen demonstrating something of their impatience in a wave of strikes and demonstrations over delayed demobilisation.

At top level the trade union leadership worked closely with the Attlee Government, staffing important cabinet posts and the boards of new nationalised industries. The latter was a co-operation which extended for some years to a large section of the rank and file and was not actively undermined until the Cripps 'austerity' policy and the wage-freeze of the 1947–50 period, which met with growing opposition.

Concentration on the export drive highlighted strikes in the docks, bringing the Government into conflict with workers whose need for change in an industry notorious for bad conditions was far from satisfied.

This in its turn merged into the Left-Right struggle in the trade union movement. The key point was the battle between the leadership of the Transport and General Workers Union, (led by Arthur Deakin, while Ernest Bevin was at the Foreign Office), and a frustrated and increasingly militant rank and file.

The 'strike problem' moved into its post-war prominence in the headlines. The number of strikes increased, though full-time officials at the Ministry of Labour never tired of pointing out that only one or two per cent of the labour force were involved. Indeed most of the strikes in this period involved few men; they were sectional disputes over piecework rates in the coal industry, disputes which almost vanished in the 1960s with the introduction of a new wage structure.

In 1950 the Ministry of Labour revised its way of cataloguing strikes, and introduced a new category – 'vehicles'. The boom in road transport, the rapid expansion of the car industry with its fluctuations of output, its high exports and profits, its complex structure but often ramshackle organisation, and the militant response of its new labour force, shifted the focus of attention to motor strikes. The traditional industries of labour struggles, coal, railways and textiles, went into a decline that continued through the 1950s and 1960s.

The 1950s saw the beginnings of a new kind of industrial action,

13. 'Household cavalry here, corporal, reporting for unloading duties.'
Giles' dock strike cartoon, *Sunday Express*, July 24, 1949

165

strikes to establish the right to work. This was another expression of the conclusions drawn from the years of the Depression,
and foreshadowed the more complex industrial battles of the
1960s.

RT. HON. GEORGE ISAACS, JP, DL
*Former Minister of Labour, and general secretary of the National
Society of Operative Printers' Assistants*

Shortly after the General Election in 1945, I was told by the chief
Labour Whip, William Whiteley, to be at No. 10 Downing Street
at 3 o'clock in the afternoon, where I saw Clem Attlee.

'You sent for me, Clem?'

'Yes, George. I'm going to sentence you to a period of hard
labour.'

'What is it?'

'The Ministry of Labour.'

'My God,' I thought. But then I thought 'Why not?', and that
was all there was to it. After that, things piled on top of one another
so fast it is difficult to separate one from the other.

I remember our repealing the Trades Disputes Act of 1927.
That was one of the first things we did. We considered in the
Cabinet whether it should be revised, amended or repealed, and
one or two, chiefly the lawyers, wanted to play around with it.
They thought there were some things that might be worth
keeping. But Ernie Bevin and I thought, this will take weeks of
arguing. So we turned the balance in the Cabinet for repeal. In the
debate in Parliament, the galley proof of that inflammatory
Daily Mail editorial at the start of the 1926 Strike came into play;
Bevin flaunted it at Churchill. (see page 87).

At the Ministry I found that my years of trade union experience
gave me confidence in dealing with the work. There was a thing
or two that I was able to point out to my conciliation officers. And
I never intervened and met the unions as Minister of Labour
until my subordinates had failed and everything had been tried
that could be tried.

Toughest of all was the docks. There had been a history of
trouble. Attempts to overcome this had not yet succeeded and
there was a feeling among the older men, and some of the younger

men, that the only way to get anything was to stand up and fight. Some just had the intention of creating trouble. The Dock Labour Board was working nicely but hadn't settled down quickly enough. The rule was still 'One out, all out', and if half a dozen stopped on the first ship, people on the second ship wouldn't know, when they came out, that perhaps the men on the first ship had gone back. It was a heritage of days long ago. An uncle of mine had to go through it. A gang leader would have a dozen cards, for jobs, and he would chuck them into a crowd of dockers who would then have to fight over them. Today it's different. Then all a man could lose by going on strike was a few days' pay. Now he has house, television, washing machine on hire purchase. By moving dockers out of the congested areas and rehousing them, by spreading them out, we brought down some of the belligerency. They have to remember all the good things they have now, and want to hold on to; good luck to them.

But times were changing. There were plenty of times when trouble stirrers didn't bring them out. But when they did, and when the Cabinet met to discuss sending the troops into the docks, the Prime Minister insisted that it was the Minister of Labour's decision. In the Cabinet he would say 'It's your decision.' And I would say 'Send them in; we have to get the food out.' I remember one case where a soldier was trying to handle a crane and an old docker said, 'Here, son, this is how you should do it.' In the old days the dockers would have fought those troops.

The changes to mechanical handling in the docks caused trouble for it took a long time for the older dockers to realise that this would not do them out of a job. The great thing was to do it without creating redundancy, to do it by natural wastage.

And, of course, as the older workers have gone from industry, so have a lot of the old type of employer, the big mine-owner for example. The feeling has grown on both sides that it is possible to reason things out. The young men of today are quite willing to fight if necessary, but willing to talk it over; they are more educated They have a lot to lose. I came out of school with little education. Today you are dealing with a different type of man. In the old days I could shove my view over and the men would say 'All right, George, if you say so.' That wouldn't do for today's trade unionist. You were moving into a sphere of reason and argument instead of thought. You had to sit on the extremists on both sides,

167

the 'Teach them a lesson, fight at any price' people. You have to answer those on both sides,

There have been big changes, but they did not come all at once, or quickly enough for some people's liking. That was the main problem when I was at the Ministry.

ARTHUR KAHL
Branch official of the Transport and General Workers' Union, at Liverpool docks

The dock strike in October 1945 actually started at Birkenhead over a cargo of timber for making pit props. The men came out saying the firm wasn't registered. The Birkenhead men were out for a week. Men from the Liverpool controls were sent to work in Birkenhead and of course they wouldn't do it. I pleaded with the regional officer to let the Liverpool men get work in Liverpool and not send them to a place where there was a dispute. But he told us, 'Work in Birkenhead.' One morning at 8.30 they refused to let men in at the Southend Dock, and within an hour and a half the whole line was out to a man. At noon we all met in a park; there was no organisation attached to it. It was suggested that we all go back to our controls, elect two men per control for the strike committee and then meet in the Independent Labour Party rooms. We were out for six solid weeks and people from other ports came up to contact us. There were 20,000-odd men out.

At one meeting a man came up on the platform and said we weren't giving the Labour Government time to get established. Well, we weren't against the Labour Government. In fact we didn't allow Communists on that strike Committee. Mind you, the Press still called us all Communists.

We were out six weeks and the Transport and General Workers' Union (it wasn't like it is now) would have no truck with us. Deakin was in charge and the Reds used to go for him. But Ernie Bevin, who had been leader of the TGWU and was at the Foreign Office, unofficially worked behind the scenes to get a committee of local church people to bring about a settlement. The idea of a committee of inquiry was put forward and the Evershed Committee was set up. It awarded us three shillings a day, from 16 shillings to 19 shillings, the first time in history we'd had a rise of three shillings a day, *and* improved holidays.

The Government had to bring in the Dock Labour Board. Previously dockers had to deal with 185 different employers. You could work for eleven different firms in a week and go to eleven different firms for wages. But even under the Dock Labour Board, we criticised the union leadership for allowing the Dock Labour officer to rule the roost, even though the workers' side had equal representation. A great deal of the trouble in those years came about because the union wasn't militant enough on our behalf. The union officials would tell us, 'You can have this – you can't have that.'

We were still dictated to by the executive committee in London. The finest thing that happened to the industry, when it did finally happen, was the shop stewards' movement. We asked the union for shop stewards in 1945, and put a resolution up to the biennial delegate conference. But Arthur Deakin made a big speech against it, and the lay members nearly all put their hands up against the resolution, even though they had shop stewards themselves in the factories.

JACK DASH
Retired rank and file leader of the London dockers

In 1945, we had decided to battle for the dockers' Five Point charter by working to rule and ending piece work agreements. This can hurt the employer. He loses half to two thirds of his production and he still has his wages bill. Sometimes the employers will welcome a strike, because it may weaken us. There was a terrific attack on us by the Press, but in spite of this they couldn't break us. Finally, the employers refused to engage us unless we went back to the piecework agreement. They locked us out. In the end there were 83,000 dockers out all over the country.

Everybody thought that the Labour Government would bring the employers before some sort of judicial body. After all, wartime regulation No. 1305 was still in force. Strikes were illegal and so were lockouts, in theory anyway. Finally, though, the Government did intervene and got the employers to sit down and discuss the Five Point charter. We were asking for 25 shillings a week (pre-war it was 16 shillings) and we got 19 shillings, the highest award up to that time. We got guaranteed national holidays and better facilities.

ARTHUR ATTWOOD
Former LAC, RAF; leader of demobilisation movement

On the big RAF station at Drigh Road, seven miles into the desert from Karachi, we had organised a camp discussion group, with speakers like John Saville, now of Hull University. I spoke about the history of the trade union movement, and once about the dock strike going on back home, which the papers were saying was a stab in the back for the Labour Government. The funny thing was that before very long they were saying the same thing about us.

I had been an electrician all my life, working mainly in the contracting industry. Altogether I worked for 74 employers. This was partly typical of the old saying that 'He who works and does his best, goes down the road with all the rest', and partly because I was active in the union and the contracting employers ran a black list. To organise workers in contracting you have to work fast before the employer breaks up the job, and, though I was still a fairly raw and immature union member when I joined up in 1942, I'd begun to gather some experience that stood me in good stead in the Forces.

With both wars at an end in the summer-autumn of 1945, the authorities were more relaxed and there was a fair amount of freedom in organising educational and current affairs discussions, usually with a bit of entertainment, gramophone recitals, a word from the padre, and so on. In the early part of the year we ran a mock election, with Labour, Liberal, Tory and Communist candidates. We would go round in the evenings along the lines with a mike on the back of a lorry, and all the candidates speaking. Half way through the Communist candidate withdrew in favour of the Labour man, who won by an overwhelming majority. We were busy, too, making sure that the men's proxy vote went home for the General Election; the part the service vote played in Labour's landslide victory has been well recognised.

During the end of 1945 considerable bad feeling on our station

170

developed, mainly due to the slowness of demob. It was now months after the war had finished and the delay was aggravated by the worsening of conditions. Increasingly more overtime was laid on, for various pretexts; bullshit parades which had disappeared on active service began to reappear and one in particular proved the last straw, a commanding officer's parade in best blue. You can imagine the effect of wearing the heavy best blue uniform in a humid climate leading up to the monsoon with a temperature of 100 in the shade. Normally we wore light khaki drill, and most blokes had put their blue in the bottom of their kitbag when they went on the troop ship. On top of all this, the food was bad and we were still living in the same decrepit, tattered tents we had lived in for years.

At some point a chalked notice appeared on the walls of the camp. It said simply '7.30 tonight'. A rumour got around of a meeting on the football field and as dusk fell several hundred men drifted over there and assembled in the shadows. Some 30 people spoke, in pretty blunt language, and because they were getting at cross purposes, one airman was chosen as chairman, to put together all the suggestions. An airman asked how the meeting could be sure that their grievances would reach the CO, and he was told that the MPs were bound to be around and would make sure the CO knew.

As a result of that meeting, on January 19th, 1946, all the men on the camp converged on the parade ground in khaki drill instead of best blue and surrounded the CO. A group of us, including myself, put our grievances to Group-Captain Williamson Jones, who said that he would arrange for the Air Officer Commanding to visit the camp.

That night, while I was out of the camp with some of my friends, a small group of men voted for a strike. The risks were obvious, for that afternoon paratroopers of the King's Regiment had been brought into the camp. So the following day, another meeting was called, with about 1,000 men there. I spoke against the idea of a strike, and we agreed that we would put the following points to the AOC; speed up demob, removal of bullshit parades, improvement of food, and to ask that we be allowed to send a petition to Prime Minister Attlee. Finally the meeting rejected the notion of a strike, which in any case had been proposed to take place just before dinner time!

Next day in the cookhouse, a warrant officer climbed on a table and told us the AOC was on the station and wanted to meet a deputation of the men. He then began to assemble a deputation, a procedure the men were decidedly cool towards. At two o'clock we called our own meeting, the first one in broad daylight and elected a deputation of 20, which saw Air Commodore Freebody, the AOC, and presented the complaints to him. He listed them, gave us a pledge of no victimisation, agreed to tell the Air Ministry about the demob grievances, to allow the petition to Attlee and to cancel kit inspections. He insisted on the weekly parade, but agreed that conditions of work and parades should be eased. We went back and I reported back over the mike to the lads; that was used against me later.

We knew that there had been demonstrations at other stations, and the lads were in touch with one another by radio and telephone. It was only later on that I discovered how many stations were involved, and that Drigh Road was the first.

Our petition to Attlee, which was signed by over 1,200 men, apart from 500 odd men who wrote individual letters to their members of Parliament at home, said:

'We the undersigned airmen of Drigh Road, India, are gravely dissatisfied with the slow rate at which demobilisation and repatriation are proceeding. Although the war ended five months ago there are still thousands of us without any indication as to when we shall see our families and friends again. Why is this? We have not been convinced by recent official reasons.

Why cannot demobilisation and repatriation be speeded up? Is it because faster demobilisation would flood the labour market at home? We expect full employment from the Labour Government we are proud to have helped elect.

Is it because British policy in India and Indonesia require large armed forces? If so we demand a reversal of this policy.

Is it because the government wishes to talk tough to other powers? We deplore such an attitude in the United Nations.

Is it because of obstruction from any quarter? We expect the Government to overcome such obstacles. You can be sure of our full support. We have done the job we joined up to do and now we want to get back home, both for personal reasons and because we think it is by work at home that we can best help Britain.'

The effect was quite profound. Thanks to our efforts and those of our families back home, demob was speeded up and in the coming months, the population at Drigh Road was changed quite drastically. Easy chairs appeared in the rest rooms and canteen. New tents sprang up like mushrooms. Evening work stopped and we went on a 36-hour week. I went along with Sergeant David Duncan, who had been active in organising the educational and current affairs discussions on the camp, to an official court of inquiry. Eventually I was told that I could go home under Class B release, which would mean demob but I would still be liable for direction of employment.

Just at this moment, though, SIB men began to arrive in camp, posing as airmen. Later on they came out into the open and began questioning men. The day before I left camp I was hauled up but told them I would make no statement, because we had received assurances of no victimisation. Sergeant Duncan kept a detailed record of the way the SIB men went about their work.

The padre was asked for a list of Communists on the camp, a list of all trade unionists, a list of the people active in the discussion group, and the speakers and candidates for the mock election. The SIB men said they were doing all this on instructions from the Foreign Office. (There was some talk in the Press at home of our petition being a stab in the back for Bevin's foreign policy.) Any man who admitted he had attended a meeting or demonstration was told he was liable for long imprisonment unless he gave information. One corporal was asked how his wife would manage for ten years without an allowance. Another was told cheerfully, 'It probably won't be the death penalty now that the war is over.'

I went down to West Bombay to await my boat home. By now I was being paid out in English money, but was taken off the boat list three times. One night, in Worli Transit Camp, Bombay, I was hauled out of bed, charged with incitement to mutiny and taken to Kalyan 50 miles away where I was held in an Army detention barracks and my book with friends' addresses in it was taken away from me. For five days I was kept in solitary confinement. I was offered the services of an Indian Pilot Officer as Defence Counsel. He was more overawed than I was, and was in any case below the rank of the officers of the court martial.

When I accepted his services I was very near to a state of collapse with strain and isolation. What I did not know was that Sergeant

173

Duncan and my mates in Drigh Road had been raising hell. They had collected 4,000 rupees in 48 hours from the lads in camp for my defence, and had alerted Labour MPs and trade unions back home. D. N. Pritt, KC, who was then in Parliament, had taken up the case, and they had engaged civilian counsel for me in Bombay. But the telegram they sent me, telling me this and urging me to stick it out, never reached me. An express letter, despatched ten days earlier reached me three days after I had accepted the Indian Pilot Officer as Defence Counsel. When this came, I rejected his services and demanded to be taken back to Bombay.

In Bombay the camp commandant was very hostile to me. He must have been nervous, because slogans were appearing on the camp walls, saying 'No Boats, No Guards', in other words no men would go on guard duty unless demob was speeded up. When the trial eventually started in Bombay, my friends were down there; I had been in touch with them, getting news of the stir at home. Prosecution witnesses claimed to recognise my voice as the chairman of the first meeting. But on May 14 the court martial was adjourned, the principle of condonation was established and the pledge of no victimisation proved. I was released. But higher authorities demanded the re-convening of the court martial and I was re-arrested. I collapsed and was taken to hospital. While I was there, I heard on the radio, that there had been a protest meeting at the Memorial Hall in London, with trade union officials and Labour MPs speaking.

The court martial was concluded and the findings sent to higher authority. But after three or four months I was released and sent home.

This time they were only too anxious to see that I got my mail. With the feelings stirred up at home about my case and that of other lads who had been jailed, the attitude of the authorities changed. They never explained to me why I was released. When higher authorities set aside court martial verdicts, they never say why.

That November there were questions asked in Parliament about 'disaffection' in the Air Force and the Secretary of State for Air, Geoffrey de Freitas told the House that during January 1946 there had been incidents at 22 stations in India, the Middle East and South East Asia. They all took place in the last ten days of the month, and first on the list, January 19, was Drigh Road.

ARTHUR W. J. LEWIS
Labour MP for West Ham North; former official of General and Municipal Workers' Union

When the hotel workers in London, starting with the Savoy Hotel, came out on strike in 1947 I think there was still a good bit of the war-time spirit among them, the *esprit de corps* developed among people during the Blitz. A lot of them had been in the forces and this had given them confidence.

They needed it, for there had never been such a strike in the catering industry, nor has there since. In fact the catering workers were considered impossible to organise. Ernie Bevin said to me at the time that he had tried for years and it couldn't be done. There was some arrogance about that – what he had tried and failed at, no one else could do. So I determined to do my best. I was then the youngest trade union official in the country, as well as one of the youngest MPs. I took over a small branch of the Municipal and General Workers Union. I'd worked in all sorts of trade and industry, but this one was completely different.

A good deal of the industry was casual labour, including men who came in off the streets to do washing up for a bite of food and a warm. There were men of all races, colours and creeds, many unable to read or write English, unorganised and not knowing the first thing about trade unions. Some were very poorly paid, most were very shabbily treated. A minority did well: there were hotel head porters on £1,000 to £1,500 a year, (with £6,000 now), mainly from tips, and *chefs de cuisine*, pastry chefs on £800 to £900. There were in fact both rich and poor and to cope with them trade union organisation had to be different, using unorthodox means and methods.

I decided that the biggest and best hotel was, as it is now, the Savoy and that if I could get organisation in the biggest and best, then the rest would follow. I used to go round to the back entrance, the staff door, send in leaflets, try and get them to meetings. Eventually a number joined, waiters and kitchen staff, and I tried to get the management to recognise the union. They adamantly refused. I couldn't get letters answered; I tried the Ministry of Labour Conciliation Department without success. Then one of our leading members, an Italian waiter, named Piazza, was summarily dismissed for alleged misconduct. We carried the campaign to all hotels and restaurants in West London. Thousands and thousands came out on strike, hardly a one of them in the trade union movement. The Hotel Owners' Association of the day dug in their heels. Only the Grosvenor House managing director agreed to meet me and discuss recognition.

The fact was that the whole industry was chaotic. Hours and working conditions varied widely, though they were mostly bad. The lack of facilities was terrible, with bad shift and split duty terms; staff were treated like cattle, having to eat their food, usually left-overs as part of wages, standing up in any old corner; there were poor washing and toilet facilities. In one luxury establishment the staff had to go out and use the public toilets. There was a bitterness and hatred of working conditions; walk in, walk out, was the usual way. But now we were all out together and were going to stay out. The *esprit de corps* was terrific. It used to be said that British waiters resented Italians, but British, French, Spanish and Chinese were on picket together like the United Nations. And the highest paid, the managers and *maitres d'hotel*, the head porters, they all supported it. They believed in justice for the poorer paid. We had one demonstration to Hyde Park, when the whole West End was at a standstill; it was reckoned that over 80,000 were on the march.

Since the hotels had oil-fed central heating, we next tried to get the oil tanker men to stop delivery, with the help of the Transport and General Workers' Union. The Savoy did manage to get some oil in on blackleg lorries. We tried to persuade them not to go in, and when they would not agree, I and the other pickets lay down on the road. At first they were reluctant to arrest me but in the end they did. There was nothing about it in the law on picketing, but they charged with me obstruction. The Establishment can get you, right or wrong.

In Parliament, the Labour back benchers were unanimous in their support of me and some helped us on the picket line. Some Labour Ministers told me privately they supported me, and some, not of the trade union school, rather looked down their noses. Naturally the Tories, particularly the ones who used the luxury hotels, didn't like it. Even today, when they can't think of anything else to throw at me, they shout, 'Lie down, lie down.'

I suppose I'm one of the few MPs who has led a strike while

being in Parliament and some of them thought it wasn't quite the thing. And it was an official strike, one of the few in that period, though the top union leadership were not enthusiastic about it and let us down in the end. I think they resented me but I've always thought I was as good as any man or woman, but not any better, and if I have people to lead, I'd rather lead them from in front. If we had had the full backing of the official trade union movement, we would have got a lot more than we did.

As it was we achieved minimum standards and the applying of wage board levels, and the Restaurant and Hotel Owners' Association had to recognise house representatives. There was a rush of people into the union, and I began to recruit new members in places outside London. Some of them wanted me to set up a separate catering workers union, but I didn't want to split the union. Later on, a certain antagonism against me developed among some of the officials. Some of them became bitter about me holding the two jobs and eventually I was got rid of; legally, but unfairly, dismissed. After that a good deal of the membership we had brought in fell away. But it was a good time, while it lasted. Without industrial action things would never have changed.

COUNCILLOR FINLAY HART
Retired shop steward at the Clyde shipyards

In 1947, we ran into serious difficulties with fuel shortages, shortage of generating plants, and terrible weather. This, coupled with a turn in Government economic policy under Stafford Cripps, began to erode a good deal of the sympathy there had been from 1945 onwards. Looking back on the amount of co-operation we gave the management and the Government for the sake of production, I think we were extraordinarily patient. It created some strange situations. In 1947 a heavy fall of snow put our yard and other yards on the Clyde out of commission. Snow was falling and being driven by the wind into the sheds. The management wanted the snow to be cleared, the men wanted to go home. I convinced my department we should clear the snow, and so you had the spectacle of the welding department, the most militant group of men in the place, shovelling snow, while other departments walked out jeering. Some of the lads dropped their shovels, but we persisted,

M

and in the end won most of the departments and indeed whole yards for carrying on.

Now the management, while it was a matter of production, were as friendly as could be. But it was clear that on wages and conditions they had instructions to fight you tooth and nail and the joint production effort, which had been born in the war and carried over, began to fizzle out. Not that joint production during the war was all that easy from their point of view. They tried to make trouble for me on one occasion, for going early to the canteen; in fact I was going early simply to attend a production meeting.

After the war, when the time came for the hours to come down from 47 to 44, the engineering industry went over to a five day week. But in shipbuilding the employers insisted on a five and a half day week. They claimed that we had to make the most of every daylight hour; because of the power shortage and cuts, the five day week meant working part of the day in the dark. So on the Clyde, for nine solid weeks, we worked the five days and then went on strike every Saturday, until we got the five day week in line with the rest of the country.

The Cripps Budget in 1947 put cigarettes up one shilling from 2/4 to 3/4, and the feeling of resentment was such on the Clyde that if there had been a Tory Government in, there would have been a strike. I was convener at Blyth and there was a terrific argument among the men. They were fuming. And of course, other things were going up. Stafford Cripps was claiming the need to cut down on dollar imports. In the end there was no strike, because of loyalty to the Government, but the price increases helped stimulate the demand for higher wages.

Indeed from that time to this, I do not think the Clyde has known a tranquil time. Unemployment began to creep in. By 1950 some yards were on their last orders and only the outbreak of the Korean War and the re-armament boom kept things going, and then when things were falling off, the Suez War in 1956 and the blocking of the canal brought more orders. Between fighting to keep the wages up to match the cost of living and fighting to get the Government and employers to provide stable employment instead of these booms and slumps, I cannot recall any year when we were not organising some movement or other – token stoppages, half day stoppages, lobbies and demonstrations – mostly unofficial.

And when it was not wages or hours, there would be running

battles over the tea break, a running fight which has gone on since the early days after the First World War. The men would get the apprentices to make tea and along would come the manager and tip over the fire with the cans on it. I've been in dozens of small strikes over the management failing to provide facilities or time to make tea. You would be given a small disc, called a check, which would be taken off you for some misdemeanour and you would be fined, half an hour's loss of pay, or something like that. Managers would get their foremen together and make a raid down the ship over tea-making and gather in all the checks. Afterwards, as senior shop steward, I would have to interview the management and tell them that unless the checks came back, the men would hold a meeting outside. In all the wage negotiations from that time on, they have always tried to introduce an official tea break for which the workers would not get paid. In engineering shops with line production, they have been obliged to sort this out, with tea trolleys, but in ship-building, they have always tried to get round it.

To these pinpricks you can add the complications of demarcation disputes that blow up from time to time, and which the Press always exaggerates out of all proportion. The fact is that life's experience leads to a very simple approach on the part of the tradesman. In the old days marine engineers used to do so much by hand, and now so much is done by machine, by men who have not served their time. The craftsman tries to keep his hold on that particular operation, at all costs, for every technical innovation just increases the chronic insecurity of the whole industry. If a man can monopolise a certain function he is secure, he can stay in the yard, and keep his job.

Towards the end of the war I wrote a pamphlet advocating the amalgamation of blacksmiths, boilermakers and shipwrights,[1] for the arguments between these trades have bedevilled ship-building. At Blythswood, we worked out a programme to cut out demarcation disputes between shipwrights and platers. The rank and file accepted it, the full time officials rejected it. But amalgamation helps overcome these divisions, as does the recognition of the rights of the other fellow. Every step in that direction eases the

[1] Since achieved, these unions joined together to form the Amalgamated Society of Boilermakers, Shipwrights, Blacksmiths and Structural Workers in 1963.

demarcation problem, every increase in unemployment under-mines our efforts.

One of the most heartening things during the UCS 'work in'[1] has been the way in which the lads of different trades have got together. You have not heard of demarcation disputes, for the lads have seen what they have in common and not the differences.

FRED HOYLE
Former branch official of Transport and General Workers' Union at Avonmouth docks

To support your fellow worker, whoever he is, has always been one of the best principles of trade unionism. For that reason, what-ever the cost of it, I can look back and say I have no regrets about the part I played in the dock strike of 1949. It was not for more pay, nor better conditions, nor was it against victimisation of our own people. It was in answer to an appeal from another union, a seamen's union, from another country. And our reward for sticking to our principles was, as it often is, to be abused in the Press and other quarters.

In June 1949, vessels were arriving in the docks of this country which were involved in a dispute with the Canadian Seamen's Union. This union's officers appealed to British dockers not to work these ships and the dockers responding, refused to unload them. The vessels were declared 'black' and tied up to the quay side. This happened at Leith, Liverpool, London, Southampton and Avonmouth. Now in all these ports, except Avonmouth, the TGWU recognised the dispute and the dockers were permitted to work all other vessels, though they were not working the ships involved in the CSU dispute.

At Avonmouth, however, events were different. When the ships, *Montreal City* and *Gulfside* arrived, the union and its members decided to hold a secret ballot to decide whether the men should work them. The union supplied ballot boxes, ballot

---

[1] Faced with liquidation of the company and heavy sackings, the workers at the four yards belonging to Upper Clyde Shipbuilders Ltd, organised a 'work-in' from 13 June 1971, until 1 May 1972 when Govern-ment financial aid and other moves ensured that the sackings did not take place.

papers and supervised the ballot. The result was a majority vote not to work these vessels and the men decided to form a strike committee. Each morning they had a meeting in which they stated they were willing to work all other vessels in the port, but not the two vessels in dispute. This was all that the Avonmouth dockers asked for, but this the Avonmouth employers denied them. It came to our notice that the chairman of the strike committee was trying to get the men to unload a banana boat, hoping by so doing to break the deadlock. But realising he was toadying to the employers, the men removed him from the strike committee and appointed a well known local character, Joe Doody, in his place.

Dockers have always been in the forefront of militant protest for improved wages or conditions, or against victimisation or injustice. But this strike, which our local dockers interpreted as a lockout by the employers, as our men were willing to work vessels not in dispute, but were not allowed to, was unique as a gesture of solidarity to the seamen of another country. Our members accommodated the striking seamen in their homes and they were a fine lot of men, good living, good characters.

After the stoppage had been in effect for two weeks, in response to an appeal by the employers, the Labour Government sent in troops and naval mechanics to run the local docks. The situation for the men was now getting serious. The police anticipated trouble, the men's meetings were disorganised. They claimed that the union officials should have been fighting on their behalf instead of leaving them to their own resources. At one meeting which was particularly rowdy and disorganised the men appealed to me to take the platform. I explained that I was a branch secretary of the union and though a minor official I could not take part in an unofficial stoppage of work. But things got so bad that one morning I was impelled to jump on the platform, and appeal to them. They listened to me. The die was cast and I was their new leader. I addressed each mass meeting, wrote articles for the local Press, and addressed letters of appeal to the Prime Minister, the Minister of Labour and to MPs.

As was now evident the employers were using the dockers of Avonmouth as their guinea pigs, hoping that if they could compel them to work the vessels in dispute, other ports would follow suit; we decided to appeal for support from these other ports where vessels were tied up. Two members of our strike committee journeyed to London and Southampton. I went to Liverpool and Leith. In Liverpool there was already a minor dispute in progress. A coaster, the *Dromore* had been diverted from Avonmouth, and the dockers refused to work her. I stayed in Liverpool for three days, making appeals for support and at the end of it the whole of the Liverpool dock labour force was on strike in sympathy with us.

I then went to Leith, but was not successful, for it was evident the local officials had been getting at the men.

Meanwhile our local dockers were remaining solid in their determination not to give in to the employers' demands. They realised they were to be made the scapegoats, and at every meeting the show of hands to continue the stoppage was unanimous.

However, at the start of the fifth week of our local stoppage, I was informed that in other ports men were now working the ships in dispute. I raced up to Liverpool and realised it was true. Returning I informed our strike committee; realising that, being only a small port, we could not fight alone, we decided that our men had sacrificed enough. We put the decision to them, to continue the stoppage or return to work. The show of hands was a majority for return and they went back that day. We obtained a statement by Arthur Bird, the Docks National Group secretary, that there would be no victimisation for anyone who had taken part in the dispute.

However, when we returned, I was not called for work for many months. To use the expression of some of my militant friends, 'I took the can back for everybody.' At a meeting of the union's disciplinary committee in Bristol I was banned from holding office for two years. My action in support of the men ruined my career. I had been branch secretary and next in line for a full-time union appointment. This future after many years of study and hard work was now ended. For the next seventeen years I continued in employment as a rank and file docks tally clerk and retired at sixty-six.

I paid a high price for loyalty to principles. Union officials tried to turn the men against me, by stating that I was a Communist. In fact, I'm a very deeply religious man and have spoken from the pulpits and platforms of our churches for many years. Despite all the victimisation, the strife, the pettiness and even the hatred, I believe that moral principles ultimately prevail.

JACK DASH
Retired rank and file leader of London dockers

When the Canadian ship *Beaverbrae* came into the London docks during the Canadian Seamen's strike, the lightermen's and stevedores' unions refused to work it. But the employers said to everyone in the docks, 'Work that ship or no ship at all.' So we were locked out for the second time since the war.

It was one of those disputes which stand out since the war, because they were about trade union principles. Another such strike was the Roberts Arundel strike of 1966, and another the 'work in' at UCS.[1] As such these disputes are a challenge to the Establishment, and the means employed in 1949 to try and compel the dockers to work the Canadian ships showed that they recognised it as a challenge.

An even bigger challenge was coming in the docks. In 1951 a strike was taking place in the northern ports, being led by the Liverpool part of the National Portworkers' Committee. Since the 1945 strike we had made big advances, not only in working conditions, but in our own organisation. The dockers' committees in the different ports had made pledges of unity to one another. Because of this pledge, the London dockers' rank and file committee called a meeting in the Royal group of docks, where 12,000 dockers worked. Only 400 came.

On Friday evening, the leaders of the Portworkers Committee were at a meeting in the White Hart pub, at the Stepney end of the Rotherhithe Tunnel. They were deliberating how to extend the stoppage. While they were talking the door burst open, and a group of men walked in.

'What port are you from?'

Of course, they weren't dockers, but plain-clothes men. The committee were all arrested and put on trial for organising a strike. Since Order 1305 from the wartime days was still in force, this was in theory illegal. This was, however, the great *faux pas* of Hartley Shawcross, the Attorney General. One day there were 400 men

[1] See page 180.

out on strike; the other men were unwilling to join in because they did not see eye to eye about a claim, and there was no chance of extending the strike. The next day, on an issue of principle, the arrest of the seven committee men, the whole of dockland was out.

The Port of London Authority had felt so confident the day before that it had prepared dismissal notices for all the men who were out. Now everyone was out. The slogan was 'When they're in the dock, we're out of the docks.' Every time the seven appeared at the Old Bailey, we struck. And they had to acquit them. Because those seven men had the courage to face five years jail, the legislation which had been in force for 11 years was removed. It was an augury for what could happen with the Tories' Industrial Relations Act.[1]

CHARLES BLACKLEY
Secretary of the Manchester District Council, National Union of Railwaymen

When the railwaymen came out in 1951, Order 1305 was still in force; this meant that the union could not call out the men officially. Instead the branches of the National Union of Railwaymen, and in Manchester the district council of the union, took action unofficially. We held a mass meeting in the Railwaymen's Club on the Rochdale Road, where a district official explained the difficulty that the union leadership was in. The goods and cartage men had already struck. They sent the balloon up and had a big contingent at the meeting, and were calling for supporting action. We formed a Manchester strike committee including all grades; drivers, signalmen and plate-layers.

Once the Manchester men were out, there was a snowball effect all around the country, bringing out men from all the other districts. They couldn't prosecute us all under 1305, and since the union officially hadn't issued a call for a strike, they couldn't pillory the union. The union executive committee was sitting tight, but after about four or five days we had a telegram down

[1] Became law on 28 February 1972, setting up Court of Industrial Relations and providing for legal sanctions against unions and members in certain cases of industrial dispute.

from Unity House in London, from the general secretary, saying, in effect, 'Thank God for Manchester.'

By then it would have been difficult to have held back the members, even if the executive committee hadn't been ready for a strike, particularly the poorer paid men in the goods and cartage, who kicked off. The effect of three or four years wage freeze in a period of rising prices was frustrating to say the least, and while the businessmen were climbing on the post-war band-waggon, the workers were being left behind. The organised part of the working-class, the trade unions, had been hamstrung for years with 'Don't rock the boat' calls from Attlee. I'm amazed that the wage freeze went on for so long, for those workers that observed it, or were held back, were really soaked. Indeed you can say that this was one thing which led up to the Labour defeat in 1951. This lack of confidence in Labour had already led to a big loss of seats and votes in 1950.

I threw myself into this particular strike with enthusiasm and was elected branch secretary. I later became the secretary of the Manchester District Council of the NUR, from which point I've seen the whole history of the Beeching carve-up of the railways. In the 1950s the Manchester District covered 92 branches in most parts of East and South Lancashire and some parts of Cheshire, with 28,000 members. After the rationalisation drive on the railways, the district had 37 branches with 12,000 members. Nationally, the Union's membership went down from 400,000 to 185,000. It was the last major wages strike that the NUR has seen, although there have been threats (always averted by wage increases at the eleventh hour), and there has been spasmodic unofficial action.

It was the Beeching cuts which achieved what nothing else was able to achieve, when in 1963, the three main unions, railwaymen, loco-men and clerks, joined together for a day protest strike. In Manchester the three unions had a joint committee and on the day we completely stopped the railways and marched with the union banners through the city to a mass meeting. It is one of the tragedies of the industry that we were not able to overcome the division between the three railway unions.

In the 1950s the antagonism between the NUR and the loco-men was at its worst. It grew over disagreements about differentials in wage rates, with drivers always trying to preserve the difference as

185

soon as the porters' wages were lifted a couple of per cent. The fact that both unions could see their membership going down increased the tension. When the loco-men came out on strike on their own in 1955 the drivers in our union, the NUR, found themselves placed in an invidious position, as the union was saying that officially they should go to work. There is still some bitterness today, at a personal level, with ASLEF and NUR drivers meeting in the canteen and refusing to speak to one another.

Perhaps the worst of that period is over now and relations are better.

WILL PAYNTER
Former general secretary of the National Union of Mineworkers

While I was general secretary of the National Union of Mineworkers I saw the industry contract. In 1958, we had 710,000 members. When I left in 1968 the number was 350,000 and now it is 250,000. And in the first decade from 1945 to the late 1950s the industry was in a peculiar position, with a scarcity of coal. The miners moved up the wages league from 84th position to the first three, along with the printers. Demand was in excess of supply for a time, and they were even importing American coal.

The chief feature of the period was not the extensive strike of the pre-war years, but the short, unofficial strike involving a small number of men, and it would be a piecework issue. You have say 30 lads at a coal-face, on piecework. Suddenly they come up against rocks or ironstone that slows up the work. They call up the overman: 'What'll you give me for that?' 'Two and sixpence.' 'Bugger that.' And the dispute takes the men off the face. It may only involve one man, but they all come out to see the manager, to secure a settlement, and then go back.

Often you would have the piecework men out and the day wage men would be sent home. The day wage men tolerated this for many years, not being involved in either dispute or settlement. Then suddenly, you got the tit for tat strike developing. Once the piecework men got back to work, the day men would come out. They'd even let them go down the pit and then walk out. When I was President of the union in South Wales this became a problem. I must say that I did not believe these sectional strikes were a

186

good thing, for they very often divide workers against one another. In fact, sometimes management will provoke them for their own purposes.

Of course, with the introduction of the national wages system in the late sixties, the unofficial strikes dropped to one sixth of the previous figure. With the national wages system the piecemeal unofficial, sectional strike has begun to give way to the national strike.

DICK KELLEY
Labour MP for Don Valley; Former Yorkshire miners' pit official

Work on the face is the most variable thing you can have, apart from fishing. No two days are alike. One day the going's soft, one day it's hard; one day the power will break down, another day the roof will need shoring up. On piecework this means the earnings fluctuate rapidly, and it's a constant battle to keep the level up. The men are intelligent enough to realise that taking direct action is the only way to increase earnings.

This daily struggle was always the way of the industry under private ownership; the trouble when the pits were nationalised was that the ownership might have changed, but management could go on in the same old way. This has to be taken into account when you are discussing the frame of mind of the men. And militant action is important to educate the management out of that way of thinking, to make them realise that their job is to get the coal out and not to push the men around.

I don't think, though, that any working man can be made 'militant' simply by being led along by vocal elements. A man may have a big mouth and for a while others may take notice of him, but after a while they find there is no substance in him. In my experience, both while I was down the pits and since I've been an MP for a mining constituency, most strikes have been fully justified. The Press gave the impression that the miners were a lot of scallywags holding the nation to ransom. And there is no doubt that a shortage of fuel gave the men a sense of power. But in the past, privation and starving kids gave the management a sense of power and some think that they could still do as they did in the days when those were the prime consideration.

187

We've had to drum into the management's head that they have to behave differently and treat men as human beings, not as scallywags thrown into the pit because they had nowhere to go.

GEORGE BOLTON
Scottish miner, and pit official

At the back end of the war, our family moved from Lanarkshire to Clackmananshire, along with other families. The Lanarkshire coalfield was on the wane and all sorts of loose promises had been made about the pit we came to, the Devon pit, that there was coal for 50 to 100 years.

When I left school I went straight down the pit, where my father was the lodge chairman. My brother also went down the pit for a while, but then he became a professional football player. After I'd been down the pit for seven years, we began to see something new, the deliberate closure of pits. Previous closures had generally been due to exhaustion, but these new closures in the late 1950s were because of 'over-production' nationally. One day in 1959, it was announced over the television that the Devon pit was to close, along with 15 others, because of a surplus of coal. It came like a bombshell, because though closures were in the air, no one had suggested that Devon was due for closure. The reaction was bitterness; it was a catastrophe for those who had come through from Lanarkshire.

Devon was not the only pit involved, of course, and men from the pits took part in demonstrations, including a lobby to London. I took part, but it was quite clear that if this was all that was done, at the end of the day Devon would be shut along with all the others. Devon after all was showing a profit, but still they were closing it. I was a member of the pit committee, and I argued that we should try something spectacular. I won the vote in the pit committee for a stay-down strike and this decision then went to a mass meeting of the membership. It was not a light decision, to stay down for what might be an indefinite period; the men's health would be involved. But a comfortable majority was given for a stay-down strike and a notice to that effect was posted at the pit. It was interesting to see that, though the management knew all about it, unlike with previous stay-downs, they took no steps to prevent it. They could have said that no one is to go underground. But they did nothing, as though they were neutral.

On the day, I was one of the first to arrive at the pit (which was a change), and for a while I was worried in case no one turned up. One or two came and went back, and I began to panic. But eventually 57 turned up. There were 200 on the shift but we had agreed that only those who were willing should take part. The youngest was 18, the oldest men were in their fifties and could recall the pre-war struggles. We went down the pit and the agreement was that the remaining members of the committee who stayed on the surface should, through the pit delegate, have the power to call us up, but that no one else could do it.

We turned the first corner, about 100 yards from the pit bottom, and stopped there. There was an air of tension and people tended to shout at one another and be irritable, but eventually we all began to settle down. It was agreed that two of us, Tam Dalyell and myself, should be in charge. Our first decision was that if anyone showed signs of strain or distress, we could order them out of the pit. We sent two out, one on health grounds, the other because his child was in hospital. I had just had a spell in hospital myself and some thought I should go up. But I decided that come what may, I'd stay down.

We were down for $52\frac{1}{2}$ hours, like seven shifts rolled into one. The biggest problem was cold. It goes right through your bones, no matter what you do. There was some lighting. The lads on the surface were well organised and lots of local people gave food which was sent down at regular intervals. One lad, Tug Wilson, said, 'I hope it lasts for ever, I've never fed better in my life.' He used to put a girder on his back and walk up and down with it to keep fit. We had the papers sent down to us, we played cards and dominoes. and we were ready to stay down for a long time.

On the surface the support was terrific. Some 28,000 men had come out on strike in the coalfield, and pits were coming out one after another. But after $52\frac{1}{2}$ hours the pit committee called us up. The Coal Board had agreed to meet a delegation of miners in Edinburgh to discuss the closures. But the net effect was that the pit still closed. It is my personal feeling that the decision to call us up was a blunder. We had done something that had caught the imagination of the public, and if the British coalfields had been involved it might have changed the course of things in the pits.

A movement had begun with collections in the factories, a movement which was growing when we came up.

But it was worth doing. I would argue that our stay-down played a part in the decision to have the Long Annet (Fife) power station fired with coal. Many men who would have been sacked were employed in the pits supplying Long Annet with coal.

There is a thread of militant action that runs from that time in 1959 to the present day and the UCS 'work in' of 1972.[1] In fact men at the Bogside Pit, one of the four Long Annet pits, were among the first to strike, ten years later, when the Wilson Government tried to introduce the 'In Place of Strife' anti-trade union law.

J. W. (BILL) JONES
Former London busmen's leader; member of Executive Committee of the Transport and General Workers' Union

Losing ground all the time; that was the situation of the London busmen by the time the last big movement came along with the 1958 bus strike. Before the war, at the height of the rank and file movement, busmen were near the top of the pay league. If you went in for a mortgage (it was £750 when I bought my house) and said you were a busman, they'd practically handcuff you to the desk. Today, they wouldn't want to know you.

The change for the worse, I'm convinced, began to come in the Second World War, when the militants made a mistake over the industrial implications of the fight against fascism. We had a strong leadership at rank and file level, but because of the war we did not fight as hard as we should have done for wage increases and other conditions. I was a guilty as anyone else. We didn't see the relationship between winning the war and preventing the employer from exploiting our goodwill, innocents that we were. As a result we lost the right to improve the living standards of our people, improvements they were entitled to because of their contribution to the war effort. Only one good thing came out of it all, and that was equal pay for the women. The management wanted to offer 90 per cent of the male rate, but the men insisted.

So, throughout the forties and the fifties we were losing ground when other people were advancing; our industrial strength was

[1] See footnote on Page 180.

being eroded, and we were being further weakened by the turnover in the labour force as we slipped down the wages table. Young men would come on to the buses and before they had a chance to get interested in the trade union movement, they were away to somewhere else where they could get better wages. With such a labour turnover the ground was like sand beneath you.

I remember once at Dalston garage I saw the manager come into the office. I'd been away for three weeks. He said, 'By the way, Driver Brown has handed in his resignation.' 'Driver Brown? I don't know him.' 'Oh, of course, you were away when he started.'

The other factor that weakened us was the situation in the Transport and General Workers' Union, first under Bevin, and then Deakin when Bevin was in the Attlee government. Bevin did his best to break up the rank and file movement before the war, after the war Deakin brought in the political bans and proscriptions at the 1949 biennial conference. It took us years, in the long run longer than we thought, to get our political rights back. I think this period did more harm to the bus section than to any other. It began to come to an end after about seven years, when Frank Cousins took over, but by then a great deal of damage had been done.

So when we came out in 1958 to try and recover lost ground on the wages front, there were some doubts as to whether the strike would be solid. But it was, and the men and women kept it going for weeks. The weather was beautiful. And whatever the Press was like, there was no real public hostility to us. We were out in the West End selling our literature to the people there and there was a lot of goodwill. But we were vulnerable in that it was the first strike against the Government's policy to limit wage increases. We were like the postmen under Tommy Jackson[1], we were fighting the Government and we could not win unless we had the trade union movement actively behind us.

The question came up, whether to extend the strike by calling out the petrol workers, or having the power men bring the Tubes to a standstill. I put it to Cousins at the time 'Either you extend it, or you end it.' Cousins asked the TUC if they'd back him if the

[1] General Secretary of the Union of Post Office Workers. The UPW led a seven week strike of postal workers in January, February and March of 1971, for a 15 per cent increase. A court of inquiry under Sir Henry Hardiman, however, awarded the postmen 9 per cent.

strike were extended and they said no. The strike was not as effective in a way as the strike in Coronation Year, 1937, because of the advent of the private car. This is one of the difficulties of the new situation that has developed since the 1950s for the busmen. Strikes on the buses are almost non-effective, particularly when you give warning that you are coming out. Strikes have got to be looked on as a science, much as the unions do in Italy. The real modern form of struggle for London busmen is the guerilla strike, where you don't tell the employer when and where and how many garages will be out. You cannot live in the past. Public transport is in a different situation now, with millions of cars about. That is one of the biggest changes on the post-war scene, and you just have to take account of it.

LES BUCK
General secretary of the National Union of sheet-metal Workers

After the war we soon began to see changes in the pattern of production in the motor industry, big changes, with even bigger changes to come, and that meant a change in the pattern of industrial disputes. I think it's true to say that our strike at Duples Motor Bodies in North London in 1950 was something of a trail-blazer. Duples was before then one of the old style coach building firms, and though there was trade union organisation and a works council, they didn't recognise shop stewards, and striking was an unknown factor for a good many of the men. Indeed one of the first things I had to combat was the old piecework master system, an affliction of the motor industry from the old days. It was really a form of the 'lump.' with one ganger contracting, say, to make all the sliding doors and paying out the workers in his gang, or more correctly living off their backs.

In short, it was not a place where you would expect much militancy. I had been blacklisted before I came there and had been in the shop for a couple of days before someone tipped off the foreman and he said to me, 'If I'd have known who you were, you'd never have got the job.'

As I said, the firm worked on old-fashioned lines. Every morning and afternoon the managing director and manager did a circular tour of the place. The manager had a notebook and if they saw anything they didn't like, they called the foreman. If they thought it flagrant, the bloke was sacked on the spot. Then changes began. A new engineer came in, re-organising production, breaking it down into a batch system with batch ordering of material in advance. Up to then the usual practice was to build according to customers' requirements. When the batch system was first brought in, it slowed the factory down, and it was preventing our people earning reasonable wages. There was a series of meetings with the management and it became clear that the engineer saw us as an obstacle to his plans. Eventually the management got fed up of the argument and began to postpone and cancel meetings on one pretext or another.

In June there was a strike in the metal shop, when all the shop stewards had been sacked. The company said they were redundant. A little later the company tried again, but this time with a little more caution. They told the district officers of the various unions that large-scale redundancies would be inevitable and that these would include the whole of the shop committees and shop stewards. This was the usual slack period in the coach building industry and we had some difficulty in convincing the unions that this was a second attack on union organisation. When we warned them that the management was thinking of sacking five out of six of the men in the factory, some trade union officials just refused to accept it.

In the end the management solved the problem for us by suddenly refusing to talk to the trade union officials and on October 19, 1950, we were all out on strike. It was a long and tough strike and needed a lot of organising, but the enthusiasm of the men meant that the whole business was a lot easier than the trade union work I have faced since.

We made our strike HQ in an ex-service club within sight of the factory and on the wall we had a chart, like a company structure layout, showing how our strike committee functioned, finance, pickets, publicity; from the start everything seemed to click. Local business people, who felt they had a financial interest in us, were helpful. Local cafes offered us special terms, and one even laid on oilskins and tea for men on picket duty, on a bulk basis. Old trade union members, pretty staid people whose main interest in life after work was to go home and work in the garden, became involved and active. We appointed a special team to deal with social security. Some of the local officers were looking down their noses at the idea of giving benefit to strikers' dependents, but we sorted that out.

Other chaps who would never have said boo to a goose went out to speak to trade union branches. We had over 100 men on this, with a dozen cars; we got round to 1,200 factories asking for support and £12,000 was raised in two months. One group even bluffed their way into an aircraft factory and held a meeting in the works' time. But the most remarkable was the persistence of the men who chased round after black goods which the management were trying to get in or out of the factory. One bloke on his motor bike trailed a black load all the way to Norwich.

We hit the national Press when Sir Ian Orr Ewing got up in the house of Commons to ask the Minister of Labour 'the extent of Communist influence'. We got in touch with him, he met us and we were able to put a very different picture to him. We had meetings with Labour MPs. Some were not so directly helpful but all in all we effectively closed up that line of argument.

Every week we had a mass meeting, because it was imperative to keep in touch with our people. It was always well attended. Some officials said that 'this kind of strike' (a direct strike against sacking in an industry that always worked on hire and fire methods) would only last three weeks. The company, taking advantage of this kind of attitude, met the officials and it seemed that they were prepared to recommend we go back to work on the basis of discussing how many redundancies there would be. But the strike committee told the officials that this had to be put to the mass meeting. It was rejected and afterwards one bloke told me, 'If you had recommended going back on those terms, I'd have considered throwing my chair at you.'

So we soldiered on. And the spirit remained high. Not one worker went elsewhere and took a job, except in certain cases of great hardship, where the strike committee gave permission. From the very first meeting I explained that we were on strike, but that meant we were in business, in business to get our jobs back. We intended to have those jobs back, not any old job. The strike had now lasted nearly till Christmas and the issue went before an industrial tribunal under Lord Terrington. We had little idea what to expect and you can picture our consternation when we saw the KC in his pin-stripes representing the other side. Wally

Roberts, an official of the vehicle builders, represented our side. At the start their KC told the chairman that there were people outside handing out leaflets, attempting to influence the court. But Lord Terrington told him that this was not the first occasion a striker had given him a leaflet. It was not unusual as far as he was concerned.

Some confusion crept in when it came to the real point; such a tribunal had never been asked to say who is in the right on a question of redundancy, the employers or the workers? There was an adjournment and we went into a side room. Along came the counsel for the other side and it became clear the company was in some difficulty with the main production period coming on. The KC then became a sort of negotiator, running from room to room. We didn't leave the place until nearly midnight, by which time the KC was saying he didn't know who to charge for his fee, us or them.

A resumption of work for everyone was agreed, with loans for any men in difficulty, and there was a period of some problems until work picked up again. We put forward our proposals on how things ought to run. The engineer, whose changes had started the whole business, left the factory.

It was, I believe, the first strike of this kind against mass redundancy which was successful. Pre-war experience suggested that men would never stick it out for so long. But in fact one old chap said to me afterwards, 'It's been a wonderful time, and it's with some regret that I'm going back to work.' We prepared a pamphlet about the strike and thousands of copies were sold up and down the country. And I think largely on the strength of all this, I was later elected president of the sheet-metal workers' union, the first time a member had come straight from the shop floor without having been an executive committee member or a full-time officer.

Duples' experience was, I think, passed on; it proved useful later on in the fifties in other car factories, when this battle over whether management should be able to sack people as they liked without challenge came right to the forefront.

DICK ETHERIDGE
Shop stewards' leader at Austin Motors

After 1945 came a big upheaval in motors. There was a huge demand for the early models; if you had an Austin you could get twice the value. It was a sellers' market and it could have been a free-for-all industrially. But unlike the period after the First World War, the shop stewards established themselves after 1945, kept the negotiating rights and the 100 per cent trade unionism which had been won during the war. New methods of production had come in during the war too. Things moved more quickly and the management began to find it easier to deal with the shop stewards for the sake of smooth running. The size of the factory, with 25,000 men, all organised (before the war only about 2,000 out of 18,000 were in the unions) made it imperative to be able to negotiate on the spot with someone. There were 600 shop stewards and the works committee became essential to both sides. The shop stewards know as much about the place as management. In fact, you have only got to think of the place as a small town and you can see how absurd it would be not to have some kind of workers' organisation.

From 1948 on in various departments there were small strikes, over new people being brought in who weren't in the trade union. But they were generally quickly settled and it was in the early 1950s that the real struggles began. There were rationalisation changes, and then came the first redundancies. I went in on the instructions of the shop stewards and said we'd have no sacking. We came out in 1951, but the men voted around 50–50 to go back, and we lost that one, though we did achieve something. We struck, in effect to avoid the shop stewards' organisation from being broken up, which was the object of the redundancies.

We went back more or less intact. No strike is ever lost, unless it is led to the point of annihilation. You gain in the long run, even if you are apparently beaten in the short. You have to have a long view; it is a strategy, to know when to retreat, if necessary, for the employers will often let a strike go on to the point of annihilation.

Conflict is in the very nature of the motor industry. It works at high pitch to get high production. The inspection wants the quality right. The foreman wants the production right. The rate-

196

fixer wants the price right. They are all in conflict with one another and all of them are in conflict with the operator. Nothing wrong with conflict, provided it is constructive. No other industry has such a high level of intensity, efficiency or level of production. They talk as though we get money for nothing. But take it from me productivity is high. High production brings its tensions, not only on the tracks, but in the heat of the stamp shop, conditions are such that men need a rest. If an issue is important, the men want a quick decision, a quick solution. If they don't get it, then you get a row.

So organisation is the key. We had decided after the 1951 strike that if anyone got the sack we would strike. We did not always get the support of the men in those days. When the British Motor Corporation challenged us in 1956 by sacking 6,000 men, 3,000 of them at Austins, the strike we called was not automatically backed. The idea of the right to work was new in those days. If you said the gaffer was not to be allowed to give you the sack, men thought you were daft. They thought it a good idea in theory but not in practice. The unions backed it officially. We had already told them we were not going to give the gaffer the right to sack.

The first day, only 2,000 were outside the gates. We decided to go on the gates and it very quickly became rough. One bad feature was the transport section, who were taking vehicles in and out (today they are one of the most militant sections). Well, our lads know what to do with vehicles and they started to take them to pieces. The police came in, in force. I had the door of one truck open to talk to the driver, when one police officer got hold of me, one of the special police holds, and had me down on the ground. Suddenly like magic he let me go. One of our lads, a former paratrooper, put a certain hold on him. The men and women lay down in the road and stopped the trucks.

It was rough for a while, but by the second day we started to build up. The news came, this number shop was was out, then that one. We got together and marched round the place, singing what became our Austin's anthem 'Keep Right on to the End of the Road', and the departments came out one by one. In the end we won and we marched back, as we'd come out, dropping the workers off at each department, singing to the tune of 'Marching through Georgia'. 'Hurrah, hurrah, we've beat the BMC.' We were out for two weeks, followed by two weeks' holiday. They agreed to make redundancy payments and to take people back as things picked up, which they did; probably everyone who wanted to come back did.

In 1951 after the first redundancy strike the management were most abusive to me. They invited me to leave. In 1956 we went back cock-a-hoop and the gaffers were very polite to me.

LES GURL
Oxford shop steward at Morris Motors; secretary of British Leyland Trade Union Executive Committee

We had a rough time at Morris Oxford during that 1956 BMC strike. Out of 7,000, only 1,000 had come out. We knew though that Pressed Steel nearby had blacked everything, and we kept mass pickets on the place; every day, when the others were going in, they would stand and boo, and sometimes fights would break out. After a week of this, Jack Thomas, a leading Transport and General man, speaking at the daily meeting, said that we'd tried for a week to convince the others that working men should not be thrown away down the river like driftwood. He suggested that, at closing time that night, we should line the roads out of the plant, in silence with heads bowed, and hold our union cards in the air. The annual holiday was just about to start and the blokes came streaming out in between the two lines of our blokes. It had an immediate effect. Men got off their bikes, went up to the line to speak to people that they knew and promised that when they came back, they would not go in to work. But before their holiday was over the unions had settled the strike.

The thing was that it got our toe in the door over redundancy. It turned the British Motor Corporation into a militant 100 per cent firm and gave us a redundancy agreement by which no one leaves the plant without the case being vetted by the shop stewards. In my department only myself and one more came out in 1956; when I went back I turned my shop steward's card in and told them I didn't want to represent them any more. But in the end I took my card back and within 18 months there wasn't anyone outside the union.

Throughout the fifties and early sixties we made sure that the work was cut down whenever redundancy threatened, to keep the men inside the gates. We cut back and cut back until sometimes it was almost two days' pay a week, until things lifted up again. But we kept the men's jobs right through until the middle sixties when Wilson and the Labour government started urging a 'shake out'.

All the time there was the running battle over trade union membership. There were dozens and dozens of stoppages to get 100 per cent until things settled down. But the running trouble was the insistence by Morris on sticking to rating people by methods that had been in existence since the 1930s. We weren't having men sweating their guts out on the line on 1930s piecework agreements. And here again the union was not going to give any lead. The Press were saying all the time, 'When are you going to discipline their members?' But we wanted to know when they were going to serve their members.

Before we sorted matters out, the rate-fixer would come down the line, give the rate for the job, timed it at a ha'penny a minute. This meant at 7/6d an hour, he had to take three minutes on the job to get his 7/6 an hour. We had hundreds of strikes; at one time it was estimated around 400 strikes in a year altogether. We said we would do the job at a steady rate and if the rate-fixer didn't like it, then he could do the other. We had a big tussle when they started on the Farina. But out of it came an understanding from the company that a man would do a reasonable hour's work and not sweat his guts out, and no longer be scared when the rate-fixer showed up. We got a fair price for the job and when a man had a problem the steward would sort it out. You could have a young lad in, new to the job, fresh off the milk round. He'd tear into it and the rate-fixer would make a bad time for it. Then an old bloke would go on it and have to sweat to hold the time. I used to take the cases all the way through and made myself unpopular. But all the same production went up. In the early 1950s it took a year to get a rate put right. After these battles, we could get it put right in 24 hours.

One thing that strengthened our hand through all this time was organising the joint committee, bringing together the leading shop stewards from all over the BMC. Now it's called the British Leyland Trade Union executive. Before this was started, in the days of the Morris Group, with 20 factories spread over England and Wales, at different rates of pay, work was being moved from factory to factory wherever it was cheapest. The shop stewards in each factory would never know if there were redundancies, whether there was a real shortage of work or the company was up to its tricks. We tried in the early days to get the company to recognise the committee and the reply was always the same; the company would recognise the committee when the unions did.

At that time William Carron was president of the AEU and he was dead set against such combine committees. Leading stewards were threatened with losing their cards by him. And it wasn't simply Carron. The other unions weren't too happy. They didn't mind if the combine committee was all one union; it was the rank and file leaders of all the unions combining in one industry they didn't like, although no trade union official ever had anything to fear from us if he was doing his job. Later on in one big strike over the sacking of a Morris shop steward, when the TGWU were under new leadership, their officials came to me as secretary of the combine committee to get in touch with Birmingham and organise the blacking of Morris products.

When Morris merged with Austins in the BMC it was only natural for me to get in touch with Dick Etheridge at Austins and from there we went on as the BMC committee, and later as British Leyland. Some union officials see committees like this as a challenge to their power. But I think they point the way for the trade union movement by overcoming the divisions between men in different trades and unions.

REV. SIMON PHIPPS, BISHOP OF HORSHAM
Former industrial chaplain

My experience working in the motor industry on a completely freelance basis filled in a general feeling that I had previously, of the need for sympathetic understanding of the man on the shop floor, which is where all the pressure points meet. There is ig-norance in all walks of life but it seemed to me the onus of ignorance was on the anti-union side. Calls from the Press for union officials to 'discipline' their members look singularly ignorant from inside the factory.

It seems to have been recognised by the new type of leader, by men like Jack Jones,[1] that union officials are servants of their

[1] General Secretary of the Transport and General Workers' Union.

members, not there to tell the shop floor what to do. Changes in the industrial situation have shifted the point of tactical power to the shop steward, and he knows it. And indeed, in the conditions of the motor industry with all its pressures, the shop steward is being pressed from all sides.

From what little I saw of strikes, I would hesitate to generalise. But as to their being caused by greed I should not have thought the shop steward was any more greedy than anyone in another way of life. People do get led against their will. You can get a wrong 'un, an irresponsible person abusing his power, but he can only take root and have influence if the situation is allowed to develop in that way.

As an industrial chaplain, moving about freely with the blessing of both sides, I was often struck by the lack of sophistication about management, the lack of supervisory training at the foreman level, and the foreman bears the initial brunt of all the everyday clashes. Despite all the technical advances of the industry, management-labour relations seemed to be on a rough and ready basis, with – in those days anyway – very little academic thinking on the subject.

At the same time there was an odd, tough sort of mutual trust and understanding. One old-school manager was standing by the factory gate watching the chaps go out, and he said, 'There they go, the bastards, the salt of the earth.' And no doubt they would have said the same about him.

I was struck by the speed with which management labour relations would recover after what seemed a really damaging confrontation, like the Standard strike of the mid-1950s, the mass sacking of men, then taking them back. But that was largely an outside impression. Inside, the management and men understood one another better than it appeared.

BILL WARMAN
Midlands District secretary of the Sheet-metal Workers' Union

The Standard strike in 1956 was, I think, one of those big redundancy strikes of the 1950s, like Duples and the BMC and others, which helped force the hand of the employers and

government. They made it clear that we were not going back to
the old days of hire and fire, when the right to a job didn't exist.
The strange thing to me is that in those days there was all the talk
in the Press and on television about the 'I'm all right, Jack' spirit
in the factories and among the shop stewards. If 'I'm all right,
Jack' had been the rule, then the men in those factories could
quite easily have let the 'redundant men' go down the road.

I started at Standard during the war. I was a sheet-metal worker
and, even in the tough days before the war, the shop organisation
(which is traditional in my trade) protected us a little bit. Now,
you could say that those were the 'I'm all right, Jack' days. If
there was a strike, each shop would come out or stay in inde-
pendently. It was their own battle and they got on with it.

I can recall one strike in the thirties when the vehicle builders
came out and we wanted to support them, but our local secretary
persuaded us against it. During the war, though, we began to
break through that attitude. In Standards I recruited people into
the Transport and General Workers' or the Amalgamated Engineering Union, whichever was appropriate, as long as they were union
members. Our aim was 100 per cent trade unionism and we
achieved it. We had such a degree of shop organisation in Standards
that the committee met in the firm's premises in the firm's time.
And still does today. I was chairman of the committee until 1958
and my experience was that the activities of committees like ours,
with all unions working together, did a lot to spur union amalgamation after the war. Any trade union official worth his salt will
encourage a powerful shop stewards' organisation and won't be
jealous of it. I know, as a full-time official in the Midlands, that
after you have got organisation in a small factory you have to nurse
it for a couple of years. But in the big factory with the powerful
organisation the work goes on its own.

The strength gained by the shop stewards during the war really
came into play, though, after the war. The Midlands motor
industry was largely a piecework industry unlike Fords, and the
big arguments developed over piecework as the new models came
in. Every job has been broken down so much into so many
operations that the men would have lost out completely without
strong shop organisation. So there were a good many skirmishes
before 1956 when the crunch came. The company then had four
factories, at Canley, Fletch Hampstead, Massey Ferguson and

Mawdesley Road. They wanted to make changes at Canley Road and this meant a lot of redundancies.

We fought back and the company climbed down. Then they wanted to completely re-tool the tractor factory, automated transfer machinery. To carry this through they wanted to close a factory, and make a couple of thousand redundant. We reckoned the job could be done without sacking men. What was interesting was that men who were not affected, like the Canley factory, could easily have said 'I'm all right, Jack', but they didn't. While we were in conference and the company were announcing the list of redundancies, they had already posted it in the factory and were giving notice to the people. We got up and walked out.

After mass meetings, we struck. We put pickets on the gate for a fortnight, but no one attempted to pass the picket. There wasn't a single blackleg. The union officials took the matter through procedure, to the central meeting of unions and employers at York. The officials recommended a return to work and said they would give strike pay. We were faced with defying the unions. We went back to work and a lot were made redundant and there was a good deal of bitterness afterwards. But one good thing came out of it. When the crunch came at Austin later that year, the unions this time made the strike official and the men won out. The officials had begun to realise that if they accepted redundancies, then they were going to lose members and become isolated. They had not believed the employers would go that far, but they soon found out.

CYRIL TAYLOR
Former divisional organiser of the Amalgamated Engineering Union

I was divisional organiser of the AEU at the time of the Standard strike. Before the company began introducing transfer machines for the Ferguson tractor production, it had been the knife and fork method. The company had consulted us. They wanted to close down one third of the factory at a time while the new machinery was put in, a costly and time-consuming process. These people would be stood off for six months. In the meantime two thirds would carry on with the old method until the next third was ready for the change, and so on.

Now the men were very much against anybody being stood off.

They said the work should be divided amongst the men and not one third stood off. The management said it couldn't be done. I was very much against the strike. I spoke against it and made myself very unpopular with the men. Though in the end they had to go back.

There is always this contradiction between full time officials and shop stewards. Sometimes you get stewards who resent the interference of the official and try to prove he doesn't know his job, doesn't know the local conditions, or that he's collaborating with management too much. There is this feeling of hatred for management. But once you are a full time official you recognise that the management is employed by the company to do their job and if you want to get anything out of them, then you must show them you can be straight. So many shop stewards and some full time officials think you have to hate the management if you're going to do your job properly. That applies mainly to the Communists, who never show any friendly feeling to management; their way is to fight to the finish and if you can't beat them, snub them.

Full-time officials are the custodians of agreements, and there is a method, a procedure, for dealing with complaints which in the engineering industry was laid down after the 1922 lockout. It's a complicated machinery. First the man tries to solve his own problem, then he goes to shop steward, who goes to higher management, then reports to a full-time official. Then if matters aren't settled you have conferences at various levels, works conference, then a local conference, and finally the central conference at York, which is always held on the second Friday of the month. Now cases are coming to York from all over the country and local officials are only there to give advice. I know it's frustrating to the people down the line who have to wait, but I don't see how the whole procedure can be gone through any more quickly.

But where you get the frustration, there you get the unofficial strike, because the men are not prepared to wait. Once they are out on unofficial strike, they apply to the full-time man to make it official. In the old days the principle was that you did not come out until you had the official sanction. Nowadays that is turned upside down. Of course all this journey up to York is frustrating, but I don't see any better way of going about it.

CHARLIE DOYLE
*Former Battersea power station shop steward, and rank and file
power workers' leader*

Procedure. That was the word. Do your job and file a grievance.
Then it went to the district joint industrial committee and then
the national JIC, and everything had to be minuted. Every
time you wanted to deal with a question – often months old – you
had to dig up minute so and so. You'd find out the answer was
'No'. By that time you'd forgotten what the hell the question was,
but the answer was no.

In the docks, they'd blow a whistle and come out. In the power
stations since nationalisation you went through the machinery, and
you went by the book, a big book like a bible. They were all
trained since vesting day to treat the book like a bible. One time,
when I was chairman of the works committee (management and
workers' side alternated) I threw the book across the table to the
station superintendent and told him, 'I'm not interested in the
goddamn book.' He threw his arms in the air. Here was a chair.
man of the works committee who actually didn't believe in the
bible.

It seemed to me that the whole thing revolved around this
business of carry on with your job while you file a grievance and
wait. We had to put an end to that and have a strong negotiating
position to settle grievances on the spot. So we decided to have a
one day strike. This meant shutting down the plant. Now you
can't do that irresponsibly. Complex machinery, turbines costing
£5 million apiece, can't be shut down at once. After all it was
supposed to be our plant as much as the superintendent's. Our
big problem, though, was getting all the men to agree. Battersea
was one power station where the bonus from pre-nationalisation
days stopped on vesting day. So some old timers got it, newer
people didn't. We had to convince the old boys they wouldn't
lose their bonus. We had a mass meeting and there was a big
argument. One leading man in the opposition says to the meeting,
'If you do like Doyle tells you, you're like a bunch of sheep.
When the vote came, there were 12 against out of 800, and a little
bloke at the front turned round and said, 'Hurrah, the sheep won'.
And so we had our one day strike.

Afterwards the lads had a whip round and raised £50 so that we could get in touch with other power stations. This we did and set up a joint organisation of shop stewards with its own newspaper, *The Power Worker*. Later, three of us were suspended after an argument over whether the management should be able to call meetings to explain a new type of agreement with the union. They took each of the three separately and marched us out of the gates. But there we met the men leaving work. Word got round and before they came to the meeting to discuss the suspensions next day, they'd shut the plant down automatically.

Basically the men would listen to the shop stewards, because they knew us, could trust us and because what we did, we discussed with them. We had five unions in the station, engine-men and fire-men, transport workers, ETU, AEU and the general and municipal workers. That was 800 people. I was in the ETU which had 80 members, who were divided into six different branches. I could go to my branch, where most of the union members were in engineering and contracting and I could put up anything I liked. The branch would pass it send it up to the union head office, where it could go in the waste-paper basket. But inside the plant, when we called a meeting, all the 800 men attended and we all knew what we were talking about.

The structures of the unions and the structure of the industry were in conflict; often the branches were far removed from reality and for the average bloke on the shop floor, the steward represented that reality. As a militant I often had to argue with other militant workers who were in fact anti-union. They would follow the shop stewards' committee through anything, but they hated the leadership of the unions.

This came out in the work to rule in 1963. Now the power station workers had plenty of grievances; excessive heat and excessive dirt, and danger. When the steam goes through the turbine it is condensed river water, so when the water goes back to the boiler it not only retains a lot of heat, but there is a lot of muck. This has to be cleaned out every now and then. When it was your turn you opened the door which was like a submarine hatch, and stuck your head in; the heat was like a flame. You had to take everything off to go in, with a lamp and a pail and pick up the slimy muck with your hands; there was everything from eels to french letters. You hang almost upside down, scoop like mad and pass the pail back to the bloke behind you. I used to come home half dead, coming from heat into cold, put my donkey jacket on and shiver like mad. Power stations also always have tremendous draughts.

But of all the grievances, the most prevalent was overtime. There was a terrific amount of overtime and a lot of squabbles about payment for certain types of overnight work, such as for day men who had to stay overnight, or skilled men who had to stay over if a turbine broke down. In fact power stations run on overtime, and this became an important factor when we decided on the work to rule. Work to rule didn't start in the electricity industry, but it was adapted and used much more than in any other. It suited the purpose without breaking the terms of your contract. The biggest part of it was a ban on overtime. Each turbine would have four drivers, one for each shift. If one driver works a 12 hour shift and the next driver doesn't show up, you can't ask the first to work another 12 hour shift. So you call in the man who is on his day off to come in on overtime call. If there were an overtime ban and the next man didn't come in and the turbine had to be closed down. The work to rule would never have been effective if the work had not been organised in this way.

When that work to rule started, the Press did a worse job on me than was done in America in the worst days of McCarthyism. The *Daily Mirror* had a headline 'The Worst Hated Man in Britain'. At home we had bomb threats, threats of acid in the face, and even a brick through the window. I was used as a whipping boy because I edited the journal of the national shop stewards' committee. We called the work to rule in January, the coldest time of year for a simple reason. In summer, when it's warm and power demand is low, the management bears down on us. In winter when power demand is greater, we bear down on them.

We were after a substantial increase (ninepence an hour) and they offered tuppence ha'penny. Negotiations had been going on for a year and without the work to rule we would have been nowhere. The remarkable thing was that the more I was attacked, the more stations joined the work to rule. The more stations came out the colder it got, the harder the attacks and the more and more militant the men became. The men knew that the Press were distorting the issues. They knew they had a case and the more the pressure was on the more they stuck out. I remember one chap parading outside the Electricity Council offices with a poster 'Prepare to meet thy gloom.'

We did not get our increase, because they didn't want to give the impression militancy pays off. But in the year that followed there were many improvements made; in fact the skilled men ended the year two pounds a week better off. The workers knew this and they knew why it happened. It happened because they had taken direct action, against the management and against the wishes of the union leadership. (I noticed that in the official work to rule in 1970 the union followed our lead from 1963.) Those who stirred up feeling against the power workers didn't realise that they were letting them know the work to rule was having an effect, and knowing that, they were ready to put up with any amount of hostility, to get what they were entitled to.

CHAPTER SIX

1960-1971

Motivated Men

Contemporary reporting gave the 1960s a general air of frivolity, extremes of fashion, a relaxing of moral restraints; a frothy surface to a society enjoying unprecedented prosperity. In the future, more sober estimates may record it as a decade of widespread economic and social change, insecurity and struggle.

At the top, there was pressure for the 'balance of payments'; juggling with the Bank Rate, up and down from $4\frac{1}{2}$ per cent to 8 per cent; experiments with one device after another to control wages; industrial concentration on a colossal scale, with takeovers building industrial giants whose balance sheets could swallow the budgets of small nations. At the bottom, for the first time in history, over 10 million people were in the trade union movement, nearly one in two of employed people, in an age when trade unions were 'unpopular'; the growth of giant unions, with half the membership of the TUC's 150 unions packed into the top five or six.

And between 1960 and 1970, nearly 28,000 strikes, just over a quarter of the total in the 90 years covered by this book. Workers on strike whom some thought had forgotten or never known the meaning of the word; seamen on official strike for the first time in 55 years, postmen the first time in 50 years, dustmen, teachers, bank clerks. Strikes in mining dwindled to around 150 a year (from over 1,000 a year) but, as forecast by former leader Will Paynter (see Chapter Five), a change in quality rather than quantity. In 1969 and 1970 the number of men involved in the strikes rose, leading to the first national official dispute for 46 years.

A new trade union leadership emerged, personified by the heads of the transport and engineering unions; there was also a new relationship with the rank and file, trying to heal the breach of the previous decades between shop steward and head office. New breaches opened: the Labour governments of 1964–70 saw little

of the close cooperation at the top with the unions which the
Attlee governments of 1945–51; enjoyed. The remark by Mr
Harold Wilson about 'politically motivated men' inspiring the
seamen's strike of 1966, a shallow view in itself, had a deeper
meaning for the trade union movement than was realised at the
time. The close of the decade saw the Labour government trying
(and failing) with its White Paper 'In Place of Strife', to introduce
legal restraints on unofficial strikes.

This move was followed through by the Tory government
which took office in 1970, and introduced its own Industrial
Relations Bill (which became law on 28 February, 1972). This
provided for an Industrial Relations Court with power to impose
legal sanctions against the actions of trade unions and their
members in certain cases of industrial dispute. It opened up the
possibility that disputes between employers and workers, even on
a local level, could escalate into clashes between organised labour
and the government.

So the 1970s saw strikes against restrictions of trade union
rights, as well as strikes against unemployment which had grown

14. 'Just think: when the movement began, a man could be imprisoned
for trade union activities!'

Eccles' cartoon, *Morning Star*, September 1968

steadily throughout the sixties; protests which took on an increasingly political-industrial character, bringing with them new forms of action: factory occupations, 'sit-ins', 'work-ins'.

The twelve examples of industrial dispute given in this chapter can only inadequately reflect the changes of the 1960s which will certainly prove to be the most significant decade of the century so far, foreshadowing even greater changes in the future.

JIM SLATER
Official of the National Union of Seamen

Two national strikes in ten years, after fifty years without one; the seamen had a lot of leeway to make up. No one outside the industry can understand the opposition they had to face before 1960. They had to face the British ship-owners, who are a powerful enough bunch on their own, combined with the power of the government through the Merchant Shipping Act. Often they had to face them individually, in ports overseas, facing loss of pay, being left stranded, or being jailed, often without the education or legal knowledge to cope with what they were being charged with. As if that were not enough, there was a third party seamen had to contend with, their union. In fact in many cases they wouldn't go to the union because they didn't want to increase the number of their enemies.

All this was my own personal experience in 26 years' seafaring, of this kind of treatment with no redress. Once my ship was boarded in the Persian Gulf by pirates. We lost all our gear and got no compensation. The first thing the local police asked when they arrived was whether anyone had been killed, because on the last occasion those who had resisted had been tied back to back and thrown in the water.

But I'll give you an example of what used to happen, which any seaman will recognise as typical. In any other industry, this would have been a strike. It was in the 1950s and I was bosun on a ship sailing from Blyth. When the time came for sailing I saw we had three or four men less than on the last voyage and went to the old man to tell him the crew objected. It was mid-winter and you need every man and all your wits about you. Men short meant longer hours, less sleep. And it would be no use complaining when the

211

ship got out to sea. The old man said that as far as he was concerned the ship was manned to Board of Trade requirements and he was sailing irrespective of our opinions. 'As far as I am concerned', I replied, 'We are short-handed and we are refusing to sail.' He became bombastic, called all hands to the bridges, called up the mates as witnesses, got out the log book and said his piece; hereby instructed – disobeying a lawful command – under the Merchant Shipping Act, etc. We'd lose double pay for every day the ship stayed in port, and the charge for the cost of delay. There was some argument, and the old man admitted that industrially we were under-manned, but maintained it was the BOT minimum. Anyway, we didn't sail. Next day he was finding it difficult to get men – no bloody wonder I said – and that night he said he would sail whether or not numbers were made up. He claimed that the two deck boys on board made up for the men. I rang up the union district office to make sure about this and was told that boys could not be classified as men. I thought that settled that. But I was mistaken.

Next day the old man said he'd get the union down and would we stand by what the union official said. I agreed, and we were all battened down and waiting when a man told me the union official was on board, though he was midships with the captain first. He came aft later and the first thing he said to me was: 'It's wrong of you to hold up the ship. The old man's prepared to forget the logging if you sail tonight.'

'Is this ship properly manned?' I asked.

'Yes,' said he.

'You bastard,' I shouted. 'Get off this ship.' Two older seamen saw him down the gangway and threw his briefcase after him. 'Right,' said the skipper, 'from now on it's between you and the judge.' It went on, to and fro, for nine days. He tried to get men to pay off from other ships, but even though they weren't in the union, they were reluctant to do it. He said he would order tugs with every tide and charge us. Even without tugs we were £30 down apiece. The lads were worried and I'd begun to feel sorry for myself. I wrote a letter to the *Daily Mirror*, putting forward some of the injustices and the next day the old man added three to the crew and we sailed. The captain was furious by then, but it was a tip-top ship and a bloody good crew; he knew it and didn't want to lose us.

When we got to Copenhagen he told me he'd had a message from the company to say that they would forget the loggings and charges if we gave an undertaking never to repeat the action in Blyth. Well, inside I could have jumped for joy, but I flannelled a bit. I held a meeting of the men in the mess room and told them – look they're trying to get off the hook. You are in the right. They are asking you to sign an undertaking to commit a felony because that ship was under-manned and they know it. OK, they said, whatever you say. So I went back to the captain and said, 'We'll permit you to wipe the record clean and forget the matter'. He swore, but I'd guessed right. They had no leg to stand on, though they were quite prepared to exploit the Merchant Shipping Act against us. So we got away with that and our success made quite a stir in the north-east ports.

That kind of individual act was the build-up to 1960, when the National Seamen's Reform Movement came into the picture. There were all sorts of wild allegations about men being sent to Australia to be trained as agitators. It goes down well with the ignorant side of public opinion. But by 1960 there was enough feeling in the industry for trouble, agitators or no.

I was on a ship approaching the Irish Sea when the old man, a decent old boy, told me he'd heard on the radio that some seamen at Liverpool were on unofficial strike. Next day we heard they were out at other ports and some were coming out on the Tyne. When we docked in Londonderry there were more reports of men out in the north-east. Well, I was a married man with two kids. The wages were deplorable and every effort to improve them was being met with five shillings, ten shillings. We were dropping more and more behind the industrial average. I thought it over, and told the skipper that when I got to Blyth I'd go on strike. He said, 'Don't be silly, it'll all be over in a few days.' Well, if it was still on, I'd be out. I had a word with the crew and then the old man called me up again. 'Look I want to keep this crew together. I'll pay you off and take you all on again afterwards.' But it didn't work out like that.

In Blyth I went down to the strike meeting. There were two blokes just back from Liverpool reading out eight recommendations which seemed to me like a proposal for a return to work. I shouted from back. 'We came down the gangway for a 40 hour week and four pounds a month. Our whole crew came off for those

two points. What's the good if you don't want to fight for them?'
The upshot was they asked me to come on the strike committee,
'to help'. And I did, though I knew no more about striking than
they did. After about 10 days more there were all kinds of panic
stations and a meeting between the union and the Maritime Board
was in the offing. The unofficial committee decided (I know it
sounds naïve, but remember there had been no strike for 50 years)
to go back and call the men out again if they were not satisfied.
The men went back, and some of us stayed on shore. (I was
chairman of the unofficial committee by then and in the interim
the Seamen's Reform Movement was getting going all over the
country.)

The Shipping Federation tried all kinds of dodges to get me out
to sea again, threatening to ban me from the shipping pool if I
refused an offer of work. In fact they got me to one ship at Middles-
brough under the pretence it was coast-wise, but when I got on
board I found it was bound for Russia. Once I was out of the
country I'd had it. So I walked off the ship.

By this time the interim period of negotiations was over. We
had got nowhere. So we set the date for another walkout, and on
that day the men came down the gangways like one man; it was
marvellous. They stuck out for seven or eight weeks. There were
all kinds of threats to put us in jail, to take out injunctions, but they
never tried them in the north-east, because we asked for volunteers
to put down their names to take the leaders' places. I argued that
they couldn't jail us all. The men stuck together; we had some
terrific meetings and marches. They were disciplined, but there
was Sir Tom Yates, the union general secretary at the TUC
meeting on the Isle of Man, puffing his cigar and saying, 'I don't
represent that rabble.'

But whether he liked it or not, we were seamen and union
members. Eventually he said he'd meet me at union HQ. I took
one young seaman with me as witness because there had been so
much distortion in the Press. Sir Tom Yates sat in there for seven
and three quarter hours.

He began, 'Let's start from the beginning. Why are you on
strike?' Well, what can you say to a question like that?

I said, I'm working an 80 hour week for £8 a week. Did you
know that?'

'No,' he said.

'I've been to sea since I left school. Now I'm a married man with two kids. They've never had a holiday. This suit is 6–7 years old. I've had it two years. A relation gave me a pawn ticket to get it.' I pulled my shoes off and put them on the table. 'They've been cobbled four times. I'd like a holiday for my wife and kids, I'd like a new suit, and I can't wait to get a new pair of shoes. But I haven't a snowball's chance in hell of getting any of them on the present wage.'

Well, out of that unofficial strike in 1960, despite all the abuse of the Seamen's Reform movement, improved pay and conditions *and* the strengthening of the union were the results. With the retirement of the old guard from the union executive in 1962 there was a new influx of serving seamen. I was elected, though I'd a battle first to get back into the pool, for they barred me from work for 14 months after the strike. The British Shipping Federation has complete control of the industry in that way. But I won through and I was one of a number of new men on the executive. It was a real upsurge, with the rank and file taking part in the union as they never had done before, and the union gaining respect in TUC circles as never before. That all came out of the strike.

When the 1966 strike came, after a number of threats and promises, it was official. The rank and file had discovered that sea-going men could be elected to the Maritime Board which negotiates pay and conditions. So for the first time the talks were taking place with more active participation of sea-going men. It shook the heirarchy, and it shook the shipowners. The combination of militant serving seamen, with the experience of long-standing officials, and the unanimity of the 48 men on the executive made a formidable force. This is what made it all the more amazing when Harold Wilson made his speech about the union being under pressure from 'a tightly knit group of politically motivated men.' All I can assume is that he was misinformed and misled. Which is frightening when you think that the head of the country, the Prime Minister, could be so misinformed.

We were motivated all right, all of us, by conditions in the industry. How else could the men have stuck it for 47 days? They came out 100 per cent, and I can tell you they were most reluctant to go back. They took everything the Press could throw at them. When the executive took the majority resolution to go back (with some concessions on hours and holidays) I had to go and speak to a mass meeting in the north-east; the biggest cinema in South Shields was packed. I had voted against the decision to go back, but the decision had been taken and I had to abide by it.

The tension at the meeting was tremendous. Blokes were mad with anger at the decision; they were ready to come out again unofficially. I told them that if they did that I would have to resign from the Executive Committee to be with them. Now you cannot manipulate and stage manage people like that. This is something neither the Establishment nor the Press can understand, because they are not close enough to the men to know how they feel and what it is they want.

BRIAN MATHERS
Midlands regional secretary, Transport and General Workers' Union

Strikes on wages, strikes on redundancy, strikes on victimisation. These are the labels that are put on strikes and often the observer outside the trade union movement can be misled. You have to look below the surface. In my experience in years in the Midlands, during which time the whole face of industry has changed, many strikes have one root cause – frustration.

When a man feels that the process he's engaged in has no meaning for him—nothing that he can say is really his contribution; faced with the monotony of work in new processes, which treat people like mice on treadmills, many strikes are what I would call exhaust valve strikes. Add to this the frustration of what is known as 'procedure' in the engineering industry; it is not unusual for four months to go by from the time the problem arises on the factory floor before it reaches 'central conference' at York. Management say they have the right to manage, to bring in wholesale changes at the time it suits them; workers, if they are aggrieved, must 'go through procedure'.

The workers' answer to this is the strike. Now the Press keep demanding that the unions 'discipline' their members, but that's a superficial view. You have to look below the surface. In life the ordinary man or woman has so little say, there are so many people telling them what to do; the union is their only voice.

There was a strike in Wolverhampton which illustrates this

and, although it involved only one factory, it caused something of a change in our industrial relations in the Midlands. Before this strike in 1964, immigrant workers would join the trade unions, but take no part active in them. Many work people from rural communities in India, not speaking English, thought the unions were like paying national insurance. But one day in Wolverhampton a Jamaican chap came to me and said, 'Look I was in the union back home. But in this factory, where it is mostly Indian labour, there is no union and the foreman rules with a rod of iron.' I gave him some forms and he came back to me with an Indian whom he introduced as a community leader. We chatted and he asked for 500 application forms. Now I had heard such stories before, but I was astounded when two days later, all the forms were filled in, signed and one week's subscription paid.

They had a meeting, elected shop stewards and, since the firm worked under national agreements, we had no trouble on recognition. But a fortnight later, the West Indian chap came in and said he'd been sacked. The foreman had accused him of threatening him with a hammer over a piecework price. Now he was an inoffensive sort of chap and it seemed incredible to me. I told him he should go back and ask his mates if they were prepared to stand by him. The next thing I heard was that the factory was at a standstill and the employers' association was complaining of an unofficial strike. Meetings were held in a Sikh Temple where I had to remove my shoes, cover my head with a handkerchief and speak through an interpreter.

After three weeks the employers' association suggested a peace formula; the shop steward was to be suspended with pay while the case went through procedure. When this proposal was put to a meeting through an interpreter there was pandemonium. When this quietened, the strikers replied – yes they'd accept this provided the foreman was suspended as well. I began to suspect that there was a good deal more below the surface of this strike than had appeared. And so, finally I asked one of the leaders of the men to tell me what was going on. After talking to some of his friends he told me a fantastic story.

For a long time the foreman had been extracting money from them. If there was a vacancy for a fork-truck driver he would offer it to a labourer on the basis of £5 now and so much a week. There were plenty of examples, and with the help of the

P

Birmingham Community Relations Officer, statements were drafted and signed. There were hair-raising stories of people taking gifts, bottles of brandy, shoes for his wife, to the foreman's house. I presented the statements to the Chief Constable of Wolverhampton. After a complex series of happenings, ending with the foreman attempting suicide and going into a mental home, the shop steward was re-instated. Now men at the factory could get down to the business of improving the conditions of work, and since it was foundry work, they were extremely heavy, dirty and distasteful conditions.

I believe it was one of the first such successful actions by immigrant workers and its example spread through their community to other factories. It brought other immigrant workers into union activity and the Indian shop stewards later on played a big part in demonstrations against the Industrial Relations Bill.[1]

This is just one of the changes in this area of the country over the past 10 years which has brought 76,000 new members into the Transport and General Workers' Union and lifted our membership in the Midlands to over a quarter of a million. Over these years a good many major agreements have been made without strikes, of course, but they have been made because the strike sanction is in the background. The employers know it is the alternative, and so do we. Any agreements that we can reach freely and without pressure, and they are many, are the result of experiences on both sides, with the strike as the ultimate weapon.

JOHN GREEN
Shop steward of Amalgamated Engineering Union at Roberts Arundel, Stockport

The way the Roberts Arundel firm in Stockport was run made our strike in 1966 inevitable, though none of us knew that it would last 17 months before the firm gave in. The fact was that although men were in the union, Roberts Arundel was considered the least militant factory in the Stockport area. Well, the firm turned everyone into militants and after the 17 months was over, 90 out of the original 145 were still on strike.

The fact was that the American boss, Pomerantz, who had

[1] Became law as Industrial Relations Act – See footnote on Page 184.

218

taken over the old firm (Arundel Coulthard) a few months before the strike, was against unions. He always reckoned he would talk to us provided we were represented by a clergyman, doctor or solicitor, but never by the unions. But even Pomerantz admitted that the managing director, Cox, was a 'bit rough'; to stop men making tea, he smashed up the cups and tore out the electric points from the walls. That was the kind of management we had to contend with.

A few months after the takeover, they moved machinery to Preston and said the factory there would be the machine shop, while Stockport should be the fitting shop. Fifty were made redundant. Then, after a while, he announced that Preston was closing down and the machinery was coming back. But this time, instead of re-employing the redundant men, women were going to work the machines.

The whole business went 'through procedure', and the firm was warned that they should not employ any more women while this was being done. But they did. So, just a month before Christmas (and it was clear they had chosen this time for it to happen) we came out, 145 of us. After three days a letter came from the employers' federation, saying they would hold the firm to the issue; it was agreed we should go back to work. On the day the unions met the boss again, letters were already in the post sacking the lot of us. On December 6th, the dispute was made official.

At first we thought it was just the local management and that by the Spring when the American boss came over there would be a settlement, but when March came, it was clear he wouldn't deal with trade unions. In fact an advert appeared in the local papers inviting people who 'appreciate working in an atmosphere free from trade unions' to apply to Roberts Arundel. He offered the blacklegs more than he was prepared to pay the union members and in this way he succeeded to keep the factory open. He brought people in from all over the place.

Well, to their credit, a lot turned back when they saw what was going on and read our leaflets. But some did go in and work. He was offering them 11s 6d an hour against 10s 3d he offered to us. It was nauseating to see that some did go in. Never mind about the trade union angle; just the human angle, to go in and take another man's job. He swanked a lot about the production he was getting, but there was nothing to it. The blacklegs were having the time of their lives in there, going and coming just as they liked, spoiling and scrapping work. Cox, the managing director, at first said it would be a seven day wonder.

For the first six weeks we had to rely on collections from local factories. I went to collect benefits for my wife and children. It was humiliating, it made you feel you were begging, though it was only what you were entitled to. At first the bosses were very arrogant, trying to get the police to book men for picketing. One boss in his car tried to run over the pickets' posters. Another tried to provoke them by walking up and down and getting in their way. When Christmas came, one chap was playing his accordion and we were singing carols in the street and one of the bosses boasted that we'd still be singing in the streets 12 years from then.

It became clear that even when a new manager was put into the factory there wouldn't be any negotiations. So we stepped up the picketing. All the engineering factories in the area were called on for support and AEU members made a levy of sixpence a week, which is what kept us going throughout the strike. People from other factories came down and helped us on the picket line. Students came down from Manchester University and helped us. They wrote a pamphlet explaining the dispute and sold it. It all counted because as the strike went on there were some terrible Press distortions about us. They wrote that we were getting £29 a week from the union and people believed it and some of them insulted the men on picket; men who had worked there for 40 years and were out on strike on a principle of union recognition were called beggars and parasites. The fact was that all we got from the AEU levy was shared out among members of other unions, foundry workers and plumbers who were on strike with us; it worked out at £15 a week (that was against a normal wage of £17 a labourer and £22 a skilled man).

By 1967 the firm were threatening to close down. We didn't believe it. We really began to step up the efforts to have stuff going in and out of the factory blacked. We chased the firm's vehicles from Dunfermline to Dover, and got them blocked at the docks. When they tried the roll-on, roll-off ferry we went to the seamen's union and got that stopped. Once we followed a lorry to Derby and lost it down a country lane. We tracked it down and found a little packing place where they were transferring the load to another lorry and then on to the docks. But in the end we stopped it.

Nearly 400 firms stopped dealings with Roberts Arundel. A lot of people may have said that all the talks about negotiation, even up to government level, brought about a settlement, but what really counted was the blacking of the goods, and the help we got from the other trade unionists.

Moral Re-armament came into the picture (through Bill Carron, who was President of the AEU before Hugh Scanlon). They were all pals together it seemed. There was a big meeting at York and some sort of agreement. Next day we learned that it meant the blacklegs would stay in the factory and we would be taken back over 12 months. Those who defended trade unionism would be left on the streets. Vic Feather had numerous meetings with Pomerantz and couldn't get anywhere with him. So did Ray Gunter, who was Minister of Labour then. We told Vic Feather we didn't want to stay out two Christmases, but we had to in the end.

There were big demonstrations. The unions had a half day strike in Stockport. They marched through the town and round the factory and quite a few windows went in. The police banned demonstrations near the factory. There was another big turn-out on May Day and another one in September. Pomerantz kept coming over and going back. He had factories in four countries and he told the Press he was the 'Great White Father'. He used to tell us that when we lobbied him to go home. He was adamant he wouldn't settle. He still hates trade unions to this day.

But we resolved to be as obstinate as he was. We always knew that in the end he would have to come to terms. And when we had all the material in and out of the factory tied up, that was the turning point. When the end finally came, in the Spring of 1968, it was a relief, of course, but it came as a bit of a shock and people couldn't believe it. We got full recognition of the union and shop stewards, full agreements on wages, terms and conditions of employment. All the blacklegs had to go.

We won in the end, thanks to the generosity of other trade unionists. But it is a terrible thing that a man should be forced to stand on the streets for 17 months for his principles. I can remember some of the older blokes standing by the wall in the freezing wind in winter-time, coughing their hearts out. Do people think a man does that for fun? Some seem to have the idea that just because a man's on strike he should walk in the gutter. And some people think that because a man's been on strike he should be treated like a criminal. We weren't allowed to put an unemployed stamp on our cards, so after the strike I had to work 12 months and then another five before I was in benefit. They punished me another 17 months for that 17 months on strike. It was like saying the employer was in the right.

Well, I know we did the right thing. It's a funny thing but I'd lived for more than 30 years, and always been a trade unionist while I worked. But it was only then that I realised properly what it was all about.

JOHN POTTER
Strike leader at Pilkington's, St. Helens

Before the Pilkington's strike in St Helen's there had been general apathy and frustration. There were six factories, with 9,000 members of the Municipal and General Workers' Union; all in one branch, with an average attendance of nine. There was 'consultation' over wages and conditions through the Joint Industrial Committee, but JIC. had become a dirty word to most people. Pay talks would bring a penny an hour more, or a penny ha'penny, while only 11 miles away Fords of Halewood were getting three and four times as much. Then a row developed over miscalculation of bonus in the sheet works. The shop stewards had approached the management a number of times and been promised it would be 'looked into'. Four or five weeks more passed and then the lads on night shift got fed up, marched round the factory in the middle of the night and then marched round another factory, stopped outside and told the day shift they were out. Next day there was a big meeting with a couple of thousand people, and all sorts of proposals flying about. Someone said never mind £18 a week, what about £25 for 40 hours. They knew what Fords were getting from the Press and television.

This was a Sunday morning and the union officials rather took exception to meetings like this. One organiser came and stood on a barrel to speak but he was heckled down. They marched round and all six factories came out. The next day there was a branch meeting and a number of us tried to get the officials to extend the strike to other factories outside the town. The general committee, the JIC representatives, were pretty well discredited.

222

The strikers wanted to stop supplies going in and out of the factory but the officials wanted to keep the plant ticking over. So a rank and file committee was formed with a few of the stewards and this met separately, running marches and demonstrations. In the branch rooms we found this old banner of the Glass Flatteners screwed into the roof. They said, 'You can't march with that, it's not been out since 1921.' But we dragged it out and marched to the Pilkington offices; there was the JIC inside and 4,000 outside. Now you don't need to be a brilliant negotiator to negotiate an increase with that kind of strength.

But they kept telling us that the firm wouldn't negotiate under duress, until we got fed up with this kind of patter. By now they had got completely out of touch with the strikers. All they could say, when we wanted them to make the strike official, was to tell us to go back. They refused every time. We were now having big meetings, with several thousands on the football field; every time they suggested 'Go back' they were howled down.

One day I got a phone call from a journalist asking for my reaction to a 'deal' that had been negotiated, two pounds a week with strings. The Press had been told, but not us. The rank and file committee rushed round, getting leaflets out, saying why we should not accept under these conditions. The officials got the shop stewards together at a meeting in the branch rooms where a majority accepted the offer. But when they came down to the mass meeting in the park with the offer, it was booed as a sell-out. There was accusation and counter-accusation. The officials were out of their depth and in the end they were dragged off the platform and chased out of the park. It was clear that the union had now lost all control over the strike, and that we were not just fighting Pilkington's, but fighting the union and the president, Lord Cooper.

At this stage, Vic Feather and the TUC intervened, and a court of inquiry was convened, through Barbara Castle at the Department of Employment and Productivity. I was there with another shop steward, people from Pilkington's and the union. This was the first time we had met face to face; the rank and file committee had been recognised. When we got back from the Court of Inquiry a mass meeting had been called to discuss the terms Vic Feather had worked out. The general line was that we could come to some agreement, but we should go back to work. I was against this and so were four others; I felt that if we went back to work we lost our bargaining power. But next day at the mass meeting, the return to work was accepted and we led everyone back.

One of the main points of the agreement was that there was to be no victimisation and that 27 truckers at the Pontypool factory were to be re-instated. But in fact that agreement was never effective. At work the rank and file militants began to be watched and followed, and life was made unpleasant for them. Now the rank and file committee had been elected at mass meetings where the union officials had been rejected, but we were still ready to work through the union. But they would not have us. We tried to get new elections of shop stewards, but the officials said that this would have to wait until there had been an inquiry into the running of the union. They knew the old lot would have been kicked out.

Everything was suspended. They brought in other union officials to conduct an inquiry. But in fact it was just killing time while getting rid of us. The inquiry recommended the union branch be split up into six branches. But in the meantime more and more people were getting disgusted and opting out of the union. At work, more of our people were being shifted round to other jobs on less pay. The men from Pontypool were still not re-instated. The rank and file committee were fuming at the way things were going and went to the TUC about it. It was agreed that Lord Cooper would meet us at the TUC. But when we sat there round the table, waiting, a phone message came to say that Lord Cooper had been discussing with the Pilkington's shop stewards and was not willing to meet us.

We held our own meeting in the British Legion Hall in St Helens where a majority of people were for forming our own union. But for the moment we did not want to make a complete break and formed the Pilkington Provisional Trade Union Committee. We realised that under TUC agreements it wasn't possible for another union to take us in and so the Glass and General Workers' Union was formed. Some backed both horses and paid to both unions.

It wasn't long, though, before the firm decided to put the matter to the test. They began to pick on supporters of the new organisation and over a dispute about the filling in of a work-system sheet, they sent a three man gang home. They were obviously forcing a recognition strike. We tried to see management

224

but they refused. We agreed on a token strike and 600 came out. They got their cards, but the 600 were divided into a black list and a white list. Half were offered their jobs back as new starters, losing all their rights with the firm. The other half were sacked. Some were still unemployed 18 months later.

It was a tough time. Single blokes who were out were thrown out of their digs and lived rough, sleeping in brick kilns. They sacrificed a lot, but they responded well. At first during the strike the police were decent. Later they got rough; people were put in the cells, some fined heavily, one even got three months. The rank and file in other unions, dockers and building workers, helped us a lot, but as far as the full-time officials of the trade union were concerned, there was total disillusion. The officials resent any power held by the rank and file; they don't identify with the realities of shop floor life, and all they want to do is hold on to their entrenched position.

The ironic thing is that before that strike the lowest paid was £17 to £18 a week. Now it is over £22.

WALTER NUGENT
Branch chairman of the Transport and General Workers' Union

When 7,000 road haulage men on Merseyside went on strike in 1968 it shook some people. Road haulage is a fragmented industry with about 400 firms, some with 200 lorries but a lot with only four or five lorries; the men are extremely difficult to organise. For the full-time union officials it must have been terrifying at the time, having to deal with all those members, plus a lot who were coming into the union because of the strike. The fact is that though the Transport and General Workers Union has been changing for the better over recent years with more control by the members in the branches, there is a long way to go.

The shift among the lorry drivers started after the dockers had come out in Liverpool in the autumn of 1967 and won £17 a week. At the time, our basic pay was £14 a week, with £18 a week for lorries of eighteen tons and over. Someone put out an anonymous leaflet asking why lorry drivers shouldn't have £16 a week for a forty hour week. In those days, you needed 60 hours work a week to make a living wage and some were doing 77 hours a week. The

225

legal maximum is supposed to be 60. You need to know, too, what mileage a man is working. We say 22 miles represents an hour's work. Some will drive 28 miles an hour, which is bad for health; it's bad for safety, too, especially with the increase in lorry size. Tankers used to be 2,000 gallons, now we are hauling 6,000 gallons. Length and weight are increasing, and so are responsibilities. A young man can get on a job and flog hell out of it, but what's to happen if the older man can't or won't keep up that speed. We set a maximum of 24 mph, but we know that some are working up to 32. You need to think of this when you read about pile-ups in the fog on the motorways.

After we decided to strike in March 1968, the key point was the docks. After the meeting we marched down the dock road, the whole length, until all the garages on the road had closed down. When we came out, the busmen in Liverpool were already out; they'd had their eyes on the dockers as well. And while we were on strike a couple of thousand dockers were out as well, so at one time there were three meetings at the Liverpool Pier Head, busmen, dockers and lorry drivers. It was lucky the busmen were out and the buses were off the Pier Head or there wouldn't have been room for us all. About 95 per cent of the lorry drivers came out though thousands weren't in the union. It lasted about three weeks until the management turned tail and the £16 was agreed. Then we took on a levy of a shilling a week, to take on the firms that wouldn't pay up one by one. I suppose we did a lot to organise the employers as well; before, the local Road Haulage Association was just people who had applied for a licence.

Since then we went on first for a minimum of £18 and then for a minimum of £24 a week. As soon as our policy became widely known more men have been ready to join the union. Before that strike the average attendance at branch meetings was around 40. Since then it has been 80 or 90 and the atmosphere has improved.

FRANK CORNTHWAITE AND BILLIE SWINDLEHURST
Shop stewards at the Lansil Textile factory, Lancaster

Lansil was a family business, Lancaster Silks making artificial silks. A good many there had worked at the firm for donkeys' years. They used to say 'It's a regular wage, at least.' That was the point, it was a regular wage, but a low one; poor wages for a 60 hour week. The TGWU official would come down and say with a great air of having done something for you, 'There you are, lads, fourpence on your basic pay, threepence off your bonus.' That way, it was a nice, steady, profit-making firm. Then in the early 1960s it was taken over by Monsanto and they began to put the pressure on for more production.

They would say that whereas in the past it took 25 machines working to make a profit, now they needed 42 machines to make it profitable. They would say they only had enough production for 33 machines out of 44, so that they were working on 75 per cent capacity. But they were using a four-pound bobbin instead of a two pound, and so production could well have equalled 80–95 per cent. They were very clever and would try psychological warfare. We would notice that, before a meeting, four or five machines would be put down, out of production. After the meeting the machines would go back up. You had to have detailed knowledge of all that was going on, and over recent years there was a long succession of small disputes, chiefly over the bonus; the spinning department was usually in the lead.

It became the practice for the spinning department (Billie) and the dope house (the mixing and filtration plant) that prepared the artificial fibre mix for the machines (Frank) to work closely together. When Frank was sacked over a dispute about the use of tools in the dope house the management was told that if he was not re-instated by the end of the shift, the spinning department would stop. This made sense because the two departments were linked together by the production process anyway.

Bonus disputes would go on sometimes for months. But in 1969 we went from a three to a four shift system; the bonus system so complicated it could take you more than an hour to work it out. More machines were put in, the bobbin size increased. We tried for four months to negotiate a new bonus, until finally the work's director was rung up at 10 o'clock one night and told the night shift was on strike in the spinning department and he had two hours to change his mind. Tempers flared. Normally it takes 48 hours to put the machines down. This night they went down in two hours and by morning the gates were being strongly picketed by the spinning department. The dope house decided to back the spinning department and by two o'clock the next day, the whole factory was out. One bloke went in for ten minutes, but the foreman brought him to the gate and said, 'He'd best stay out. It'll only be worse for him afterwards.' Even the boiler shop was out, though the management said it didn't involve them.

By Monday we had a mass picket on the gate and we had decided that we would not go back until we had 100 per cent trade unionism throughout the factory. Then we reckoned we could come to some working understanding with the management. We began to put the black on lorries coming to and from the docks; one oil tanker driver tipped us off that something was going on at a nearby warehouse, owned by the firm. We rushed there, got past the security men on the gate and saw top management busy loading up a lorry with stuff to send out. The look on their faces was unforgettable. That never happened again. We increased the picketing until it was 24 hours a day and we had big help from the students at Lancaster University. They helped us to man the picket line, they brought food down to us at night and published a broadsheet for us. This was really valuable because normally to get this done through the union at Preston would take three to four days. The students did it for us in 24 hours. Once while we were holding a mass meeting at the gates a Lansil wagon drove up with the directors' car behind it. The strikers started to rock the wagon up and down and wouldn't let the directors into the factory. But the police came up and cleared the way for them.

We met the management after the strike and the first thing we negotiated was a big increase on the basic pay, particularly for the women. And since the strike the management's general attitude has changed. They will listen now. Before the strike they didn't take us seriously at the top. Their attitude was, 'If you want more money, what's wrong with working more overtime?' Now we talk direct and get things sorted out, working clothing, showers, other conditions. Since March 1971 we have had a general agreement that sews up the question of union membership. Now we know where we stand with them.

The uncertain thing in the future for us is what will happen under the Industrial Relations Act. We have a feeling that some of the union officials are getting jealous of the power that shop stewards have gained to negotiate for themselves in recent years. There's not so much of the 'You leave it to me, I'll sort it out' as there was before, and we're a bit concerned that some officials might see the Industrial Relations Act as very handy to put shop stewards in their place and give them back the power they had.

HARRIET HOPPER
Shop steward at Plessey, Sunderland

When the first strikes against the Industrial Relations Bill started in December 1970, all the women engineering workers at Plessey's in Sunderland came out. A month later when the TUC had its Day of Protest the women came out again, and this time the men joined them. This kind of feeling among the women workers has been growing in Plessey's for three or four years now.

In May 1967 we got a new divisional manager. He was going to use a new broom. He was like a whirlwind. He introduced female supervisors; he called them patrolling supervisors. Now I'm all for equality, but this kind is not on. He started them in other units, so that when it came to our turn I was ready and I told her, 'I'm sorry, but I'm not co-operating.' What we objected to was them patrolling round. One girl was bending down to get a tissue out of her bag, when the supervisor told her, 'You've to work till the bell goes.' She was lucky the girl didn't get up and punch her.

After about seven days everyone was stirred up, and we went to the management about it. They tried to claim status quo, they already had the supervisors in three units. But we refused. We went through the whole rigmarole of 'procedure'. It took about three months, and when they still failed to concede, the whole factory came out (except for the toolroom; I've never forgiven them). The net result was they stayed as supervisors, but there was no more patrolling.

We went through the same 'procedure' rigmarole, two years later, when we put in for the same bonus as the men were getting. All we got from the management was, 'We'll look at it in six months' time.' So I put it to the women, 'You can forget the whole thing or do the necessary.' So we gave seven days' notice. All the engineering union women were called out, and we expected the men to back us. We were disappointed over this, and women from the other shops voted to go back, leaving just the 42 of us from the machine shop. They said 'Harriet, we've got to go back, too.' So I said, 'You can go back. I'm stopping out. I'll see you Monday at 7.30.'

Over the weekend, I made six banners and I was there at half past seven. Altogether there were 150 out, all the machine shop plus some from the other shops. After a fortnight some got a bit sick, but the rest – 120 – stuck it out for five weeks. The weather was on our side, and some of us got a lovely tan. The school bus used to go past, with some of the women's kids on board and the driver would always slow down so that the kids could give us a cheer.

The unpleasantest part was the pub across the road, where the manager refused to serve us and told me to clear out of his pub. At first I thought he was joking, but then he started shouting, 'They ought to send you to Vietnam, or send you down the pits.' It turned out his daughter was on strike with us, and so we told her (she was only young) that if she wanted to go back we wouldn't hold it against her. But in the cafe where we would go for our breakfast, we were always stirring the waitresses up to go in for equal pay; it was all good fun. The funny thing was that with our holiday pay and dispute pay from the union we seemed to have enough to go round, though some were single women and some unmarried mothers and they really were in need.

After three and a half weeks the girls began to ask if the union was behind us, or miles behind us. We went to the district secretary and got him to instruct that any of the work from our departments was black. Next morning the skilled inspection people refused to touch the work and were sent home. So all the skilled men came out. From then it was only a matter of time before the management had to come to terms. We let them save their faces by giving us 98 per cent of the male bonus rate, though we were still only on 83 per cent of the male basic rate.

But whatever it achieved for us, it meant a good deal to the rest of the Plessey group, because they gave the same bonus rate to all the women in the other factories. I'd like to see the union go in for equal pay, nationally, but if not I reckon we have the strength in Plessey's to push the boat out. I asked all the women 'How many of you think you deserve equal pay?' and all their hands went up.

What pleased me most during the strike was that the men in the shipyards were so generous with financial support. After the strike we had £75 left in the strike fund. With other money we raised, it was enough to share out to those women who wanted their share. But we still had £50 left which we sent to the lads at G. L. Thomson's yard who were out on strike; they got back more than they had given us.

ANETTE BROWNLIE AND MARGARET MILLIGAN
Shop stewards' convener and shop steward at BSR, East Kilbride

Until the 14-week strike at BSR in East Kilbride there was always a lot of disatisfaction among the women there, but by and large they put up with anything, for the sake of the job. The management would say, 'If you don't like it, you know what you can do.' It was mainly women workers there and in the area there aren't that many opportunities for women to work, so they can't afford to be choosey.

In 1969 there was a lot of unrest over the bonus system, but there were only a few in the trade union, mainly men in the toolroom, and there was no recognition of unions at all. When the toolroom people walked out they started an agitation outside the gate, getting the women to join the union. Eventually around a thousand of the women came out on strike, but a few hundred stayed in. Then the firm started to bring people in from outside in buses and so we had two categories, blacklegs and strike breakers.

Well, we put up with this for weeks, standing at the gates in freezing rain, beginning to wonder if we were right in the head. We had a lot of support from other unions; a fantastic amount of money was coming in from everywhere, and there were big demonstrations in support of us. But they were still bringing those people in on the buses. It all seemed to be going flat and we decided we must do something about it.

Next morning some of us sat down in the road in front of the buses. At first they kept on coming and it looked for a moment as though they'd run us down. They brought in the riot police to drag us out of the way, but the thing snowballed and more people sat down. Then stones started to fly. It's a strange thing. You see violence elsewhere and you think that it has nothing to do with you. You think its terrible. But when something affects you directly,

231

when you feel this hate for someone who is stabbing you in the back, the violence that comes out in you is astonishing. Some of us wouldn't have said boo to a goose before the strike, but the things were done – fighting the police, painting the strike-breaker's houses 'Scabs live here'. Even families were divided, and a lot of the ill-feeling has lasted.

But we never doubted it was worth it. A hard core of several hundred kept it going for 16 weeks. When it came near Christmas the parsons came round, saying 'Now, ladies. Don't you think at this time of year you ought to think of your families?' And a woman with a big Belfast voice spoke up from the back, 'If you have any God in your heart, you'll go round and collect for us.'

When we went back, they split us up and tried to put us to work on any old rubbish. One foreman said, 'If I tell you to clean toilets, that's what you'll do.' So out we came again for another week, until we got our old jobs back. We got 100 per cent trade unionism in the factory and union recognition. Beforehand nothing was attended to. Now, a lot of the bosses have to grind their teeth to take us, but they have to do it.

HARRY HITCHINGS
Former convenor of the Amalgamated Engineering Union, at GKN, Cardiff

From the time the Labour government came in and Harold Wilson began to talk about productivity bargaining, we had a running battle at GKN Cardiff. The craftsmen there (I was convener) were direct victims of the kind of abortion in which a company with enormous profits demands increased exploitation before giving a niggardly pay increase. There were 300 craftsmen and around 3,000 production workers at two works a couple of miles apart, the Castle and Tremorfa works. Both the management and the full-time union officials were determined to get us to accept some kind of deal with strings.

During 1965, the government was limiting pay increases to three per cent; then came a period of wage-freeze. So productivity bargaining was presented as a marvellous way of getting more money, simply by making a few re-adjustments in the way you worked. Stories were spread around about what was going on at other steel mills, such as that Corby had got five pounds a week more by productivity bargaining. I didn't believe it and said so. They had got more because they were more militant. Steel employers are a tight-fisted lot and aren't going to give away money for nothing. But for two and a half years the full time officials went on at us trying to convince us that the only way to get more money was by productivity bargaining. We decided that the best way to get an increase was by working to our 40–hour rota; in effect it was not coming in, or staying on overtime, to replace a man who hadn't turned up for his shift. During 1968, about 40 of the craftsmen left due to low wages without overtime, among them some of the youngest; the management offered us 30 shillings a week if we would go back to normal working. They wanted to attach strings to the offer, but we rejected the idea.

In 1969 they kept on trying. They wanted to send the shop stewards away to school for two weeks in the Wye Valley, and they brought in three separate lots of consultants, but we stood out against all this, claiming we wanted a straight increase. The management replied with an offer of three pounds based on a national agreement, but GKN wanted to include the 30 shillings they'd already given us. We weren't having that. The lads began to introduce strict trade practices, then working to rota, then no overtime, until the foremen were losing their holidays because there was no relief to stand in. Eventually the management threatened to take away the original 30 shillings; under pressure from us, the full-time officials reluctantly made a claim for the full three pounds. Finally, and by this time it had come round to spring 1971, the management said that in view of the restrictions, they would cancel the 30 shillings. The lads in Tremorfa reacted to this and two of them were suspended; this produced immediate supporting action in the Castle works. I was on my rota day off, when I heard that men at both works were out on strike.

I felt this might be a try-on by the management, but the lads were ready for a fight, though they had never done anything like this. They stuck out on strike for twelve weeks. We marched through the town three times, carrying a coffin, with a fellow dressed as an undertaker and the slogan:

> *'Here lies the body of Brother Ben,*
> *Who died on the basic at GKN.'*

Q

There were some very colourful slogans, including one attacking the GKN chairman who had publicly supported the wage freeze introduced when Edward Heath came into office in 1970, at the same time as increasing his own salary by a large amount. The process workers at Castle and Tremorfa raised £60 a week for us, even though our being out on strike reduced their bonus. And I'd like to pay tribute to the GKN workers shop stewards' association, from whom we received tremendous financial, moral and active support. No one broke the picket lines and right to the end, at every meeting there were never more than 12 men voting to go back.

But through all this time the AEU executive never paid dispute benefit, which in reality makes a strike official. Some of the lads became disillusioned with the union and wanted to tear up their cards, but I and the strike committee were able finally to prevent this. The management then said they were prepared to let us keep the 30 shillings and there would be talks about a productivity increase which wouldn't be less than three pounds, but would include the 30 shillings, a now-you-see-it-now-you-don't sleight of hand formula. But they were demanding that we should work all the overtime they wanted, together with complete mobility so that they could switch us around as they liked; this was because 35 craftsmen had left during the strike and there were consequent manning problems.

I started on a Monday after the strike at eight in the morning and went to work preparing one of the main steam boilers for the annual insurance survey, a job I'd been doing for ten years. At ten o'clock I was told to commence work on the night shift in the bar and strip mill as from Tuesday, while the other boiler fitter was to be removed to the wire mill. Now we maintained that this involved reorganisation of the work which had not been discussed with us and amounted to a 'change of practice' involving a loss of two jobs. We tried to raise the matter with the departmental engineer, but all he did was to order me to go to the bar and strip mill.

I wrote a letter to the union district secretary, to let him know that the boiler job was 'in dispute'. I realised that the management were out to get me shifted and involved in accepting a 'change' before it had been discussed by the District Committee, so I felt I must do something out of the ordinary by way of protest. I took a rucksack, which I used to carry our trade union correspondence in, put in a loaf of bread, oilskin and spare pullover and I climbed up the tower over the works.

When I reached the top, 70 feet up, I lay down for a while because I had cramp. I was just getting up again when I heard the fire bell clanging. A fireman climbed up the ladder, a young fellow who used to live next door to me. Once he realised that I was not suicidal and that it was a dispute, he left, together with the police, who refused to bring me down, due to the danger involved for them and me. A bit later, a factory inspector for the South Wales area climbed up and asked me if it was safe where I was. I told him that it was safer up here than down in the works, because they had one of the worst safety records in Wales. I said I was glad to meet him, because I had been a shop steward there for approximately 20 years and I had never met a factory inspector before. Finally a doctor climbed up. He told me he had to come and see whether I was mentally affected or not. He had to come up every night while I was there and he wasn't too pleased about it. However we established a friendly relationship. His father, he informed me, had been 'a bit of a Socialist'.

Letters were passing up and down; some of the stewards wanted to have a bit of a demonstration and publicly burn their union cards because the union was doing nothing about my case. But I persuaded them not to do this. Next day they brought in the top security officer of the GKN group and security was tightened up. The works engineer came up with a burly works policeman behind him and said they were going to bring me down. This preyed on my mind and I sent a message to my wife (I threw it down to the roof of the pipe fitters' department wrapped round a bolt) telling her that the management were now threatening violence. When the local papers got hold of the story they were instrumental in getting a guarantee of safety letter from the company.

In general I had a good Press, which was not what the firm expected and I stuck it out until the Saturday morning when I got a message hidden in a chocolate cake (the police were letting food up, but not messages) saying that John Boyd of the union Executive Committee had said I should come down and take the matter through procedure.

By then I was exhausted through lack of sleep and strain, and the fear of falling. I decided to come down, only to be suspended after three hours and dismissed two days later. This was all carried out in total disregard for prodecure or contract of employment rulings. Some indication of this can be seen from the result of my appeal against the non-payment of unemployment benefit for six weeks to a National Insurance local tribunal. They unanimously found that, despite the fact that I had climbed a water tower and remained there for $4\frac{1}{2}$ days, and had failed to work shifts and refused to come down when ordered to do so, the employers 'had not shown themselves to be reasonable employers. This being so the tribunal was not satisfied that their actions were not justified in the circumstances and accordingly allowed the appeal', and I was paid my six weeks' benefit.

The union EC instructed the district secretary to demand my re-instatement, but the management refused and 'failure to agree' was recorded. The issue went to national level for discussion between the Independent Steel Employers' Association and Brother J. Boyd, union EC member. However the only employers' representation present was three executives from the Cardiff GKN plant, the personnel director, the chief engineer and a member of the industrial relations department. Brother Boyd protested about this, I was told, but the 'impartial' discussion proceeded with the very three people directly connected with my dismissal acting as judge and jury. Since then an aggregate meeting of GKN craftsmen has demanded a further meeting, this time with the Employers Association and not just GKN; so have the GKN shop stewards' committee and many trade union branches, for the purpose of discussing my reinstatement, which is still a current issue.

Meanwhile, the Final Appeal Court of the AUEW, meeting in October 1971, accepted my appeal, that our strike was according to rule and should have resulted in dispute benefit being paid. This over-ruled the EC decision and meant that every AUEW member got £75 strike pay.

LEONARD R. CHANDLER
Post Office telephonist, Guildford

At the Guildford Exchange, during the Post Office strike[1] out of 150 staff, two full-time and two part-time men and one of the

[1] In Jan-Feb 1972.

girls among the day staff came out on strike. The rest stayed in. After one week, one full time man went back in leaving me. After three or four weeks I was tempted to go back to work, and even rang up to say that I was coming in. But on reflection I decided, 'No, I'll stay out', and so I stayed out for the full seven weeks.

I think that I am a fair man, and I had found that my whole working conditions were governed by the fact that the Union of Post Office workers were working on my behalf. I worked this out for myself; from being the sort of man who keeps to himself, I took on the job of trying to show others where their loyalties lay. I had been a telephonist for 12 years and before that had been on the round and knew what a postman has to put up with. They start at four o'clock in the morning (most of them need to sleep in the afternoon), and if they are not in bed by ten at night then it is only a matter of a few hours before they must be at work again. The average postman around here would pick up £16 10s a week. With a wife and perhaps a couple of kids, with council house rents at six pounds a week, what arithmetic do you need to prove that it is not enough.

The telephonists, or the majority of them, did not belong to the UPW; they either belonged to the older rival organisation or belonged to no union. Now a house divided against itself cannot stand. That sounds very simple now but it took a great deal of searching on my part to find this truth. I felt I could not take something got for me by someone else's endeavour. If it had not been for the work of the UPW, the people I was working among would have been about four pounds a week worse off. The UPW I knew carried the most weight. It led and the other organisation followed. In ten years it had only negotiated one small increase which the UPW refused because it was not linked to pensions. So I weighed up in my mind which was the most effective organisation and I joined the UPW.

It seemed to me that when the UPW took the decision to call a strike, then it was my duty to support my fellow members. Many of those who worked at Guildford Exchange were earning extra cash to add to their husbands' wages. What was serious to the full-time staff was something else; they were not concerned, did not take the situation seriously. When I went back after the strike they treated me as if I had been ill. They were not remotely concerned about what was at stake or what it had cost me. They showed no allegiance to those working on their behalf. If only one of them would turn round and say, 'We don't want the increase the UPW has negotiated', that would re-instate them in my eyes.

During the strike we had to dig into my holiday money. My wife got a job as a typist part-time. Once or twice I went to the union for hardship money and am grateful to the union and those other unions who donated. It was a difficult time for us with three children of school age. But it was a lot more difficult for a good many others and I'm glad we stuck together. It was like being back in the army; in a tight situation, you close your rank.

My father was a postman in the old days. And now I can recall some of the things he told me. They make sense now, but it took 40 years to sink in.

ROGER O'HARA
Former strike leader at the Shell Star construction site, Ellesmere Port

In 1968 the stewards on the site where I was working were given documents about a new productivity deal. It had all the usual features of the kind of productivity bargaining being peddled at that time – discipline clauses, 'flexibility of labour', doing jobs of other trades, putting up your own scaffolding, and so on.

It was a fertiliser plant being built for ShellStar (Shell and Armour Star) on marsh land in the middle of nowhere some miles from the industrial part of Ellesmere Port, and apart from the building workers there were constructional engineers, plumbers heating and domestic engineering union people – about 900 in all. We were setting up turbines, boilers, pumps and vessels, and this new agreement was going to make a big difference to our working conditions.

But we were told that it had already been agreed by the unions. I got hold of a copy of the agreement from a shop steward and with another lad, I suppose I'd call him an anarchist, agreed that we'd get the agreement printed in full and distributed to all the construction workers. Then we'd put out another document showing all the pitfalls. Within a week we had a meeting with the full time officials of the various unions and, with the exception of the boilermakers' union official who said the agreement would have to be accepted first by his members, they all took the line that they had accepted it for us and that was all there was to it. There was a bit of a row with the lads throwing chip bags on to the platform, and in the end we all decided that we weren't going to work it.

After about six weeks the firm called all the shop stewards to a meeting on Friday afternoon. Our shop steward (AEU) was off ill, and his deputy was away in Ellesmere Port attending a meeting of constuction workers' shop stewards discussing what to do about the Bill Barbara Castle was trying to get through at that time, 'In Place of Strife'. So I went to the meeting as deputy's deputy. The firm told us that because we wouldn't accept the agreement which had been signed, sealed and delivered by the union's we were all sacked and would get our money and cards at 4.30 that night. At around 4.30 the lads were already queueing up to get paid for the week. We told them to go back and sit in the huts and wait while the stewards had a meeting.

The stewards got together and talked matters over and two ideas were put forward. One was to tell the firm we were not accepting our cards, to picket the gate on the Monday and call it a lockout and ask the building workers to support us. The other proposal was to occupy the site and sit in; if they brought the police in, to burn out the bolts on the construction and bring the whole lot down. The first course was more or less agreed. In the meantime the men had refused to accept their cards and we had asked the buses which took them back into town to hang on a while for us. We held a meeting and put the two proposals to them. The proposal to occupy the site was defeated by about 10 votes out of 400. Then the other idea was accepted unanimously. Over the weekend we got in touch with the stewards who had not been there on the day and they agreed with what had been done.

When Monday came we picketed the gate. Or rather we put a picket across the road at an island further down. As the traffic built up we explained the situation. The other workers went through, and then held a meeting and told the management that if we were not re-instated, they would be out. Later we heard the sound of a drum being beaten. We went to the top of the road and saw a mass of men marching out, singing the International. It was lockout for us, strike for them.

Next day we closed the road. We stopped everyone, even the maintenance men, the milkman and the washerwomen. No one got through. The police came up to try and get the lorries through, because the road beyond led to the Shell Refinery. But we sat down in the road and as they dragged us out from the front, we walked round to the back and sat down again. A traffic jam built up to Bebington, 10 miles away.

Then we sent out groups of men to lobby. One went to the meeting of the Confederation of Engineering and Shipbuilding Union's where we saw Hugh Scanlon, President of the AEU. Later another group went to the Labour Party Conference. They got tickets for the Conference Dance; one was in his wellington boots! They went in and one got a dance with Barbara Castle and raised it with her. All the construction workers in Mersyeside came out on one day strike to back us and 9,000 marched through the city.

Barbara Castle intervened and called both sides to a meeting at the Department of Employment and Productivity. Our stewards got themselves dressed up and went down there. They introduced themselves at the door and the DEP officials there took them straight into the conference room and served them tea and cakes, before they found out they were the stewards and not the full time union men. In the end we were told to tell them what we wanted, and we laid it down; mutual agreement instead of 'flexibility', put up our own scaffolding to a height of three feet, and so on. This agreement which we had revised then went back to the management, who accepted it and gave us two shillings and sixpence on the basic rate as well.

Every man was taken back after seven weeks and the strike made a big impression. If the men on the site had accepted this Wilsonian '20th century' nonsense in the way the full-time officials had done, they would have got rid of half the labour force. The ones left would have been paid more, but what is that but agreeing to give the sack to your own mates. But it wasn't on as far as our lads were concerned. They knew there was going to be a big blow up and they had prepared for it, saving their money. And they were ready to go even further than we did; there was even talk of blocking the Mersey Tunnel, by driving in cars from both ends.

SIMON FRASER
Secretary of the Liverpool Trades Council

When the men from the ShellStar site came down to London, Barbara Castle and Tony Crosland were terribly impressed with them and the way they argued the case against the agreement which the unions had already accepted.

This in itself illustrates one of the most important problems the Labour and trade union movement is faced with today, the gulf between people at the top and the rank and file at a time when the rank and file are taking the initiative more and more. One of the Merseyside MPs said to me, 'You know, I'm not happy about the quality of people on our local committee.' Somehow he has acquired the belief that just being up in Westminster gives him some superior quality. Yet I can show you shop stewards on any building site that could lick the pants off that man intellectually.

As with MPs, so with trade union officials, even those with Left wing views; once they leave the factory, once they go up a grade they begin to acquire the attitude, 'Just leave it to us. We'll sort it out round the table.' Almost like MPs they begin to live in an ivory tower, with a mystic belief in their own power to solve problems. For a while as officials they retain the verve and drive that got them elected. Then in the next stage you see a change; you stop seeing them at demonstrations. Then comes the next stage when they begin to wish that the demonstrations would not take place.

I would be the same myself, I know, but the organisation I work for, the Liverpool Trades Council, happens to be an organisation with no money; to exist, it has to keep in touch with the shop stewards, the activists, the men in the branch. I'm thankful in a way that my position keeps me in touch with rank and file men rather than full-time officials. If we are to be of any use at all it must be in assisting the workers in the interests of the trade union movement. Our attitude is that men in dispute should be helped by the trade union movement and if the trade union doesn't do its job then we must step in.

Four years ago, when the Merseyside busmen, who were equally divided between two unions, went on strike without warning, the full time officials told them to get out, and so the men came to us.

We helped them by standing as guarantor for a meeting in the stadium, helping produce leaflets. One is constantly impressed by the terrific amount of talent that trade unionists display when their backs are to the wall. They show talents so far undisplayed, talents for speaking, writing, the presentation of a case and the layout of material – work from the top drawer. Afterwards, when the strike is over, they are back to being bus drivers, builders or whatever they were, once more.

It is men at this level who are suspicious about the Industrial Relations Act. The full-time official is not threatened by it in the same way, but the shop steward sees it as aimed directly at him. In recent years I have become aware of the growing frustration of the rank and file with the state of affairs in politics. the feeling that whatever promises are made at election times, the same sort of policies will come out of Westminster. Coupled with this a growing taste for direct action.

This is not only on the industrial field. The people locally who wanted a play street tried for months to get the council to do something. They know the local councillor personally; he is a nice bloke, but nothing gets done. Then one day the people themselves block the street and stop the traffic; almost immediately the council does something about what seemed impossible only the day before. So there is a growing readiness for people to take things into their own hands. This to them is the participation which the official system denies them. The old ways of conducting political and trade union activity are in the melting pot and more and more people want to try something new.

JIMMY REID
Convener of shop stewards, Upper Clyde Shipbuilders

When the shop stewards at Upper Clyde Shipbuilders saw what the Government was aiming at in June 1971, that it was withholding money, that it was determined to liquidate (although production figures were on the up and up and there were orders on the books), they knew that they were up against a new situation.

The pattern of former struggles, they felt, would not be successful. And so we went through the options. The blow came on

242

Saturday 11, June 1971. We met on the Sunday and we ran through the various options. Everybody was against the close-down of any of the yards. Acceptance was not on. No 'run down', letting men go out of the gate over a period; no 'blood money', taking a lump sum to go away and find a job elsewhere. There were no jobs elsewhere any longer. A strike would mean that the yards were empty and they could close them behind our backs. A sit-in strike was not appropriate. The industry was economically sound and these days economic decisions cannot be abstracted from their social consequences. Hence the need to demonstrate. We had to take control effectively. If you allow the works to be dismantled, the assets removed, the labour force dispersed, then you are finished. And so the 'work-in' began the next week.

We tried to look creatively at forms of trade union struggle to see whether they were relevant. It is no good reacting like Pavlov's dog. You have to choose the form of struggle appropriate to your circumstance.

We knew, too, that if we were on our own, no amount of militancy could succeed. And so at each stage we made out our case. We presented our blue-print for the yards to the Trades Union Congress, and we sent our people all over the country, all over Scotland, Britain and abroad. It resulted in a tremendous solidarity campaign to an extent that quite amazed us, from the big trade union donations to the kids who organised cake sales and the widow who sent us her pension for the week. And we used the mass media. We knew that what we were doing had wider implications for the whole public, and we knew that it was a good story.

We are not saying UCS is a model for other people to use. We looked carefully at our own circumstances and decided this was the right form of action for us, whether it had been done before, or done by anyone else.

POSTSCRIPT

The year that has passed since the making of these interviews has exceeded all the hopes, fears or expectations of the future expressed in them. The number of strikes rose sharply in 1970 and 1971 – so that at the present rate the next 100,000 will be reached after 30 years, not 80.

The miners, taking national strike action for the first time since the 1926 General Strike and Lockout, scored a remarkable victory in February 1972, the lessons and effects of which are still being analysed.

As predicted by its critics, the Industrial Relations Act caused disputes involving the railwaymen and transport workers to expand to the scale of national political issues; the militancy of the workers involved, far from being abated by the legal action, has been increased.

October 1972 saw the Upper Clyde Shipbuilders' 'work in' score a notable success in its action to keep the shipyard workers in employment.

The Clyde 'work-in' has inspired a series of similar actions at other places in the country; factory 'occupations' being used not only to prevent sackings, but also to enforce wage demands.

The 1970s are likely to demonstrate more forcibly the simple truth of past decades – that strikes will continue as long as their causes in living and working conditions persist.

INDEX TO CONTRIBUTORS

Angell, Isaac, 47
Arnison, Albert, 45
Attwood, Arthur, 170–4

Blackley, Charles, 184–6
Blyton, Will, 75–7
Bolton, George, 188–90
Brown, Isobel, 95, 121–4
Brownlie, Annette, 231–2
Buck, Les, 192–5
Byrne, Joe, 40–2, 134–6, 162–3

Campbell, John, 111
Chandler, Leonard, R., 236–8
Clements, Jack, 47–8
Collinson, John, 108–9
Cornthwaite, Frank, 226–9
Crump, Jim, 128–30, 160

Dash, Jack, 169–70, 183–4
Davies, Ben, 153–4
Dickenson, Bessie, 97, 124–5
Dickenson, Harold, 124–5
Doyle, Charles, 205–8
Drury, Alf, 64–6

Eisenstone, Isaac, 36–7
Etheridge, Dick, 154–5, 196–8
Evans, Dai Dan, 145–8
Evans, Edgar, 148–51

Fineman, Sid, 35–6, 133–4
Fraser, Simon, 241–2

Gardner, Jim, 59–61
Garrard, Alf, 62–3, 90–1, 130–1
Green, John, 218–22
Griffiths, James, 30–2, 74–5, 100–3
Gurl, Les, 198–200

Hann, G. Maurice, 49
Hart, Finlay, 61–2, 177–80
Hitchings, Harry, 232–6
Hodgkinson, George, 56–9, 87–8
Hopper, Harriet, 229–31
Howell, J. F., 68–70
Hoyle, Fred, 180–3

Irons, Albert, 46, 66–7, 91–2
Isaacs, George, 39–40, 86–7, 98, 166–8

Jackson, Frank, 27–9, 52–5, 92–3
James, George, 99–100
Jeffreys Hywel (Jeff Camnant), 105, 151–2
Jeffreys, Hywel, 32–4
Jones, J. W. (Bill), 138–40, 190–2

Kahl, Arthur, 168–9
Kelley, Dick, 110, 111, 187–8
Kerrigan, Peter, 80–1, 90, 114–16

Lewis, Arthur, W. J., 175–7
Lewis, Mrs H. E., 67–8
Lewis, Dr John, 71–3, 96–7
Longworth, Jack, R., 125–7
Lovell, Bob, 81–3

Mathers, Brian, 216–18
McCullogh, Jessie, 130–1
Milligan, Margaret, 231–2
Moffat, Abe, 107–8, 141–3, 161
Mofshovitz, E., 116–19
Morgan, Megan, 103–4
Murphy, Pat, 42–5

Nettleton, Dick, 157–9
Nugent, Walter, 225–6

O'Hara, Roger, 238–40

Paynter, Will, 103, 143–5, 186–7
Phipps, Rev Simon, 200–1
Potter, John, 222–5
Pountney, Ernie, 70–1

Reid, Jimmy, 242–3
Reynolds, Hugh, 77–8, 105–7
Robson, Alex, 136–8
Rolph, Ted, 37–9

Scouller, R. E., 49–50, 88–90
Slater, Jim, 211–16
Stewart, Bob, 22–7

INDEX

Stokes, W. H., 78–80
Swindlehurst, Billie, 226–9

Taylor, Cyril, 203–4

Warman, Bill, 201–3
Wesker, Sarah, 119–21
Withers, J., 93–5
Wylie, George, 156–7

246